GOD'S
ECSTATIC
LOVE

D1608113

APOCRYPHILE
PRESS

BOOKS BY BRUCE TALLMAN

Archetypes for Spiritual Direction:
Discovering the Heroes Within
(Paulist Press, 2005)

Finding Seekers:
How to Develop a Spiritual Direction Practice
from Beginning to Full-Time Employment
(Apocryphile Press, 2011)

A Thousand Spiritual Lessons:
Wisdom and Peace for the Over-Busy, Over-Informed,
Over-Worked, and Over-Whelmed
(Kindle Direct Publishing, 2021)

God's Ecstatic Love:
Transform Your Life with a Spiritual Masterpiece
(Apocryphile Press, 2021)

TWO IMPORTANT NOTES

IMPORTANT NOTE ONE: Francis de Sales' language, like that of the culture he lived in, was not gender-sensitive, which is another reason why he deserves an update like this. My commentary is gender-inclusive, but where I quote de Sales I have not changed his wording from the original *Treatise on the Love of God* as this would sound fabricated and inauthentic. When reading these quotes, keep in mind that de Sales was well-known for his sensitivity and, if alive today, he would have changed his wording.

IMPORTANT NOTE TWO: If you have received a free digital copy of *God's Ecstatic Love* and would prefer a hard copy, it is available in that format at http://apocryphilepress.com/book/gods-ecstatic-love/ and many other online vendors. And feel free to pass your free digital copy on to others.

GOD'S ECSTATIC LOVE

Transform Your Life with a Spiritual Masterpiece

BRUCE TALLMAN

THE APOCRYPHILE PRESS
Hannacroix, NY
www.apocryphilepress.com

Copyright © 2021 by Bruce Tallman
www.brucetallman.com

Cover and interior design by Adam Thomas
www.adamthomas.net

ISBN 978-1-955821-56-8 | paperback
ISBN 978-1-949643-87-9 | epub
Published by Apocryphile Press, Berkeley, California, 2021
Printed in the United States of America

All footnotes are from *Treatise on the Love of God* by St. Francis de Sales, published in 1616 in Annecy, France. The *Treatise* was originally translated into English by Rev. Henry Benedict Mackey, O.S.B. and published in 1884 by Burns and Oates Limited, London, England. This translation, which is in the public domain, was photographically reproduced from the Third Edition by arrangement with Burns and Oates and republished by TAN Books, Charlotte, North Carolina in 2012.

Scripture quotations for everything except the Psalms are from the *New Revised Standard Version Bible*, copyright 1989, National Council of Churches of Christ in the United States. Used with permission.

Quotations from the Psalms are from *The Psalms: Poetry on Fire*, The Passion Translation, copyright 2014, 2015. Used by permission of Broadstreet Publishing Group, LLC, Racine, Wisconsin, USA. All rights reserved.

Beloved, let us love one another, because love is from God;
everyone who loves is born of God and knows God.
In this is love, not that we loved God, but that God loved us.
God is love, and those who abide in love abide in God,
and God abides in them.
We love because God first loved us.
The commandment we have from God is this:
those who love God must love their brothers and sisters also.
By this we know that we love the children of God,
when we love God and obey God's commandments.
–I John 4:7, 10a, 16b, 19, 21, 5:2

True virtue has no limits, it goes ever further;
but especially holy charity, the love of God,
which is the virtue of virtues,
and which, having an infinite object,
would be capable of becoming infinite
if it could meet with a heart capable of infinity.
–Francis de Sales

Humans are the perfection of the universe;
spirit is the perfection of humans;
love is the perfection of spirit;
and divine love is the perfection of human love.
–Francis de Sales

Totally love God who gave himself totally for your love.
–Clare of Assisi

The things we love and why we love them tell us who we are.
–Thomas Aquinas

The soul is made of love and must ever strive to return to love.
Therefore, it can never find rest or happiness in other things. It must
lose itself in love.
By its very nature it must seek God, who is love.
–Mechthild of Magdeburg

The one who desires nothing but God is rich and happy.
–Alphonsus Liguori

O my All, my Beatitude, Infinite Solitude,
Immensity in which I lose myself,
I surrender myself to you…immerse yourself in me
so that I may be immersed in you
until I go to contemplate
in your light
the abyss of your splendour!
–Blessed Elizabeth of the Trinity

We give God our time
and God gives us God's Eternity;
we give God our humanity
and God gives us God's Divinity;
we give God our nothingness
and God gives us God's All.
–Fulton Sheen

The goal of life is God!
The source of life is God!
God is the fact of life
from which all things
take their meaning and reality.
–Howard Thurman

All the great saints in history were so passionately in love with God
that they were free to love other people in a deep affective way,
without any strings attached.
It is following the first commandment
that asks us to give everything we have to God
that makes the second commandment
– to love others as yourself –
truly possible.
–Henri Nouwen

Prayer of Dedication

To the Father/Mother of Life
to Jesus the Universal Christ Incarnate
to the Holy Spirit, the Sacred Life-Force
to Paul, the Greatest Disciple of Jesus
who said "I live, yet not I, but Christ lives in me"
to Augustine, the Great Doctor of the Church
who said "Our heart is restless until it rests in God"
to Francis of Assisi, the Great Pauper
who found God's riches in all things
to Thomas Aquinas, the Great Theologian
who dominated Christian thought for centuries
to Teresa of Avila, the Great Reformer
to John of the Cross, the Great Mystic
to Francis de Sales, the Great Lover of God

and in the twentieth and twenty-first centuries:
to Thomas Merton, the Great Contemplative
to Pierre Teilhard de Chardin, the Great Seer
to Dorothy Day, the Great Worker
to Richard Rohr, my Great Teacher for thirty years

And to my children Hailey, Brandon and Alana
my trinity, my three hearts
living outside my body

this book is dedicated.

May the Great Spirit
unite everyone in
God's Ecstatic Love.

TABLE OF CONTENTS

BOOK ONE
PREPARATION FOR THE REST OF THE BOOK: THE SCIENCE OF LOVE

BOOK TWO
THE GENERATION OF DIVINE LOVE

BOOK THREE
ON THE DECAY AND RUIN OF OUR LOVE FOR GOD

Acknowledging my Seven Clergy Editors

I wish to thank the seven following ordained priests and ministers for diligently and thoroughly reviewing, theologically critiquing and editing my manuscript:

- James Schmeiser, Ph.D., D.Th., retired Roman Catholic Seminary Rector and Professor Emeritus of Contemporary Spirituality
- Reverend David R. Elliott, Ph.D., retired Professor of Western Civilization, the Reformation and Counter-Reformation
- Reverend Kevin Steeper, Pastoral Support Person for United Church of Canada Ministers
- Reverend Robert Lemon, Anglican Dean
- Reverend Elise Feltrin, United Church of Canada Minister
- Reverend Steven Dozeman, Reformed Church Minister
- Reverend Linda Johnson, United Methodist Minister

And last, but not least: Dr. Catherine McMulkin, Executive Director of the Canadian Fellowship of Christian Spiritual Directors, who gave me much valuable feedback from a spiritual direction point of view.

I also wish to thank the eight Christian laity who functioned as testers for many of my ideas: Susan Marino, Bonnie Martin, Cindy and David Berg, Mary Ann Tippelt, John Fraresso, Patrick O'Connor and James Adjan.

Thank you all for your profound wisdom and insights!

INTRODUCTION
WHY THIS BOOK WAS WRITTEN

Loving God is the most important thing in life. When Jesus was asked what the greatest commandment was, he said "Love God with all your heart, mind, soul, and strength." Or as one person translated it: "Love God with all your passion, intellect, soul, and willpower."

Jesus also said there is a second great commandment which is like the first one, that is, "Love others as you love yourself" (Matthew 22: 37-39). These two commandments sum up all of scripture, the Law and the Prophets. Everything else is commentary.

In 1983 I decided to make these great commandments the center of my life. When I pondered, "How can I love God with all my heart?" it occurred to me that I needed an expert opinion. Shortly after, I discovered Francis de Sales' *Treatise on the Love of God.* It was very profound but seemed out of date since it was published in the seventeenth century. I thought "Someday someone should do a modern update of it."

Now, God has called me to be a writer. I have had two books published which were aimed at professional spiritual directors and counsellors. One of them, *Finding Seekers,* is a bestseller in its field. Plus, I have had hundreds of articles on spirituality published in the London Free Press, the main newspaper where I live. Various people have suggested I should write a book on spirituality aimed at the general public. Because I felt God was telling me through these people what I should do, I give God all the credit for this present book. I have just tried to obey orders.

For several years now, God has been laying on my heart that the world is falling apart and this is partly because the major religion of the western world, Christianity, has been overwhelmed by all the contemporary challenges to it: modern evolutionary science, scholarly criticism of the Bible and of the church's historical record (both important and necessary, but faith-shaking), a materialist and consumerist culture, Christians rubbing shoulders with other major world religions thus relativizing Christianity, the rise of people who are spiritual but not religious, the new atheism, and so on.

If their faith survives, Christians today seem to be either anti-intellectual, anti-science fundamentalists with great passion, or broad-minded liberal intellectuals who lack passion. God has led me to believe that what the world needs now is a new type of Christian, that is, one who is both passionate and intellectual. De Sales' *Treatise* is an intellectual and passionate approach to God and a masterpiece that fits this need.

In brief, I have written this book because God led me to write it. God has called me to do my little part to try to renew our civilization by renewing the Christian faith. I don't see many Christians living Christ's Great Commandments. And I believe they don't love God with all their heart because no one taught them the importance of this, and just showing up at church for an hour once a week is not enough to transform anyone.

In my opinion and that of many scholars, the *Treatise* is on the level of other great classic Christian works such as *The Cloud of Unknowing*, *The Imitation of Christ*, and *The Spiritual Exercises of Ignatius of Loyola*, but the *Treatise* is unknown by 99% of Christians. I wrote my book with the hope of remedying that.

This is meant to be a devotional book, not an academic one, and so I hope the 260 quotes from the actual *Treatise*, hundreds of passages from scripture, and my 21st century commentary on all this will have a spiritual impact on my readers and change their hearts, minds, souls, and wills. I hope they will find their love of God growing as they read it.

I didn't want the book however to be so heaven-bound that it was no earthly good. I believe that loving other human beings is integral to loving God, and so I wanted to show how God's love and loving God in return relates to the everyday real-life issues of ordinary people. Throughout, I relate de Sales' ideas to contemporary concerns about social justice, peace and care for our planet.

Jonathan Sacks, the Chief Rabbi for the United Kingdom from 1993 to 2013, said that "Since we are living with such immense powers of destruction, God is setting us a really big challenge. God is giving us very little choice: we must love or die. That is where we are at the beginning of the 21st century."

Hopefully *God's Ecstatic Love*, a condensed version of the greatest spiritual masterpiece of a great spiritual master on the most important topic of all, that is, God's love and loving God and other human beings, will help us all in fulfilling this great 21st century challenge.

BACKGROUND

WHO WAS FRANCIS DE SALES?

Francis de Sales (1567-1622) was a Bishop of Geneva, Switzerland and is honoured as a saint in the Catholic Church. He became noted for his deep faith and gentle approach to the religious divisions resulting from the Protestant Reformation.

He was born in the noble Sales family in the Duchy of Savoy, France. His father wanted him to be a magistrate. As a nobleman, in 1583 he went to the Jesuit College de Clermont in Paris to study rhetoric and humanities.

In 1584 he attended a discussion about predestination and became convinced of his damnation to hell. A crisis of despair ensued that lasted until January of 1587 when he prayed before a famed statue of Our Lady of Good Deliverance, a Black Madonna, and dedicated his life to God with a vow of chastity. His faithful devotion to the "God who is love" not only expelled his doubts but influenced the rest of his life and teachings, often referred to as "The Way of Divine Love."

In 1588 he entered the University of Padua in Italy where he studied law and theology. There, with the aid of a Jesuit priest as his spiritual director, he decided to become a priest. In 1592 de Sales received his doctorate in law and theology.

When he returned to Savoy, his father, Lord François de Sales, secured his appointment as a senator and chose a wealthy noble heiress as his bride. However, Francis refused to marry and was ordained as a Catholic priest in 1593. He was immediately appointed as provost of the cathedral in Geneva.

As provost he set out to evangelize the area which was almost completely dedicated to the teachings of a major Protestant reformer, John Calvin. The residents refused to listen to him and at first he failed miserably and had to reside in a fortress guarded by Duke of Savoy soldiers. Several times he escaped assassination attempts.

In 1602 de Sales was consecrated Bishop of Geneva. His diocese became well-known for efficient organization, zealous clergy and well-instructed laity. He worked closely with the Order of Friars Minor Capuchin who actively preached the Catholic faith in his diocese. De Sales himself was an eloquent preacher and he became famous for his patience and mild approach. His motto was "The one who preaches with love, preaches well."

His goodness comes through in his books, the most widely popular one being *Introduction to the Devout Life* which was written specifically for lay people. The main teaching in this book for beginners is that love should take precedence over penance as the means to spiritual progress. His even more mystical *Treatise on the Love of God* was written for those more advanced in the spiritual life.

Along with St. Jane Frances de Chantal, de Sales founded the cloistered women's Order of the Visitation of Holy Mary in Annecy France in 1610.

Francis de Sales died of a stroke in 1622, was canonized by Pope Alexander VII in 1665 and declared a Doctor of the Church by Pope Pius IX in 1877. In 1923, Pope Pius XI proclaimed him a patron of writers and journalists because he extensively used his books to convert thousands of Calvinists. He is also the patron of the Sisters of St. Joseph, the Paulist Fathers and the Society of St. Francis de Sales (also known as the Salesians of Don Bosco).

The spirituality of Francis de Sales in his two main books had a profound effect on St. Vincent de Paul, and in the 19th century many religious communities adopted his spiritual approach: The Missionaries of St. Francis de Sales, the Oblate Sisters of St. Francis de Sales and the Oblates of St. Francis de Sales for men.

How This Book Was Written

While I was not yet bishop, having more leisure and less fears for my writings, I dedicated my little works to princes of the earth, but now being weighed down with my charge, and having a thousand difficulties in writing, I consecrate all to the princes of heaven, that they may obtain for me the light requisite, and that if such be the Divine will, these my writings may be fruitful and profitable to many. Thus, my dear reader, I beseech God to bless you and to enrich you with his love.

–Francis de Sales, Preface to Volume I of the *Treatise on the Love of God.*

I first read the *Treatise* in the 1980s. However, over the course of many years, in the process of buying hundreds of books and moving three times, somewhere in the shuffle I lost the two volumes of the *Treatise.* I searched everywhere on my bookshelves but could not find them.

One day in 2016 I felt the urge to reorganize my home office and decided to get rid of some old boxes full of books that were stored behind a couch. There at the bottom of one of the unpacked boxes was the *Treatise.*

I picked up the two volumes and turned them over and over in my hands, staring at them like two invaluable jewels, like treasure hidden in a field.

I opened Volume One and noticed that it was first published on July 31, 1616. To me this date was significant and seemed like some kind of sign from God as it was exactly 360 years to the day before my wedding on July 31, 1976 to my dear wife Grace, without whom I probably would not have any faith at all. God drew me into the faith through Grace and it felt like God's grace was going to draw me deeper now through the *Treatise*.

I also realized that 2016 was exactly 400 years since the *Treatise's* original publication, a lot has happened since then, and I believed the *Treatise* needed updating.

De Sales' magnum opus was written pre-science. For example, it is rather amusing to learn that he believed clams formed pearls by opening themselves to dew dropped by God from heaven. Also, as another example of the prevailing mentality, in 1615, one year before the *Treatise* was published, the Roman Inquisition concluded that Galileo's heliocentrism (sun-centered solar system) was "foolish and absurd in philosophy, and formally heretical since it explicitly contradicts in many places the sense of Holy Scripture."

However, in spite of the never-ending rise of science and the gradual decline of religion in North America and Europe, faith has not gone away. Islam is burgeoning and Pentecostalism and Catholicism are exploding in various parts of the world. Philip Jenkins, an expert on world religions, wrote in the March 2017 issue of *Christian Century* magazine in an article titled "The Catholic Surge in Africa" that, "If current trends continue, as they show every sign of doing, then by 2040 there will be some 460 million African Catholics, a number greater than the total world population of Catholics in 1950." Contrary to what is happening in Europe and North America, on the world stage religion is not disappearing, it is gathering momentum.

I have written *God's Ecstatic Love* mainly for Europeans and North Americans in the hope of sparking new growth there as well.

The growth of religion in other parts of the world is not surprising since the direction of evolution on our planet has become increasingly spiritual as God's love continues to drive the whole evolutionary process. Matter intrinsically heads toward spirit. That is God's plan and the way God set things up.

Planet Earth has evolved from rocks and water (matter) to plants (life) to animals (sensitivity) to humans (thought) to the spread of the great world religions across the globe (spirit). Evolution has always headed in a spiritual direction: from matter to life to sensitivity to thought to spirit. And love is the perfection of spirit.

Christians and Muslims already make up about 54% of the seven billion people on Earth: in 2019 there were 2.4 billion Christians and 1.9 billion Muslims. If those numbers keep growing and you add in Hindus, Buddhists, Jews and those who are "spiritual but not religious" (which includes many atheists who are interested in spirituality), eventually the entire globe will be covered over with the final layer of spirit, love and divine love.

Perhaps from all of this a "meta-religion" will evolve, a higher religion that everyone, even atheists, can agree on. If we focus not on our differences but on the major themes or values in all religion and spirituality: wisdom, joy, trust, patience, kindness, respect, justice, truth, compassion, nonattachment and of course love, then the ancient tradition, the united way will emerge that Aldous Huxley wrote about in his 1945 book *The Perennial Philosophy*.

In any case, the process of writing went like this: in 2016 I started reading the *Treatise* again and scribbling notes a couple of hours a week. In fact, I wrote 330 pages of double-spaced notes from which I made an 18-page outline as the foundation for reconstructing the *Treatise* for our postmodern age.

I wrote it over the next two years and then asked seven clergy persons from six major Christian denominations to edit it. I received very helpful feedback from a Catholic seminary rector, two United Church of Canada ministers, a Presbyterian professor, an Anglican dean, a United Methodist minister, an Evangelical Reformed pastor and the Executive Director of the Canadian Fellowship of Christian Spiritual Directors (see *Acknowledgements*). In response to their insights, I have completely revamped the manuscript seven times.

If at times the book feels a little archaic in its tone and in the words I use, it is because I intentionally wanted to capture the spirit of de Sales' original work and wake our contemporary minds up to the brilliance of a 400 year old masterpiece. For example, de Sales uses the words "complacence" and "benevolence" a lot. While in our century we may interpret these words a certain way at the surface level, de Sales gives them a much deeper spiritual meaning and I wanted to preserve the integrity of that.

The Treatise was written in twelve "books" (really minibooks). The book and chapter headings in my book follow those of de Sales. However, in addition I added the 99 Names of God on pages 21-24, the forty qualities of God on pages 238-243, and the Ninety-Nine Names of Jesus on pages 244-247.

Although culture has changed, human nature is basically the same as in de Sales' time. The first four "books" in *God's Ecstatic Love* focus on de Sales' "science" of the love of God, that is, an explanation of how God has evolved us in such a way that, whether we acknowledge it or not, human beings are naturally drawn to God. These chapters include a description of how divine love is generated within us, the progress and perfection of this love, as well as how this perfect love can decay and be ruined.

Following de Sales' outline, books five to twelve describe how to apply his science to loving God, that is, the practice of divine love. In these chapters we will examine the two chief exercises of divine love according to de Sales: complacence and benevolence; the exercise of holy love in prayer; the soul's union with God perfected in prayer; the love of conformity which unites our will to the will of God; the further uniting of our will to God's will through the love of submission; the command to love God above all things; the supreme authority of love over the soul; and final counsels on holy love.

This is an intellectual/devotional work, not an academic one. Many of the ideas in it have come from my vast reading. Often another author wrote something profound that stuck in my heart, soul and memory and I include it here, but years later I was often not able to identify the exact page number where I read it. I came across much of what is included here long before I was thinking of writing this devotional book, and so I did not take careful academic notes at the time. However, a "Heart, Mind, and Soul Bibliography: Books to Stimulate Loving God with Passion, Intellect and Depth" is included beginning on page 262. Many of the books in this bibliography are the sources of the ideas here.

Also, while writing I recorded the chapter and verse of key Bible verses, so this book is solidly and extensively rooted in scripture. There is an index of scripture verses cited on pages 256-258. The only footnotes with exact page numbers in the book are ones from de Sales' *Treatise* and are cited on pages 259-261. Everything in this book is either quotes from de Sales at the start of each chapter, or passages of scripture, or my reflections on both.

I have been influenced by so many outstanding thinkers of the 20th and 21st centuries as well as centuries before that. I cannot name them all, but some of the key ones have been Reinhold Niebuhr, Paul Tillich, Thomas Merton, Pierre Teilhard de Chardin, Carl Jung, Joseph Campbell, Anthony de Mello, William Johnston, Henri Nouwen, Ronald Rolheiser, Thich Nhat Hanh, Pema Chodrun, Ilia Delio, Marcus Borg, John Dominic Crossan, Matthew Fox, Robert Barron, Rob Bell, Ken Wilber, and most of all Richard Rohr, a well-known Franciscan priest, theologian and mystic. I have been Rohr's disciple for over thirty years, but in addition to his influence, the "flavor" of all these thinkers, if not the outright mention of them, will hopefully be felt throughout this book in my 21st century reflections on de Sales' 17th century thought.

If we are going to have a passionate and intelligent faith, one that can match the challenges of the 21st century, we need both de Sales' passionate love of God and a commentary on his text that takes into account all the important intellectual advances since he wrote his *Treatise*. That is what I have humbly attempted to offer here.

BOOK ONE

PREPARATION FOR THE REST OF THE BOOK: THE SCIENCE OF LOVE

CHAPTER ONE

WE NATURALLY LOVE THE GOOD

Love being the first complacency which we take in good, as we shall presently show, it of course precedes desire; and indeed what other thing do we desire, but that which we love? It precedes delectation, for how could we rejoice in the enjoyment of a thing if we loved it not? It precedes hope, for we hope only for the good which we love: it precedes hatred, for we hate not evil, except for the love we have for the good: nor is evil evil but because it is contrary to the good. And, Theotimus, it is the same with all the other passions and affections; for they all proceed from love, as from their source and root. 1

(**Important note:** Throughout the *Treatise*, de Sales addresses his teachings to a disciple named Theotimus, which means "God-fearer." As Psalm 111:10 says: "The fear of the Lord is the beginning of wisdom." "Fear of the Lord" means "absolute respect for God.")

In short, Theotimus, the will is only moved by her affections, amongst which love, as the primum mobile and first affection, gives motion to all the rest, and causes all the other motions of the soul. 2

Now these affections which we feel in our reasonable part are more or less noble and spiritual, according as their objects are more or less sublime, and as they are in a more eminent department of the spirit: for there are affections in us which proceed from conclusions gained by the experience of our senses; others by reasoning from human sciences;

others from principles of faith; and finally there are some which have their origin from the simple sentiment of the truth of God, and acquiescence in his will. 3

Humans naturally love the good because we are foundationally good. This may not be readily apparent, because anyone who follows the news knows of the many horrendous breaches of the good that occur on a daily basis.

However, in the first chapter of the first book of the Bible, God said "Let us make humankind in our image, according to our likeness"(Genesis 1:26) and "God saw everything that God had made, and indeed, it was very good" (Genesis 1:31).

Humans are foundationally very good. Evil is always a corruption of something that was originally good. So, good is always primary, evil always secondary.Because we are primarily very good, we love the good.

However, we tend to love things that everyone assumes are good—wealth, health and longevity. But these are false gods our culture tells us are good for us, but which let us down. How many times have wealth, health and longevity failed and then people did not know what to do?

This is where Ignatius of Loyola comes in. The founder of the Jesuit order believed that we need to learn the virtue of 'holy indifference,' that is, indifference to ourselves and what happens to us.

Ignatius taught that the main Christian virtue was total compliance with the will of God—to praise God whether God gives us wealth or poverty, health or sickness, a long life or a short one.

The teaching of Ignatius is similar to the idea of submission to the will of God in Islam. And, as we will see later, it is similar to what Francis de Sales taught. Whenever there is a coherent and repeated teaching across different religions, it is a sign there is a deep human truth founded on divine truth.

Beyond what the culture brainwashes into our minds and hearts, there are virtues that are truly good in all circumstances, such as patience, kindness, wisdom, joy, peace, fortitude and so on.

What the world needs now is a return to virtue.

Capitalism and communism have both failed us. With capitalism we are heading towards consuming ourselves out of existence. As has been said many times—if everyone in the world consumed the way the First World countries do, we would need four planets to survive. And pure communism—the rule by the people for the people—has always ironically ended in dictatorship of one form or another—as demonstrated by Stalin and Mao. The present Communist Party of China is promoting a strange blend of atheistic communism and capitalism that may succeed materially but may also kill the souls of a billion Chinese.

What is necessary is to locate happiness in virtue for its own sake. We pursue riches and fame because we are told they will make us happy. However, how many so-called 'stars' struggle with relationship difficulties, addiction or mental health challenges?

As a holy man said: "Do not pray for wealth and power and success, pray for wisdom and patience and hope when you are poor, weak and failing."

We need a kind of meta-religion of happiness, a realization that it is virtues like wisdom and compassion that bring happiness. 'Meta' means 'higher,' so what we need is a higher religion.

Jesus was teaching this meta or higher religion in the Beatitudes: beyond any religion we are only blessed (happy) when we are humble, pure in heart, peaceful and just.

All these virtues are found in every major world religion. So again, what we need is a higher religion that goes beyond any individual religion and focuses all it does on these virtues. This is what not only Jesus taught, but also Buddha, Confucius, Lao Tzu and Mohammed. As the Dalai Lama recently said, "My religion is kindness." We know in our depths that these virtues are what are truly good for us.

However, would that include all people? Many atheists, although they are not interested in God per se, have shown an interest in spirituality since they realize scientific materialism and reason, while very helpful, become dry and sterile when they leave out the human spirit.

Einstein believed the virtues of awe, wonder and curiosity are the true drivers of science. If all atheists believed this too, they would feel comfortable with a meta-religion of virtue, although they would probably prefer to substitute the words "value-system" for "meta-religion."

Whether one calls it a meta-religion, meta-value-system or meta-humanism, it is the same thing. It is a recognition that humans are naturally drawn to the good, we naturally love what is good for us, and it is virtues like wisdom, peace and love that are truly good for us.

CHAPTER TWO
THE GREATEST GOOD IS GOD

*The affections of the supreme degree are named divine and super-
natural because God himself spreads them abroad in our spirits, and
because they regard God and aim at him, without the medium of any
reasoning, or any light of nature. 4*

*These supernatural affections are principally three: the love of the
mind for the beautiful in the mysteries of faith, love for the useful in the
goods which are promised us in the other life, and love for the sovereign
good of the most holy and eternal divinity. 5*

*Divine love is indeed the last begotten of all the affections of man's
heart, for as the Apostle says: That which is animal is first; afterwards
that which is spiritual – but this last born inherits all the authority, and
self-love, as another Esau is deputed to his service; and not only all the
other motions of the soul as his brethren adore him and are subject to
him, but also the understanding and will which are to him as father
and mother. All is subject to this heavenly love, who will either be king
or nothing. 6*

*Divine love is a child of miracle, since man's will cannot conceive it if
it be not poured into our hearts by the Holy Ghost. And as supernatural
it must reign over all the affections, yea, even over the understanding
and will. 7*

*Ah! What a union of our hearts shall there be with God there above
in heaven, where, after these infinite desires of the true good never as-
suaged in this world, we shall find the living and powerful source thereof. 8*

So our soul panting with an extreme thirst for the true good, when she shall find that inexhaustible source in the Divinity, – O good God! what a holy and sweet ardour to be united and joined to the plentiful breasts of the All-goodness, either to be altogether absorbed in it, or to have it come entirely into us! 9

Before we launch into this chapter, some things need to be clarified and explained. This explanation is necessary because the chapter (and indeed the rest of the book) contains many declarative statements about "God."

However, "God" is a loaded word for some people.

For some, it conveys images of an angry old man in the sky. Atheists refuse to believe in this God and most believers do not believe in this god either.

Some may conceive of God as the "Great Spirit," "Absolute Bliss Consciousness," the "Ultimate Holy Mystery," the "Higher Power," the "Ground of Being," the "Depth Dimension of All Things," the "Eternal Now," or whatever else is meaningful to them.

Reference to "God" in this book means all these possible dimensions and more, but for the sake of conciseness and consistency the word "God" will be used as shorthand.

Also, the declarative statements about God that follow are made *as if we know all these things for sure about God.* However, they are really *faith statements about God.*

As St. Augustine wrote "Faith is to believe what you do not see; the reward of this faith is to see what you believe." And as scripture says: "We walk by faith, not by sight" (2 Corinthians 5:7); the things of the Spirit are "spiritually discerned" (I Corinthians 2:14) and "faith is the assurance of things hoped for, the conviction of things not seen" (Hebrews 11:1).

Thus, *believers do not know for sure* any of these statements about God, but they *believe* them because they *spiritually discern them to be true.* The statements just make spiritual sense: if there is a God, this is what God must be like, or at least, this is what a *healthy discernment* of God tells us what God must be like.

In the life of faith, there are "converging probabilities," that is, if you believe God is loving and forgiving, it is probable therefore that God is also patient and personal. These are faith-based extrapolations about what God is like.

God is ultimately mystery, but believers have made faith statements about God throughout history. There have been distorted views of God at times down through the ages, but Francis de Sales is offering us his *healthy discernment* of what God must be like.

Hopefully, this is enough clarification that we can now speak freely about de Sales' view of God.

The virtues that we discussed in the previous chapter, and that we recognized as our true good, are what God is.

Christians are fond of saying "God is love," but God is also the virtues of wisdom, peace, joy, patience, kindness, generosity, forgiveness, humility, justice and so on.

God is all these virtues to the maximum. God is unimaginably holy, true, beautiful, creative, free, trustworthy, merciful, kind, personal, joyful, healing, life-giving, helpful, understanding, faithful, comforting, gentle and non-violent as well as loving.

God is the greatest never-ending good. God is thus infinitely lovable. We should love God before all things.

However, there are still higher forms of loving God than just loving God before all things. Loving God before all things simply means that we make God our absolutely number one priority. We value God and place God before all things. However, a higher form of loving God is to love God in all things and all things in God.

God is in all things, so, while loving God *before* all these things, we also love God *in* all these things. We highly value all these things, not more than God, but because we see God in them all. Everything is a facet of the face of God, and we keep seeing new aspects of God by contemplating all these things. We learn more and more about God and fall deeper and deeper in love with God by contemplating all God's faces. Just as a lover cannot get enough of contemplating his or her beloved's face, so the devout cannot get enough of seeing God's infinite faces.

Why would anyone love anything before God? God literally and irrevocably has it all. All the galaxies, stars and planets belong to God. In 2017, scientists estimated that there may be as many as two trillion galaxies and we now know there are hundreds of billions of stars in most galaxies, and that on average each star has six planets spinning around it. Then there are the moons of these planets. In just one solar system, our own, Jupiter has 67 and Saturn has 62 confirmed moons.

The point is that God has created all of this—all galaxies, stars, planets, and moons. And in God's generosity, God gives them all to each of us. As St. Chrysostom wrote "God asks little of us but gives us everything."

Our true inheritance is not some piece of earthly real estate or thousands of dollars given to us by our parents. Our true inheritance, if we have eyes to see it, is the unlimited, never-ending wealth of the entire universe we receive from God.

Beyond anything material, God is our true inheritance (Deuteronomy 10:9). And God is an inheritance that will never pass away and is given to all of us fully and equally, so there can be no sibling rivalry over who gets the bigger share of the inheritance!

Why would anyone love anything before God? Everything else is passing away—galaxies, stars, and civilizations all had a beginning and eventually will end. They may be replaced by others, but only God is permanent, reliable and the Eternal Rock as scripture says, the everlasting foundation of all things (I Corinthians 3:11).

God is the only steadfast reality. Everything else has merely relative reality because it is passing away. And even this relative reality is given to things by God's grace.

God is the source, sustenance, and goal of all things. Our only purpose as human beings, our one true goal, is to become divinized, that is, to become filled with God (Ephesians 1:23, 5:18). We cannot be filled with God unless God loves us, and God does love us with an infinite love. So, why would we love anything more than God?

God is infinitely creative and beautiful. God's beauty and creativity come to us through mountains, waterfalls, goldfinches, peacocks, kangaroos, leaping dolphins, shimmering tropical fish, and the danc-ing ghosts of the aurora borealis.

God's creativity goes particularly wild with insects: fireflies, hon-eybees, iridescent butterflies, stick and stink bugs, thousands of types of ants.

God's power is displayed through hurricanes, tornadoes, earth-quakes, volcanoes, lightning and thunder, tsunamis, and through sun flares that burst forth for millions of miles.

Everything was created by God to induce awe and wonder in us mere mortals.

There is the awesomeness of human conception, pregnancy and birth from a totally cramped, dark and silent place in the womb into a world full of light and sound, the love of smiling parents and a mother's breast to suck on, feed and comfort us.

Just as a child in the womb cannot possibly imagine the world of wonders it is about to be born into, so adult human beings cannot fully imagine the even greater wonders they will be born into in the afterlife.

God created the ongoing wonders of human development, from the zygote to the baby to the child to the agonies of adolescence, to the power and competence of young adulthood, to the beauty of fall-ing in love, the passion of sexuality, the joy of creating a home and a family of one's own, the existential quandaries of mid-life, the decline of old age, the agonies of death and the glory of the afterlife.

God is the master of all these wonders, so why would anyone love anything more than God? Science can give us explanations of the mechanics, chemistry, biology and physics of how these wonders work, but it doesn't explain the poetry of them or why they exist in the first place.

On the one hand, our sense of wonder has been dulled by science's explanations, and so we have fallen asleep spiritually.

On the other hand, science keeps revealing new mysteries to us: quantum mechanics, relativity, quarks, bosons, the 'God particle' (which explains why all other particles have mass), dark matter and dark energy which compose 95% of the universe—the visible universe is only 5% of the matter and energy out there!

Science is simply a tool God uses to show us God's ever-expanding greatness, and God is the master of the whole evolutionary process. God's fiery desire to share infinite love with other creatures created the Big Bang, the cosmic fireball that became giant stars. These hypergiant stars then exploded and seeded all the elements of the periodic table into smaller stars which then joined together in galaxies.

Again, God's infinite love is driving the whole evolutionary process from matter (rocks and water) to life and sensitivity (plants and animals) to thought (humans) to spirit (the spread of the great religions across the globe).

God's infinite love is driving all of evolution to create creatures of higher and higher consciousness that are more and more capable of love.

Animals obviously love more than plants, and humans are capable of broader love than animals. A dog or horse may love its master, but a human can love not only her or his parents, but siblings, aunts and uncles, grandparents, friends, coworkers, and even people on the other side of the planet. God's goal is that each person be full of love (John 15:9-12).

Given that God wants each of us to be divinized, that is, to be completely full of God's love, to be fully alive; and that God is the creator, sustainer, and goal of all things; and that God is the giver of all things; the only permanent thing; the master of all mysteries and of the whole evolutionary process; and given that God loves us with an infinite love; that humans by their very nature are seekers of the good, and God is the absolute and infinite good, why would we love anything more than God?

CHAPTER THREE
THE NINETY-NINE NAMES OF GOD

Our relationship with God is a relationship unlike any other. Most relationships are mainly one-dimensional: the other person is our spouse, friend, father, mother, son, daughter, teacher, doctor or co-worker.

Muslims regularly recite the ninety-nine names of Allah. Similarly, the God of Jews and Christians has a multifaceted relationship with us. To illustrate this, here are ninety-nine names of God from just a few of the Psalms (in order of appearance):

Watcher over Us (Ps. 1:6)
Awe-Inspiring One (Ps. 2:11)
Bestower of Blessings (Ps. 2:12)
Restorer of Courage (Ps. 3:3)
Our True Hero (Ps. 3:8)
Our Champion Defender (Ps. 4:1)
Wonder Worker (Ps. 4:3)
Despiser of Violence (Ps. 5:6)
Welcomer (Ps. 6:9)
Our Perfect Hiding Place (Ps. 7:1)
Soul-Searcher (Ps. 7:9)
Fascinating Artist (Ps. 8:3)
Vindicator (Ps. 9:4)
Righteous Judge (Ps. 9:7)
Fulfiller of Hope (Ps. 9:18)

Helper of the Fatherless (Ps. 10:14)
Comforter of the Humble (Ps. 10:17)
Eternal Lord (Ps. 11:4)
Strengthener of Souls (Ps. 13:6)
Our Safe Place (Ps. 16:1)
Maker, Mediator and Master (Ps. 16:2)
Our Prize and Portion (Ps. 16:5)
Our Inheritance (Ps. 16:6)
Our Counsellor (Ps. 16:7)
Giver of Wisdom (Ps. 16:7)
Listener to Every Prayer (Ps. 17:6)
Our Power (Ps. 18:1)
Our Bedrock and Fortress (Ps. 18:2)
Our Pathway of Escape (Ps. 18:2)
Salvation's Bright Ray (Ps. 18:2)
The Deliverer (Ps. 18:6)
Revelation's Light (Ps. 18:28)
Our Secure Shelter (Ps. 18:30)
Wrap-Around Presence (Ps. 18:30)
Empowering One (Ps. 18:35)
Our Forever Lover (Ps. 21:7)
Faithful One (Ps. 22:5)
Our First Responder (Ps. 22:24)
Best Friend and Shepherd (Ps. 23:1)
Restorer and Reviver of Life (Ps. 23:2)
Spirit-Anointer (Ps. 23:5)
King of Glory (Ps. 24:8)
Lord of Victory (Ps. 24:10)
Invincible Commander (Ps. 24:10)
Giver of Grace (Ps. 25:6)
Our Bodyguard (Ps. 25:21)
Salvation's Source (Ps. 27:1)
Our Strength and Shield (Ps. 28:7)
Mighty Protector of All (Ps. 28:8)
Our Healing God (Ps. 30:2)

Our Stronghold (Ps. 31:3)

God of Faithfulness (Ps. 31:3)

Our Rock of Strength (Ps. 31:4)

Our Treasure Chest (Ps. 31:19)

Remover of Hypocrisy (Ps. 32:2)

Life-Giving God (Ps. 32:5)

Our Adviser and Guide (Ps. 32:8)

Promise-Keeper (Ps. 33:4)

Spirit-Wind (Ps. 33:6)

Galaxy-Creator (Ps. 33:6)

Our Radiant Hope (Ps. 33:20)

Deliverer from Fear (Ps. 34:4)

God of Joyous Mercies (Ps. 34:8)

Opposer of Evildoers (Ps. 34:16)

Our Spiritual Director (Ps. 37:5)

Bringer of Prosperity (Ps. 37:37)

God of Kindness (Ps. 40:10)

God of Compassion (Ps. 40:11)

Great and Glorious (Ps. 40:14)

The Living God (Ps. 42:2)

Our Mountain (Ps. 42:8)

Unfailing Love (Ps. 44:26)

Our Safe Refuge (Ps. 46:1)

Our Helper in Trouble (Ps. 46:1)

Bringer of Joy and Delight (Ps. 46:4)

Lord of Angel-Armies (Ps. 46:7)

God Over All Nations (Ps. 46:10)

Astonishing One (Ps. 47:2)

The Enlightened One (Ps. 47:7)

Our Forever-God (Ps. 48:14)

Our Bridegroom (Ps. 49:15)

God over all Gods (Ps. 50:1)

Wisdom-Teacher (Ps. 50:6)

Fountain of Forgiveness (Ps. 51:1)

The Sweet One (Ps. 51:8)

Fountain of Pleasure (Ps. 51:17)
Loyal Lover (Ps. 52:1)
Divine Helper (Ps. 54:4)
Rescuer from All Trouble (Ps. 54:7)
The Unchanging One (Ps. 55:19)
Measureless Grace (Ps. 55:22)
God of Mercy (Ps. 56:1)
Collector of Tears (Ps. 56:8)
Life-Giving Light (Ps. 56:13)
Grace-Fountain (Ps. 57:1)
Constant Caregiver (Ps. 57:3)
Extravagant Lover (Ps. 57:10)
Our Savior-Hero (Ps. 62:7)
Banquet of Soul-Pleasure (Ps. 64:5)
Confidence of All (Ps. 65:5)
Steadfast Lover (Ps. 66:20)

These ninety-nine names of God remind us of just how incomparably glorious and loving God is. There are many more names throughout the Jewish and Christian scriptures.

If we take a few minutes to contemplate just these ninety-nine holy names, and drink them in, it is obvious that God loves us with immeasurable love and we have to ask again, why would anyone love anything more than God?

CHAPTER FOUR

GOD IS MORE LOVABLE THAN ANYTHING BECAUSE GOD IS MORE LOVING THAN ANYTHING

The great Solomon describes, in an admirably delicious manner, the loves of the Saviour and the devout soul, in that divine work which for its excellent sweetness is named the Canticle of Canticles. And to raise ourselves by a more easy flight to the consideration of this spiritual love which is exercised between God and us by the correspondence of the movements of our hearts with the inspirations of his divine majesty, he makes use of a perpetual representation of the loves of a chaste shepherd and a modest shepherdess. 10

As soon as man thinks with even a little attention of the divinity, he feels a certain delightful emotion of the heart, which testifies that God is God of the human heart; and our understanding is never so filled with pleasure as in this thought of the divinity. 11

God has himself planted in man's heart a special natural inclination not only to love good in general but to love in particular and above all things his divine goodness which is better and sweeter than all things. 12

This love of which we speak would only tend to God as acknowledged to be author, lord and sovereign of every creature by natural light only, and consequently to be amiable and estimable above all things by natural inclination and tendency. 13

Still the holy inclination to love God above all things stays with us, as also the natural light by which we see his sovereign goodness to be more worthy of love than all things. 14

God's love is constantly all around us, but most of us have not been aware of it. We have been sleepwalking through God's love our whole lives.

If we believe, as Richard Rohr asserts in his book, *The Universal Christ*, that Christ is incarnate in the whole universe and is infinitely loving, then God's infinite love is in, and comes to us through, every created thing.

This idea, that God's love is mediated to us through all things, requires nothing less than a paradigm shift in our thinking. This is completely opposite to the notion that God is somewhere "out there."

God does indeed transcend us but in terms of greatness, not distance. Since God's transcendence has been over-emphasized in Christianity to the point where God's immanence is rarely mentioned or even thought of, it is important, if we are going to love God, to reflect for a minute on what God's immanence could mean.

The following is an extended example of the needed paradigm shift, with a few caveats. First of all, it may seem like a confusion of human and divine activity or even pantheism, but the point is to convey God's total intimacy with us.

Also, the examples given are idealized. This needs to be stressed. If life was ideal, this is the way things might be. The world we actually live in is a lot messier than what is portrayed here—there are broken marriages, families, workplaces, politics and religions where God's immanent love is not readily apparent.

However, God is immanent in the bad times, the hard times too. The cross of Christ is the great sign that God suffers with us in all the messiness of human reality.

However again, if we all were more aware of and consoled by God's immense and immanent love, imbibed it and lived out of it, perhaps this is how things would be. But again, this is an idealization, and may not even be possible given the propensity that we all have to be unloving and do unloving things.

To make this more personal and give you more of a sense of the power of the mind-shift needed, "you" and "your" will be used here instead of "we" and "our."

If God's love is mediated to you through the creation in all its aspects, then God was in your mother, God conceived you through your mother, God carried you in your mother's womb for nine months, then God gave birth to you.

God's love was more than willing to go through the anguish of childbirth for you, and God rejoiced with unspeakable joy at your birth. God was delighted to breastfeed you and to cuddle you for hours and hours.

God loved you through your father's love and his tears of joy, and God rocked you in his arms and constantly clucked and cooed to you.

God's love took you into God's home and watched over you and protected you every minute as you grew up. God loved you through your siblings, if you had any. Through your sister(s) and brother(s), God tickled you and laughed because you were hilarious.

Through your family, God played with you, fed you, and taught you to walk and talk.

God loved you through that special childhood friend, your favorite friend who you so closely bonded with. God shared intimate stories with you and played a hundred children's games with you.

God loved you through your favorite pet, your dog that was so happy to see you when you got home, or through your cat who liked to lie in your lap and purr as you stroked it. God barked in excitement, purred in contentment, and sang for you through the birds when you went outside.

God's love was all around you though you did not know it. God healed your body through your doctor when you became ill, and God taught your mind through your teachers.

God gave you the universe to explore as an infinite gift of love to you. God loved you by giving you five senses so you could see, hear, taste, smell and touch everything. And God loved you through these same senses that warned you of impending danger.

God loved you and still loves you through implanting in you a constant desire to make your life better and better. And God loved you through giving you your will, imagination, memory, rational faculties, intuition and wisdom so you could constantly improve your life. God loved you at all times by leading you from within your mind so that you could see opportunities for your growth.

God's love opened some doors and closed others. God's love for you was at times tough love. Out of love, God allowed you to go through some hard times of failure, unemployment, illness, divorce, brokenness, addiction or betrayal so you would wake up to the sufferings of others and become more humble, wise and compassionate.

God loved you through civilization—everyone working together to make a safer and more fulfilling society. God loved you through governments which created laws that protect you. God also protected you through police, firefighters and soldiers. God loved you through businesses that create jobs, better houses, cars and clothes for you.

God loved you through artists, musicians and authors. God made movies for you, danced for you and danced with you, wrote novels and plays for you. God loved you through all the movies and plays you've seen and all the books and magazines you've read.

God created beautiful buildings for you through architects and built safe roads and bridges for you through engineers.

Through your spouse God lived with you, had deep conversations with you, cooked hundreds of delicious meals for you, and planned your children's education and future with you. God's love did housework for you.

According to Pope John Paul II's theology of the body, God is present to you in your sexuality. To build on this idea, it can be said that God made love to you through your partner. God kissed you, massaged you, stroked and rubbed you, and brought you to climax, and cuddled with you as you bathed in the afterglow following orgasm.

God loved you through introducing you to God's Word, the Bible. God caused your heart to be on fire when you first read the Holy Scriptures. God loved you through your church. God was your pastor, preached sermons to you, and prayed for you through your priest or minister, and through the congregation. God gave you the sacraments.

To sum up this example of the required paradigm shift we need to make in our thinking if we are going to fully love God, God is infinitely more lovable than anything because God is infinitely more loving than anything: God has loved you, continues to love you, and will always love you in thousands of different ways, if you have the eyes to see it.

CHAPTER FIVE

THE ROLE OF FREE WILL IN LOVING OR REJECTING GOD

As it would be an impious effrontery to attribute the works of holy love done by the Holy Ghost in and with us to the strength of our will, it would be a shameless impiety to lay the defect of love in ungrateful men, on the failure of heavenly assistance and grace. For the Holy Ghost cries everywhere, on the contrary, that our ruin is from ourselves: Destruction is thine, O Israel! Thy help is only in me: that our Saviour brought the fire of love, and desires nothing but that it should be enkindled in our hearts...that the divine goodness is not willing that any should perish, but that all should come to the knowledge of the truth: and will have all men to be saved. 15

God never abandons such as he once justified unless they abandon him first; so that, if they be not wanting to grace they shall obtain to glory. 16

If humans naturally love the good, and the greatest good is God, and God loves us in thousands of ways, why do we not all love God with all our heart?

The simplest explanation is that God did not want us to be robots whose programming made it impossible to not love God. True love is not programmed or forced love.

Love is more a choice or a decision than a feeling. This is a revolutionary idea since most cultures continually pump into people the idea that love is primarily a feeling, not a decision.

This revolutionary idea is particularly true in marriage since, inevitably, there will be times when a married person does not feel loving towards their spouse. However, they can still decide to do loving things to their partner. Love is really "to will the good of the other," regardless of how you are feeling. Love is more a commitment to be faithful than an emotion. And emotion follows motion. Once you start to make loving gestures, the feelings start to return.

If our love for God was only due to our programming, if the desire to love God above all things was simply something God planted in our soul and we had no choice in the matter, it would not be true love. Love and God must be chosen and willed.

We naturally go towards the good, but love is still a choice. We can choose to go against the good, or our perception of what is good for us can be wrong. Our ego can get in the way and we can choose to do what is objectively not good for us. To paraphrase the apostle Paul "I don't do what I should do, and I do what I should not do."

Our will governs the other major faculties of the soul, that is, our reason (or intellect), our emotions and our body.

The higher faculties of the soul are will and intellect, but often will dominates reason. It is possible to present a person with all the reasons in the world why there is a God and they will still choose not to believe, if that is what they want.

In the same way, you can present an entirely forceful argument for why there is no God and people will still keep believing if that is what they have chosen to do.

Some philosophers believe that, in general, people decide what they want and then use their intellect to find reasons to justify what they want.

The will also controls our emotions. We can choose to feel peace or anger, joy or sadness, confidence or fear, pride or shame, hope or despair, enthusiasm or boredom.

It does not matter what happens to us as much as what we choose to think about what happens to us. People disabled with various illnesses are often far happier than fully able-bodied people, just as poor people frequently are more joyful than the rich.

Disability and poverty can lead a person to see through the vacuity of our materialistic world, so they operate out of gratitude not greed.

Through using our will, we can choose to love temporal goods and make them our god even though we know they are passing away, or we can choose to love the higher things in life such as wisdom, spirituality, truth and ultimately God. Love of transient goods can totally disorder one's love for eternal things and the divine order.

Will also governs our body. It obviously controls our voluntary physical movements such as our jaw when we are talking and our legs when we run. And although it cannot totally control our involuntary bodily functions such as the desire for food or sex, it can put reins on them so that we do not engage in gluttony or promiscuity.

Love, intellect and will interact with each other. Love draws us to what appears to be good, intellect decides if what we are drawn to is truly good or not, while will pursues it or rejects it and then finds reasons to justify its actions.

Our soul has inferior and superior parts: the sensual and the rational. The soul itself is spiritual but can be motivated by the will in an inferior or superior way. When the will loves through the senses alone, the soul's love can be brutish and animalistic. When the will loves through reason and intellect alone, the soul's love can be spiritual and angelic. The key is to integrate all this so the soul and will permeate all aspects of our being: body, mind and spirit. After all, God created us as whole, unified and complete beings. We are not disembodied spirits or spirits trapped in a body that is not really part of who we are.

There is as well an inferior and superior will which can be seen in Jesus and Abraham. Jesus says, when faced with crucifixion, "Not my (inferior) will but thy (superior) will be done."

Similarly, Abraham surrenders to what seems to be God's will—the sacrifice of his son Isaac—rather than submitting to his own inferior will—the safety of Isaac.

In both cases great faith was required. Faith leads us, hope sustains us and charity (divine love) completes our journey home (I Corinthians 13:13).

And even in charity there is an inferior and superior part. Complacence, the inferior part of divine love, loves God for God's benefits to the lover. Benevolence, the superior part, loves God solely for God alone. Benevolence starts in complacence, but it does not end there.

In both complacence and benevolence, the love of God is a supernatural gift given to us by God, we cannot simply will either of them. However, once we taste divine love, we never forget it and it dominates all other faculties of the soul including will and intellect, in both their inferior and superior parts.

Love of God begins with complacence—the Holy Spirit working within our soul wakes it up to God's presence and enlivens it. The soul cries out "Oh my! This is what I have really longed for all along— the Absolute Good, my Lord and my God!"

Complacence is the first spreading of the wings of the soul, but it is the wind of the Holy Spirit that gives the soul flight. True love is always about Spirit gently bringing about the union of our heart, mind and will with God and God's purposes.

CHAPTER SIX
THE NECESSITY OF GOD'S GRACE

Eagles have a great heart, and much strength of flight, yet they have incomparably more sight than flight, and extend their vision much quicker and further than their wings. So, our souls animated with a holy natural inclination towards the divinity, have far more light in the understanding to see how lovable it is than force in the will to love it. Sin has much more weakened man's will than darkened his intellect. 17

For so our human heart naturally produces certain beginnings of God's love, but to proceed so far as to love him above all things, which is the true ripeness of the love due unto this supreme goodness, - this belongs only to hearts animated and assisted with heavenly grace, and which are in the state of holy charity. 18

We love God because of the affinity of our soul with God. We are similar to God in our soul, but not the same. God and our soul are both spiritual, have virtues, reason and can understand things.

However, in other ways, the two are polar opposites. God is omnipotent, omniscient and eternal. The soul, by itself, if we include the body as an integral part of the soul, as de Sales does, is frail, ignorant and created at some point.

So, love takes place by similarity not sameness. It is similarity not sameness that draws a man and woman to love each other, and similarity not sameness that causes us to love God.

We cannot love God without God's grace. This grace first takes place with God planting in our hearts the desire to love God above all things. This desire is just latently there. We are not programmed or forced to act upon it, we can always reject God's grace. But again, humans are naturally drawn to the good, and the ultimate good is God. By this desire God draws us to God.

We are also drawn by God's grace to self-fulfilment. Everyone, if they have not been damaged by life, wants to be all they can be—their truest, most authentic self.

When the Holy Spirit by grace awakens our soul to the presence of God, we begin to intuit that, if we can become joined and united with God, then we will be all that we can be and more—there will be infinite growth in power, knowledge and love forever. When we wake up to God, we wake up to who we really can be—our true self.

While we desire to fulfill who we really are through fully loving God, we also discover that we cannot do it. We have the capacity to love God with all our heart, but we do not have the capability: our intellect is darkened by ignorance. In order to love something, we need to know it. We cannot love something if we know nothing about it. To love something fully, we must know it fully.

Ah, but there's the rub: God is the Ultimate Mystery, the All-Glorious, the Creator of billions of galaxies. Our minds at best can only know the tiniest fraction of God.

Even Thomas Aquinas, the greatest mind in the medieval church, had to stop writing once he was given a clear insight into the unspeakable glory of God. Aquinas was the author of the *Summa Theologica* written between 1265 and 1274 which summed up all theological knowledge until then. Subsequently he declared after a vision of God "All my works are straw."

Even worse than being unable to look at God except, as Paul noted, "through a glass darkly," our will is wounded by sin. As Paul also noted: "I do not understand my own actions. For I do not do what I want, but I do the very thing I hate...I can will what is right, but I cannot do it. For I do not do the good I want, but the evil I do not want is what I do. Now if I do what I do not want, it is no longer I that do it, but sin that dwells within me...with my mind I am a slave to the law of God, but with my flesh I am a slave to the law of sin" (Romans 7:15-25).

Throughout history people have been slaughtering other people, if not outrightly by genocide, then in their hearts by hatred, racism and injustice. The denigration of women through sexual abuse fueled by pornography is at epidemic levels in modern life. In fact, our lack of sexual integrity as a society has been referred to by some sociologists as "rape culture."

In any case, all of us in the western world are seduced by the capitalist ethos of "I produce and consume therefore I am," and so we have raped the planet. In our lust for pleasure, profits and possessions, we have overmined the land, overfished the seas, filled the sky with too many planes, the roads with too many cars and we have cut down old growth forests and Amazon rain forests.

Counselors know how many human hearts are infected with lust, envy, greed, anger, deceit, fear and gluttony resulting in addiction to alcohol, drugs, money, food or sex.

The seven deadly sins are still alive and well despite all our science, education and enlightenment. The ego is fully in charge in a civilization telling us that self-actualization, that is, fulfillment of all our needs and desires, is the ultimate purpose of life, and we can do it all without God.

Although we have the potential to love God fully, because of our darkened intellect and our seduced will, none of us can do it by our own power. We need the grace of God to fulfill our longing to love God above all things. We are limited, tied, bound and corrupt. So, God has to take the initiative in liberating us.

We are naturally drawn to the good and to God and "our hearts are restless until they rest in God" as Augustine said. All this is God's grace before we even have faith—this is "prevenient faith"—but our ego gets in the way and draws us off course. And so we need God's further grace to turn back to God.

Book Two

The Generation of Divine Love

Chapter One

Plan A: Incarnation
Plan B: Redemption

All God's works are ordained to the salvation of men and angels. 19

Now of all creatures which that sovereign omnipotence could produce, he thought good to make choice of the same humanity which afterwards in effect was united to the person of God the Son; to which he destined that incomparable honour of personal union with his divine Majesty, to the end that for all eternity it might enjoy by excellence the treasures of his infinite glory. 20

He also clearly foresaw that the first man would abuse his liberty and forsaking grace would lose glory. 21

But in order that the sweetness of his mercy might be adorned with the beauty of his justice, he determined to save man by way of a rigorous redemption. And this could not properly be done but by his Son. 22

He willed that thus he should make himself the companion of our miseries to make us afterwards companions of his glory, showing thereby the riches of his goodness, by this copious, abundant, superabundant, magnificent and excessive redemption, which has gained for us, and as it were reconquered for us, all the means necessary to attain glory, so that no man can ever complain as though the divine mercy were wanting to anyone. 23

Thomas Aquinas wrote that it is of the essence of goodness to communicate itself to others. And the essence of the highest good is to communicate itself to others in the highest way.

This is why God became incarnate as a human being. This was Plan A. God is the highest good and planned to become human from the start. Before the Big Bang and the creation of all things, God planned to become human to show us how to be fully alive.

God did not become a human being in the birth of Jesus as an afterthought because we sinned. God was not caught by surprise by our sin and then decided the only way to save us was to send God's Son to become one of us and take all our sins upon himself on the cross.

God did not first of all become one of us in order to die for our sins. That was Plan B. God planned to become human right from the start in order to show us how loving God is and how we can become fully loving human beings.

As many saints and mystics have written "God became human so that humans could become God." Not that we actually become God, which is impossible, but that we open up our hearts fully to God and become more and more Christ-like.

We have been made in the image and likeness of God; but while we have retained the image of God, the "imago dei" within us, we have lost the likeness of God through sinful behavior. God became human because God knew that on our own, we would not know what a fully alive, sinless human being would be like and what God was really like. We needed Jesus to show us these things.

We would need more than the Ten Commandments, we would need the walking, talking visual aid called Jesus of Nazareth to demonstrate how to do it.

Also, as Richard Rohr repeatedly says: "God did not become human to change God's mind about us, God became human to change our mind about God." In other words, God already loves us before we do anything. We don't have to earn God's already-given love.

As part of losing the likeness of God, humans had become fearful about God. In pagan circles, God was seen as Jupiter, a god of wrath throwing lightning bolts, or as Mars, a god of war. Humans needed to know that when they saw the nonviolent Jesus, they were seeing the real, authentic God.

One of the rare times Jesus displayed any wrath was when he cleared the moneychangers out of the temple. Jesus was disgusted that the temple, originally meant to be a place for prayer, fasting and almsgiving, had been turned into a marketplace of financial transactions.

God became incarnate as Jesus of Nazareth in order to show us how to be fully open to God. Jesus was human like us, but his uniqueness lay in always trusting in his complete union with God, whereas we doubt our complete union.

Jesus came to show us how to love God fully, and also how loving God is, by taking his love all the way: "No one has greater love than this, to lay down one's life for one's friends" (John 15:13).

Plan A was God becoming incarnate to divinize us, to show us how to be fully united with God. Indeed, to show us we already are fully united with God, we just need to wake up to it. God planned from the very beginning to merge the divine and human so both could fully understand each other.

God had already supplied all our material needs by creating the universe, our true inheritance. But when the time was right God wanted to supply all our spiritual needs by becoming human. Not that God had not started to fulfill our spiritual needs. God had already done that through Judaism and the law. But now God wanted to complete God's work. As Jesus said: "Do not think that I have come to abolish the law or the prophets; I have come not to abolish but to fulfill" (Matthew 5:17).

God had created a covenant with Abraham and then gave his people the law to keep them close to God. But when the law failed to do that, God sent the prophets. And when the prophets failed to turn peoples' hearts back to God, God sent Jesus.

God's providence supplies all things: both our material and spiritual needs. God created angels and humans to praise God forever, not for God's self but because praising God is the best thing for both angels and humans.

However, God knew beforehand that some angels and humans, having free will, could choose to rebel against God and therefore could need redemption.

Plan A was to become human to show us how much God loves us and how to be fully alive, and Plan B was to show us the full depth of God's mercy and the full range of God's superabundant providence by giving us salvation from our sins, mediated to us through the self-sacrificing love of God's Son, Jesus the universal Christ incarnate.

God has given us both abundant love and abundant redemption through Jesus Christ.

CHAPTER TWO

ALL OF CREATION IS FOR AND BY THE UNIVERSAL CHRIST

The sovereign Providence, making his eternal purpose and design of all that he would produce, first willed and preferred by excellence the most amiable object of his love which is our Saviour; and then other creatures in order, according as they more or less belong to the service, honour, and glory of him. 24

Thus were all things made for the divine man, who for this cause is called the first-born of every creature: possessed by the divine majesty in the beginning of his ways, before he made anything from the beginning. 25

It is important to grasp that the central doctrine of Christianity, the Trinity, was not an idea early Christians dreamed up. The doctrine of one God in three Persons was based mainly on lived experience, not logic or philosophy.

From their lived experience of the wonderfulness of the created world, ancient Jews came to believe there was one supreme God who created all things. There were also numerous prophecies of various kinds in the Jewish scriptures, some saying that God is going to become human, others that a great messiah is coming, and still others that the messiah will be a suffering servant.

Some Jews of two thousand years ago experienced Jesus fulfilling all these prophecies. Jesus was so extraordinary, curing all kinds of illnesses both physical and mental, raising dead people back to life, feeding thousands of people with a few loaves of bread and a few fish, calming the raging sea by his command, that they began to ponder that perhaps this was their God in human form.

After the death of Jesus, through the lived experience of him rising from death to life, living among them and finally ascending into heaven, the disciples of Jesus experienced an immense and powerful Spirit guiding them in everything they did.

It took a few centuries for the church to formulate all these lived experiences into the doctrine that the Creator of all things, and the fully human, fully divine, fully incarnate God, Jesus, and the immense and powerful Spirit (who they named the Father, Son, and Holy Spirit) were all the same God.

The point is not to get stuck on these names but rather that Christians have experienced the one God acting in three distinct ways in biblical times and throughout history.

Christians refer to the Father, Son and Holy Spirit with a collective name, that is, as the "Trinity" or "Three Persons in One God."

Some well-known Catholic theologians, such as Richard Rohr, now refer to the second person of the Trinity, the Son, as the Universal Christ. This Universal Christ first became incarnate in a general way in the universe and then became incarnate in a special way in Jesus of Nazareth.

After rising from the dead, Jesus of Nazareth and the Universal Christ were united in a new way, so that Jesus the Christ was now everywhere in the universe. Jesus himself said "I will be with you always, until the end of time," and three times in Revelation, the last book of the Bible, Jesus said "I am the Alpha and the Omega," the beginning and the end of all things.

The implication of this for Christians is that Jesus is bigger than the church and Christianity. The creation, the universe, is the true Body of Christ, far greater than any church. God as Jesus the Universal Christ is everywhere, as are God the Father and God the Holy Spirit. Because the Trinity of Father, Son and Holy Spirit are everywhere, there is no need for Christians to fear anything or anyone.

Christians can find the face of Jesus the Christ in all things, not just the Bible, the church, or even Christianity in general. Jesus Christ is in science, in secular human rights movements struggling for justice for all, in nature, evolution, Judaism, Islam, Buddhism, Hinduism, and in the latest theories and discoveries of physics, astronomy, biology, psychology, and philosophy. The lived experience of Christians is that they can find the one God, Jesus the Christ, in the whole world.

Also, according to scripture, everything has been made by and for and through the Universal Christ who is also called the "Word of God" in John's gospel:

"In the beginning was the Word, and the Word was with God, and the Word was God. He was in the beginning with God. All things came into being through him, and without him not one thing came into being…And the Word became flesh and lived among us, and we have seen his glory, the glory as of a father's only son, full of grace and truth…No one has ever seen God. It is God the only Son, who is close to the Father's heart, who has made him known" (John 1:1-3, 14, 18).

Again, we read "Christ is the image of the invisible God…for in him all things in heaven and earth were created, things visible and invisible…all things have been created through him and for him. He himself is before all things, and in him all things hold together" (Colossians 1:15-17).

All things, including us humans, were made by and for the Universal Christ. Since the Universal Christ made us, God loves us with an absolute love and wants us to be with him forever.

Adam and Eve loved God with all their heart as their highest good, but that love for God was broken when they disobeyed God and ate the forbidden fruit God had commanded them not to eat.

The relationship between God and humans was broken and can only be restored if we turn towards God and love God again. We cannot be with Jesus the Universal Christ forever if, of our own free will, we choose not to love him.

Jesus the Christ's mercy far outweighs the sin of humans, but still

Christ desperately wants us to freely give ourselves to him, not for himself, but because he knows that to love God is the best thing possible for us.

Our eternal life with Christ, or our eternal death without him, rises and falls on our decision to love him or not. Therefore, because Christ loves us so much, he *commands* us to love God. When one of the scribes asked him "What is the greatest commandment?" Jesus said: "You shall love the Lord your God with all your heart, and with all your soul, and with all your mind, and with all your strength" (Mark 12:30).

Normally we would say that we cannot command someone to love us, we can only invite them to do so. Love cannot be forced, or it is not love. This is true on the human-to-human level.

However, our eternal destiny, to be with or without God forever, is not dependent on human love. Christ as our Creator has the right to *command* that we love him; then we must figure out how, *of our own free will*, we can totally love him.

Christ here is like Moses, who after laying the whole law before the people of God, shouted "I have set before you life and death . . . Choose life!" (Deuteronomy 30:19). Moses commanded the people to choose life, that is, to follow the law, not for his sake, but because it was a matter of life or death for them. If they obeyed God's Ten Commandments, they would live and thrive, if not, they would perish.

It is only because Christ loves us so much and wants what is absolutely best for us, that we are *commanded* to love God with all our heart.

CHAPTER THREE
ALL IS BY GRACE

God indeed shows to admiration the incomprehensible riches of his power in this great variety of things which we see in nature, yet he makes the infinite treasures of his goodness still more magnificently appear in the incomparable variety of the goods which we acknowledge in grace. 26

The sovereign goodness poured an abundance of graces and benedictions over the whole race of mankind. 27

God, in the form of Jesus the Universal Christ, commands us to love God with all our heart, soul, mind and strength, and to love others as we love our self (Matthew 22: 37-39).

Ah, but here again is the rub: we cannot be fully united with God without love, and since we are weighed down by our own wounds, created by our own folly or that of others, we cannot fully love God on our own.

We need help to fully love God. This help is abundantly available in the form of God's grace. So, let's examine in more depth how grace operates within us.

God will flood us with the grace of blessings and pleasures if we say the tiniest 'yes' to God's help. But God always leaves us free to accept or reject God's grace. God *commands* us to love God because it is so utterly important to do so, but God never *forces* us to do so.

The Holy Spirit works only by attraction, never by force. God never fails us, but we can fail God by refusing God's grace. However, God's grace includes all kinds of allurements God dangles before our imagination to tempt us to say 'yes.'

Even before we have faith, that is, trust in God, God is working in us, helping us to imagine that if we say 'yes' we will have greater health in our body, peace in our soul, better relationships with all those around us, far greater purpose and meaning in our life. God invites us to full life on Earth and gives us hope that we will have eternal life rather than eternal death.

So again, if we reject God it is due to our willfulness. If we accept God, it is through God's grace, through the Holy Spirit inviting and attracting us until we say "Yes, a thousand times, YES!!"

CHAPTER FOUR
HOW GOD DRAWS US

Love is the universal means of salvation. 28

The visible sun touches everything with its vivifying heat, and as the universal lover of inferior things, imparts to them the vigour requisite to produce, and even so the divine goodness animates all souls and encourages all hearts to its love. 29

God does not only give us a simple sufficiency of means to love him, and in loving him to save ourselves, but also a rich, simple and magnificent sufficiency, and as such as ought to be expected from so great a bounty as his. 30

It was not by the works of justice, which we have done, but according to his mercy he saved us, by that ancient, yea, eternal, charity which moved his divine Providence to draw us unto him...For if the Father had not drawn us we had never come to the Son, our Saviour, nor consequently to salvation. 31

God *draws* us with invitations, sweetness and gentle persuasion rather than *driving* us to say "yes" with violence, fear, threats or coercion.

How could it be any other way? If we believe that the highest and best human beings are loving and wise, and that God is infinitely greater than any human being in every way, how could we believe that God is violent?

God is unimaginably good, just, trustworthy, merciful, kind, peaceful, patient, healing, humble, helpful, gracious, understanding, comforting, and forgiving, so how could God be violent?

It is important to remember that the scriptures are the word of God, but they are written by human beings. The violent caricatures of God that sometimes occur in the Bible are due to the consciousness of the writers at that time.

It took Jesus to show us the true compassion, healing and sweetness of God and this is what drew the large crowds who followed him in his time on Earth. The desire of Jesus to show us what God is really like is also what led him to die on the cross rather than destroy his enemies.

Some Christians think that rational arguments are what draw people to God. However, it is not mainly reason that draws us to God, but rather glimpses the Holy Spirit gives us into the mysteries of faith. Reason is certainly important, but it is not everything.

My friend Leon grew up Catholic, went into religious studies at university, completed a PhD in Hinduism, and then decided that all religions are irrational nonsense.

When I visited him at his farm near Saskatoon in Saskatchewan, I didn't know that he had become a hardened atheist. He had completely shut his heart to God and made "Reason" his new god.

In several weekend-long debates over whether there is a God or not, in which my main argument was how amazing reality is, it all came down to one thing for Leon, that is, "Reality just happens to be this way."

I replied that "In my mind it is far more rational to believe there is a supreme, all-knowing, all-powerful, totally creative, totally free Intelligence that is behind all the wonders, complexity, lawfulness and beauty of the universe than to believe things just happen to be this way. It takes far more gullibility to believe this all just happened by chance than to believe there is a God. Belief in God is far more rational than atheism."

However, in spite of all my best rational arguments, I was not able to convince Leon. In fact, if anything, the debate just drove us both deeper into our own positions. This is because faith is more a matter of will than of reason. People decide what they want to believe and then find reasons to justify that belief.

Our intellects become convinced about the reality of God not so much by reason as by the Holy Spirit stirring our imagination to picture the possibility of a life of eternal meaning surrounded by saints, angels and faithful ancestors praying for us; a life on Earth lived in harmony and integrity with all other human beings; inner visions of peace and joy and the glory of God.

Faith, hope and love are all gifts of grace, all infused into our hearts, imaginations, will and longings by the Spirit that is at work within us before we even know it. "Prevenient grace" is a theological term which means that our will starts to become "complacent," that is, begins to be open to the will of God, even before we have faith. God leads us in all sorts of ways through people, music, art and the glories of nature; ways that our heart knows before we even consciously understand it.

Before that we are walking with our back towards the sun. It is through tasting, no matter how subtle, the sweetness of divine love, that turns our head around. As we sense the rays of the Holy One shining upon our face, shining through us, shining through our heart and soul, the cold will of unbelief starts to melt.

The dove of our spirit that was encased in ice begins to thaw and be freed. All we need to do on our part is spread our wings, the wings of imagination God gave us. It is the wind of the Holy Spirit that carries us away.

Like two lovers, our fingertips and those of the hand of God caress, and our heart flies away.

CHAPTER FIVE
TURNING TOWARD GOD

God sends us the favourable wind of his most holy inspirations, which, blowing upon our hearts with a gentle violence, seizes and moves them, raising our thoughts, and moving our affections into the air of divine love.

Now this first stirring or motion which God causes in our hearts to incite them to their own good, is effected indeed in us but not by us; for it comes unexpectedly, before we have either thought of it or been able to think of it, seeing we are not sufficient to think anything towards our salvation of ourselves as ourselves, but our sufficiency is from God. 32

God loves us first and kisses us first. According to Bernard Lonergan, a brilliant Canadian theologian and Jesuit priest, the last thing God does before God sends a soul into the world is to give it a kiss, a kiss of God's perfect love, unity, beauty, goodness and truth.

This first kiss by God is the beginning of sexuality, and from then on we long to find perfect love, unity, beauty, goodness and truth in a soulmate. When we first kiss our soulmate, our heart cannot get enough of it, becomes more and more excited and is led into sexual union, orgasm and eventually if we are fortunate, into one of God's greatest gifts, that is, children.

However, even our soulmate and our children cannot fully satisfy our longing for the greatest love of all, union with God. Tasting God's kiss of perfect love, unity, beauty, goodness and truth, our heart responds wholeheartedly and our whole being follows. If our ego does not block anything, we will love God with all our heart, mind, soul and strength as Jesus commanded us to do.

Love of God requires getting our ego out of the way, or in traditional terminology "repentance." However, let's not think of repentance in the narrow sense. For most of history, many Christians have limited themselves to morality. As important as moral behavior is, Christianity is more about transformation through mysticism and contemplation.

Jesus declared that everyone should engage in "metanoia." It was Saint Jerome's inaccurate translation from Greek to Latin that changed "metanoia" into "repentance."

"Meta" means "higher" and "noia" means "mind." Therefore, when Jesus calls for metanoia, he is not just calling us to repent, to not do evil things, he is calling us to go to our higher mind or our true self, to be the best version of our self, which is impossible without God.

We cannot be completely fulfilled in God without the help of God's grace. When Jesus says "repent," he means "turn around," turn towards God with all your heart, mind, soul and strength. He is saying "Totally surrender to God in every area, every aspect of your life, totally get your ego blockages out of the way, be your best self, and let God into every nook and cranny of your life." This includes your moral life but goes far beyond it.

Does this leave any room for loving our self? Yes, as long as we are loving our true self. Our true self is the God-image, the "imago dei," the divine love in which we were made. We were made in the image and likeness of God and we may have lost the likeness by our sinful behavior, but the image of God remains.

Our true self, like God in whose image we are made, is all the virtues of love, peace, kindness, patience, trust, goodness; in short, every good quality that shines out of people at their best.

It is absolutely holy and good to love this self. By loving our true self, we are praising the God who created us, and we are growing in all the virtues that constitute our true self, the virtues mentioned above and also commitment to truth, justice and reconciliation.

However, growth in all these virtues is not possible without God's grace, and so the commitment must be to be open to God's grace even before we love our true self, so that all of God's graces flow to and through the true self. Repentance, metanoia, turning towards our true self without first loving God is empty and futile.

It is possible to have knowledge of God, but not love God. In fact, this is the situation of many Christians today: they know about God, but they do not love God above all things. They love themselves, even their small self, their ego, more than they love God. Their ego, an illusion, predominates.

The ego is who we think we are based on what the world tells us: we are our job, gender, name, nationality, our role as spouse or parent. Many Christians love their own external person, which was created by society, not the soul of who they are, which is love and truth.

People inside and outside the church may know God, but not love God. Spiritual directors fairly often hear from their directees (people taking spiritual direction) "I am worried I am really just a *fan* of Jesus, not a *follower* of Jesus, a spectator, not a disciple. My faith does not seem to require anything of me except for showing up once a week at church."

The apostle Paul wrote "knowledge puffs up, but love builds up" (1 Cor. 8:1) and "if I have prophetic powers, and understand all mysteries, and all knowledge, and if I have all faith, so as to remove mountains, but do not have love, I am nothing" (1 Cor. 13:2).

Therefore, even if religion scholars, theology teachers, pastors, clergy, bishops, or popes have all knowledge of God, but do not have love, they will not make it into the reign of God. This is why Dante placed even popes in his *Inferno*.

Even if we repent and turn toward God only so that we can love our true self, the ego is still in charge. The ego, like the devil, is incredibly subtle and devious, and can weasel its way into our every motivation.

Therefore, the best repentance is the most pure and single-minded. It is done out of love of God alone. It is not concerned with what rewards it will get for loving God, or for how its love of the true self will grow, or how it will grow in virtue, patience, kindness, humility or any other virtue.

The sole motive of the true lover of God is to love God for God alone because God is, and always will be, more lovable than anything, even all archangels, saints and prophets. God is more lovable than all the rewards of heaven, and more lovable than even heaven itself.

Before we go any further, let's briefly review why God is more lovable than anything.

First, everything else except God is passing away. Nothing except God is permanent. Everything is a shadow passing in the night. Nothing has any substance in and of itself. Everything is insubstantial dust compared to God.

America had a beginning like any other nation, it was born, will fade, and eventually die. The Roman Empire lasted about 500 years, the Greeks about 400. The Persian, Egyptian and Babylonian empires have come and gone, as have Chinese and Mongolian dynasties. The saying "The sun never sets on the British Empire" no longer applies. After 200 years it has dwindled down to almost nothing.

Perhaps Texas or California or Florida or New York State will leave the union and the rest of America will break up. Or perhaps there will be a civil war between conservatives and liberals, or between rich and poor, or something else will cause America to fall.

In Canada, separation by Quebec or Alberta could divide the country in two.

In a couple of hundred years or less our present home will likely be gone. Some new developer could even raze it to the ground in the next twenty years. Perhaps the home we grew up in is already gone.

Our spouse and children, if we have them, will eventually die, as we will.

When the Andromeda and Milky Way galaxies collide in a few million years, as astronomers say they will, our sun and its planets may not survive. Earth may be flung into space by itself, separate from the sun. Our sun itself will implode when its fuel runs out and it can no longer sustain the nuclear explosions that currently keep it inflated. After it implodes it will explode in a supernova and incinerate planet Earth.

We may consume all the resources on the planet and die out as a species. Climate change may wipe us out or we may be taken over by robots. This is already happening in many ways. Many economists and technologists believe that with self-driving vehicles replacing the need for drivers of trucks and cars, and also with artificial intelligence taking over even professional fields like law and medicine, we will soon be facing unemployment rates of 40%. One can only imagine the riots that might happen. Work may cease to be a permanent fixture of the average person's life.

The point is that nothing is permanent except God. Meanwhile, the Psalms tell us in various places that God is:

Giver of blessings (Ps.2:12)
Our perfect hiding place (Ps. 7:1)
The unshakable eternal one (Ps. 11:4)
Our only safe place (Ps. 16:3)
Our maker, mediator and master (Ps. 16:2)
Our true inheritance (Ps. 16:6)
Our deliverer from death (Ps. 18:6)
Our savior from despair through grace (Ps. 25:6)
Our healer (Ps. 32:2)
The adviser and director of our life's path (Ps. 32:8)
Always faithful and true to God's promises (Ps. 33:4)
Our radiant hope (Ps. 33:20)
The liberator from all our fears (Ps. 34:4)
The giver of joyous mercies (Ps. 34:8)
Unfailing love that can be found anywhere (Ps. 44:6)
The holy lord and king reigning over all (Ps. 46:10)
The soul's sweetest thing (Ps. 51:8)
Our savior from all bad things (Ps. 54:7)
Full banquet of pleasures (Ps. 64:5)
The utterly trustworthy one (Ps. 65:5).

Given that everything is passing away except God, and God is all those glorious things just mentioned, why would we love anything more than God, the One who is infinitely more lovable and loving than anything?

CHAPTER SIX
HOW GRACE LEADS TO LOVE OF GOD

Mark then how the Eternal Father draws us: while teaching, he delights us, not imposing upon us any necessity; he casts into our hearts delectations and spiritual pleasures as sacred baits, by which he sweetly draws us to take and taste the sweetness of his doctrine. 33

Everything positive that happens in us happens by the grace of God.

Some people say they don't believe in God because they don't believe God intervenes in human history.

But here is the good news: God does not have to intervene because God is always here already. God is everywhere for all eternity, so God does not have to intervene, to come swooping in from outside the system.

As theologians such as Paul Tillich say: God is Being-Itself, so all being is God. And God is also Becoming-Itself, moving the whole evolutionary process from beginning to end, from Alpha to Omega. God is Love incarnate in the whole universe, leading it to evolve from rocks and water (matter) to plants (life) to animals (sensitivity and feelings) to humans (thought) to the great religions spreading across the planet (spirit).

God is leading everything on our planet in a spiritual direction from matter to spirit, but we can always resist and oppose this guidance, as every war does, whether the war is within ourselves, our family, our community, our nation or internationally.

The unstoppable movement of evolution towards creatures who are more conscious and more capable of love all happens by the grace of the God who is always there, enticing everything onwards until its full flowering in human beings. God does not have to *intervene* because God *is* our constant internal drive to become more conscious and loving beings.

This is similar to Carl Jung's notion that all of us constantly strive to become "individuated" (fulfilled). Whether we know it or not we are all trying to become who God created us to be, our own unique, unrepeatable true self.

God's delights, appeals and inspirations to goodness that constantly happen within us are all meant to lead us on to loving God, which is the best fulfillment for us.

As Paul wrote, charity or love surpasses faith and hope as the main theological virtue. These three virtues are the essence of what scripture is pointing us toward, but love is the greatest of all. If we do not have love, all our knowledge, gifts, and acts of self-sacrifice are meaningless.

Charity or love of God loves God above all things and this love of God makes one supremely happy, but all of this is the gift of God in the first place. We cannot produce the love of God on our own.

God spends eternity contemplating God and God's creation, falling deeper and deeper in love with it all. Just as children are one of the greatest gifts of married love, out of love God wanted to produce God's own children who could fully share and participate in God's joy. So, God created the human race, and led us through various stages to knowledge of the one true God. All this is God's grace, God's gift to us which culminated in God's supreme gift, Jesus the Christ.

CHAPTER SEVEN

ON THE PROGESS AND PERFECTION OF LOVE

Doubtless, Theotimus, we are not drawn to God by iron chains, as bulls and wild oxen, but by enticements, sweet attractions, and holy inspirations. 34

Before we consider the perfection of love, let's unpack in a new way what Jesus meant when he said, "The greatest commandment is 'You shall love God with all your heart, mind, soul and strength.'"

Jesus also declared that "No one can serve two masters" (Matthew 6:24). He left no room for divided affection or allegiance. Since there is only one God and this God is supremely valuable above all else, this God demands supreme loyalty.

However, in our material state this greatest commandment is impossible to obey. No human being with a fallen nature, wounded heart and clouded intellect can possibly love God with all their heart, mind, soul and strength every waking moment.

This commandment proves beyond doubt our inability to obey the law. To disobey any of the Ten Commandments of God is to sin. This one command to love God with all our heart, since we constantly do not completely fulfill it, puts us in a constant state of sin.

Jesus continually reminded the Pharisees of their inability to keep God's law. He was trying to get them to see their utter spiritual bankruptcy and their need for a savior. Without cleansing of sin by the cross and the power of the Holy Spirit working within them, even for those who think they are pure and holy, loving God wholeheartedly is impossible.

Christ commands us to love God absolutely, but he never expected us to work up this holy love by our own efforts. He knew that, by our self, we are not capable of such love.

It is important to realize here that when God makes a demand, God's intention is to meet that demand for us.

Our love for God originates from God not us. It comes from God's love acting within us. "We love because God first loved us" (1 John 4:19). God infused us with God's love, and this generated within us our love for God. Without the Holy Spirit acting in us, loving God is impossible.

God's infused love within us can also move us to pray like the man who prayed "I believe Lord, help my unbelief" (Mark 9:24). Similarly, we could pray "I love Lord, help my unlove." We can ask God to help us in areas where we don't love God with all our heart, mind, soul and strength.

We must begin in loving God by seeking God's power to do the impossible. God specializes in doing the impossible. God leaves what is humanly possible up to us.

As a spiritual discipline, we can try every day to say to God "I love you," and we can also pray "Lord, help me to love you more each day." God wants us (for our sake) to love God absolutely, and prayer gives God an opening within us through which God can motivate us to love God with our whole being,

Over time, most believers witness God's compassion, mercy, grace and faithful love for them through all their struggles, trials and temptations. And this creates an ever-deepening love for God that grows and grows.

Our spiritual instincts (which are the Spirit working in us) tell us that we cannot love God if we don't know God. Getting to know God through studying God's Word should therefore become our first priority.

Knowing God's Word, the Bible, makes us even more eager to pray, obey and honor God in all things and to share God's love with others. It is through these spiritual disciplines of prayer, study and sharing God's love that the love of God grows and matures within us, to the glory of God.

Sharing God's love with others, besides letting others know that God loves them with an everlasting love, mainly involves striving for social justice and fighting systemic evil. We cannot authentically love God without caring about our fellow human beings. This is why Jesus said the second Great Commandment, "Love others as you love yourself," is similar to the first Great Commandment, "Totally love God."

CHAPTER EIGHT
ON LOVING GOD WITH ALL OUR HEART, SOUL, MIND AND STRENGTH

Pious discourses and arguments, the miracles and other advantages of the Christian religion, make it extremely credible and knowable, but faith alone makes it believed and acknowledged. 35

You have heard, Theotimus, that in general councils there are great disputations and inquiries made about truth by discourse, reasons and theological arguments, but the matters being discussed, the Fathers, that is, the bishops, and especially the Pope who is the chief of the bishops, conclude, resolve and determine; and the determination being once pronounced, every one fully accepts it and acquiesces in it, not in consideration of the reasons alleged in the preceding discussion and inquisition, but in virtue of the authority of the Holy Ghost. 36

To conclude then, Theotimus, this assurance which man's reason finds in things revealed and in the mysteries of faith, begins by an amorous sentiment of complacency which the will receives from the beauty and sweetness of the proposed truth; so that faith includes a beginning of love, which the heart feels toward divine things. 37

What does it mean to "love God with all your heart, mind, soul and strength"? Let's look at this part by part, starting with the heart this time.

As Proverbs 4:23 says "Keep your heart with all vigilance for from it flow the springs of life." From the heart flows our will, all our desires, passions, affections, perceptions and thoughts. And without these properly aligned, living a life of love is impossible.

We tend to think of our heart as simply the seat of our emotions. But in the Bible, the heart is our whole inner person: not only our emotions but our mind, will and conscience.

When our heart is turned away from Christ by sin, preoccupation, temptation or love for worldly things, our heart is covered by an opaque veil. We can no longer properly see God, nor can the "imago dei," the inner mirror of God, accurately reflect God.

When we turn our heart to God within us, the veil is removed, and we can see the glory of Christ. We see Christ's beauty, virtues and wonderfulness and Christ infuses God's love into our heart so that our love for God grows: "And all of us with unveiled faces, seeing the glory of the Lord as though reflected in a mirror, are being transformed into the same image from one degree of glory to another; for this comes from the Lord, the Spirit" (2 Corinthians 3:18).

Along with our heart, we are called to love God with all our soul. In the Torah, the first five books of the Jewish testament, the "soul" refers to one's whole being as a living person, which includes and goes beyond one's heart: "The Lord God formed man from the dust of the ground, and breathed into his nostrils the breath of life, and the man became a living being" (Genesis 2:7). "Living being" used to be translated as "soul." Without "ruach," the breath of God, the Spirit within us, we would not be nor have a soul.

Moses starts with a call to love God from within, and then takes that to a higher level by saying that everything about us as a person is to declare God as our Lord. We are to love God with our passions, hungers, perceptions, and thoughts but also with how we talk, what we do with our hands (our livelihood), how we utilize our talents and how we respond to challenges—*our entire being is to display that we love God*.

Loving God with our whole being includes loving God with our spirit, the immanent part of our being, the part where we receive and contact God. This is where God comes to live in us when we accept Jesus the Christ as our savior. In our spirit we can have companionship with God and spend time in God's presence.

What is the difference between the spirit and the soul? Our soul is made up of our mind, our emotions and our will as well as our outward behavior: how we talk and act. It is our whole person, our connection with the creation and reality. Soul is the unifying principle of our physical and intellectual being. The deepest part of the soul is the spirit. Spirit is given to us, the energy of life that we share with God.

God created the soul so we could express God to others, but often, because of the fall into self-consciousness, we simply express our self. We have our own opinions, our own feelings and our own decisions apart from God. God is put on the backburner of our lives.

When we turn our heart to God, we begin to not only love God with our heart but also with our soul and spirit. God's thoughts become our thoughts, God's feelings become our feelings, and God's decisions become our decisions.

As God does this transforming work in us, we spontaneously glorify God. And as we spontaneously express God, others see Christ expressed in us and come to know God.

Just as the spirit is the deepest part of the soul, so the mind is its leading part and directs the rest of our being. But our mind can be distracted by so many things. One American psychologist calculated that the average person thinks 60,000 thoughts a day!

However, God wants our mind to be set on the Spirit where God dwells within us. The apostle Paul wrote "To set the mind on the flesh is death, but to set the mind on the Spirit is life and peace" (Romans 8:6). By "the flesh" Paul usually means "the heart, soul and mind that cuts itself off from God" not the physical body. Although he was speaking to Greeks and Romans who thought matter was bad and spirit was good, he was not himself a dualist.

There are many ways to set our mind on the Spirit. One is through centering prayer or Christian meditation where we focus our mind on God's presence or on a sacred word such as "Jesus" instead of on the 59,999 other thoughts coursing through our mind. This prayer is not meant to replace other forms of prayer. It simply puts those other forms into a new and fuller perspective.

Every time our mind gets distracted by these thoughts, we gently bring it back to the name of Jesus or to God's presence. As Thomas Keating said: "The thousand distracting thoughts we have in a twenty-minute Christian meditation session give us a thousand opportunities to return to God."

Another simpler way to set the mind on the Spirit is to read the Bible with an open heart. Daily reading of God's Word enlightens, cleanses and renews our mind and has great benefits for our entire soul, spirit and even our body.

That brings us to the final part of Christ's command, that is, to love God with all our strength or might. The word "might" or "strength" is translated 298 times in the Jewish scriptures as the adverb "very." One interpretation is that it means we should love God with all our "very-ness." The Greek translation of "might" is "power." The Aramaic translation is "wealth."

Thus, the might or strength of a person is not just who they are, their will or their physical strength, but everything they have at their disposal, all of their resources. The call to love God therefore involves honoring God with everything God has given us: our spouse, children, home, work, co-workers, intellectual pursuits, hobbies, technology and most importantly our time.

We can honor God with our family time, work time, volunteer time and leisure time. There should be no aspect of our life that is not devoted to God. Whether we are practicing our spiritual rule (the schedule of our spiritual practices throughout the day) or at work or church or playing or watching sports, our conduct should show that the love of God reigns in us. This is similar to what Brother Lawrence suggested in his classic *The Practice of the Presence of God*.

What God is commanding is wholehearted, whole life allegiance and exclusive commitment to God that impacts not only us but our whole community in terms of all our relationships. Every closet of our life needs to be opened and purified by the grace of God. We cannot be one way at church, and another way at work, at home or on the Internet.

Authentic love for God must start with God-oriented desires, thoughts and feelings that permeate all our speaking, actions, ways we spend our money and the types of entertainment we choose.

Our love of God must include what we do with our body, our five senses and our sexuality. When we turn our heart to God, receive and communicate with God in our spirit, experience God in our soul, set our mind on God, our body and our sexual behavior will follow.

In short, we will love God with all we have, with our entire being, with every aspect of our life. This is what it means "You shall love the Lord your God with all your heart, soul, mind and strength."

Eugene Peterson, in *The Message*, his translation of the Bible into the language and nuances of 21st century speech, puts the Great Commandment of Jesus this way: Love God with all your passion, prayer, intelligence and energy."

CHAPTER NINE
THE PROGRESS AND PERFECTION OF LOVE CONTINUED

When God sees the soul overthrown by sin he commonly runs to her succour, and by an unspeakable mercy, lays open the gates of her heart by the stings and remorses of conscience which come from the divers lights and apprehensions which he casts into our hearts, with salutary movements, by which, as by odorous and vital liquors, he makes the soul return to herself, and brings her back to good sentiments. 38

If the soul thus excited add her consent to the solicitation of grace, seconding the inspiration which prevents her, and accepting the required helps provided for her by God; he will fortify her, and conduct her through various movements of faith, hope and penitence, even until he restore her to her true spiritual health, which is no other thing than charity. 39

Since God is infinite, and since it is God who causes love of God (charity, caritas) to grow, charity can grow and grow infinitely. There are no boundaries to its potential to growth, except sin.

Sin, or "missing the mark" as it is translated in our post-modern, post-truth world is a lot more serious than our relativism and situation ethics would have us believe. In its essence it is turning our back on God, the source, sustenance and goal of all things, the One who is infinitely more lovable than anything.

Of course, there are degrees of sin. The Roman Catholic Church has always distinguished between "venial" (non-mortal) and "mortal" sin, but sin is really a continuum from doing things that might slightly dampen our relationship with God such as a spontaneous judgment in our mind about a person from a different culture, to all-out rebellion against the Holy One in the form of leading people into an unnecessary war or even genocide with unbridled rape, torture and terror.

A classic example of this unbridled rebellion, besides the Holocaust, was the massacre of one million Tutsis (about 70% of the Tutsi population) and systematic rape of 500,000 women by Hutus. The killing was done by brutally hacking men, women and children to death with machetes and burning others alive. This is not just "missing the mark."

In some ways this face-to-face death-dealing may be less sinful than a military officer sitting at his or her desk somewhere in Europe or America and destroying a family or whole community somewhere in Iraq, Afghanistan or Syria with the flip of a switch connected to weaponized drone technology.

At least with face-to-face combat we would see the terror on the face of our "enemy" and hear their screams, and because of this, possibly feel some remorse. The officer flipping the switch or pressing the button may not have any pangs of conscience since "I was just doing my job."

The ultimate in this type of impersonal killing would be to start a nuclear war, a threat constantly hanging over all our heads like Damocle's sword.

In any case, if we don't get climate change under control, we may go beyond the "sixth great extinction" in which scientists tell us we are living, to the destruction of all life forms on Earth. We may by our greed and over-consumption go beyond destroying millions of other creatures to destroying our own species.

Sin is a vast continuum ranging from an uncharitable thought to the extermination of all life on our planet.

Mercifully though, God is always there, in the thick of things, in the center of our hearts, minds, souls and spirits arousing pangs of conscience whenever we go astray. Even the drone commander, particularly if they have a spouse and children, must occasionally think of the terror they are raining down on other families.

Beyond pangs of conscience, God is constantly wooing us, always inviting us to follow the Way, the Truth and the Life so we reclaim the path of love. Whether we are on the path or not, God is our constant lover reminding us of all the delights of following God's ways: a clear conscience; peace of mind, heart, and soul; a greater awareness of all the beauty and diversity of the creation from honey bees to orangutans; better mental health; better relationships; better marriages; and better sex as well as all the other benefits that psychologists are now starting to prove come with believing in a Higher Loving Power.

Although sin may abound in our world, grace abounds even more (Romans 5:20).Grace is a regular ongoing facet of life because the Holy Spirit constantly permeates everything.

The media mainly reports on disasters such as homicides, floods, famines, and government corruption, and although people often do suffer, most of the time many people will have had a reasonably good day and will be reasonably well taken care of. If 999,999 people in the province of Manitoba had a relatively good day, but one person was stabbed to death, who would the media tell us about? Goodness is the constant, unreported background of all our lives.

Good is always foundational, evil is always secondary. Most of the time our businesses, governments, education, health care and legal systems are doing their job of employing, producing goods, feeding, clothing, educating, healing and protecting us, but all of this is so commonplace we are not conscious of it.

We only notice the media reports on aberrations. Media focuses our attention on the negative aspects of life, and thus becomes a kind of mental pollution that overlooks the grace of God, the blessings that are constantly there.

God is always trying to move all of us from within to take care of our loved ones in our personal lives and to care for others through our work. Most of all, God is trying to draw us closer to God every day. God wants more and more intimacy with us. So again, it is God's work in us, not our own effort, that preserves us in charity, in love of God. All we are called to do is cooperate with the transforming movements of God within us, constantly leading us to new heights.

Ideally, God wants us all to be fully alive; to eat, pray and love; to live, laugh and love; to dance and fall in love; to have great families with as many children as we can afford; to have many grandchildren to delight in. If we are single, a vowed celibate, or unable to have children, God wants us to be fully alive in the relationships we do have, particularly our friendships.

God wants all of us to be fully educated; to have meaningful work that we love; to seek restorative justice, peace and full life for everyone; to have broad minds; to be lifelong learners; to use all our skills and talents; to have a wide variety of interests; to do well financially and share our largesse with others; to heal one another; to have a vibrant social life; to support culture and all the arts, creating great novels, poetry, sculpture and paintings; to enjoy great food; to have a rich intellectual and spiritual life; to know the scriptures well; to belong to thriving religious communities.

God wants us to be filled to the brim with enjoyment and fun; to participate fully in sports or to fully enjoy watching sports of all kinds; to revel in music, song and all the simple pleasures of life, the thousand enjoyable things that happen to us every day whether we acknowledge that it is all coming from God or not.

This is what God wants for us. As Psalm 16:11 says: "You show me the path of life. In your presence there is fullness of joy; in your right hand are pleasures forevermore." Or as Jesus declared: "I came that they (all people) may have life and have it abundantly" (John 10:10). That's what God wants for us!

CHAPTER TEN
THE HEAVENWARD GROWTH OF LOVE

Now, not only shall each one in particular have a greater love in heaven than he ever had on Earth, but the exercise of the least charity in heaven, shall be much more happy and excellent, generally speaking, than that of the greatest which is, or has been, or shall be, in this failing life. 40

In heaven, Theotimus, the loving attention of the blessed is firm, constant, inviolable and cannot perish or decrease; their intention is pure and freed from all mixture of any inferior intention; in short, this felicity of seeing God clearly and loving him unchangeably is incomparable. 41

God ardently wants eternal life for all of us. God wants us fully alive now and forevermore. To reject God now and forevermore is a burning folly: to see the sacred bush of this life consumed by the fire of impermanence and think that is all there is.

The false, secular self thinks the self is all there is and that it can do without God. However, it will find at the end of life that all the illusions it wrapped around itself to convince itself it was real—all its passion about the false gods of wealth, power and possessions—will be like a fire that burns all these idols up when the false self comes to physical death.

Jesus said, "Do not store up for yourselves treasures on Earth, where moth and rust consume and where thieves break in and steal;

but store up for yourselves treasures in heaven…for where your treasure is, there will your heart be also" (Matthew 6:19-21).

Here on Earth we see darkly. There is no perfect union with God in this life. So, rejection of God even by believers is always a possibility. This life at best is only betrothal to God, the engagement, not the marriage.

Here on Earth, natural truth can be grasped by reason. Science can show us so much, but this is still seeing darkly, seeing only partial truth. Science cannot show us God or God's plans.

To grasp supernatural truth, we need faith and grace. But we cannot produce this faith and grace by our own efforts. They are gifts from God alone. But God wants to lavish on us the gifts of faith and grace. God's love, faith and grace are perfectly given and always waiting to be perfectly received. God dearly wants us to love God, not for God's sake but for our sake, because loving God is absolutely the best outcome for us.

On Earth, God feeds us most powerfully with God's love and grace through communion. But the eucharist is just a foretaste of the heavenly communion where God will feed us directly God's self without any mediating elements such as bread and wine.

Just as a nursing mother feeds her baby directly with herself, with her own milk from her own breasts not the breasts of others, so God will feed us directly with God's own breast, not the breast of the church. But for now, God has given us God's breast, the church, to feed us heavenly food on Earth, the spiritual body and blood of Jesus the Christ.

CHAPTER ELEVEN
THE EASE AND PERFECTION OF LOVING GOD IN HEAVEN

This perfect conjunction then of the soul with God, shall only be in heaven, where, as the Apocalypse says, the Lamb's marriage feast shall be made. In this mortal life the soul is truly espoused and betrothed to the immaculate Lamb, but not as yet married to him. 42

But in heaven, the marriage of this divine union being celebrated, the bond which ties our hearts to their sovereign principle shall be eternally indissoluble. 43

The afterlife, the heavenly life, life without boundaries, unbounded life and love, goes beyond betrothal to marriage. Finally, and totally, "My beloved is mine and I am his" (Song of Solomon 2:16).

Marriage to God in the afterlife is an unbreakably secure relationship of being loved and of loving, a never-ending immersion in deeper and deeper love.

And this never-ending growth in loving God will be easy, far easier than on Earth where everything rusts, changes, and falls apart eventually. Even though Jesus said that he would make easy and light the yoke (responsibilities) of those who are burdened on Earth (Matthew 11:30), in heaven loving God will be even more easy, delightful and free of all impediments. This freedom will happen because as Jesus said: "You will know the truth and the truth will make you free" (John 8:32).

In heaven our intellect will be directly united to God's truth. There will be no knowing the truth darkly, no hesitation, no second guessing, no shadow of doubt. We will be mainlining truth.

All our senses will be ravished with the beauty of God. We will see directly the glory and infinite perfection of Jesus the Christ. We will hear the heavenly choirs, see millions of flaming angels and archangels hovering in joyful abandon around the Lord of Hosts, taste the ineffable goodness of God, smell the exquisite perfumes of incense and wildflowers, and lie down with our resurrected bodies in the glorious fields of the Lord.

As we grasp God's incomparable wisdom and truth, our happiness will be an always overflowing fountain. The desire and longing for God that consumed us on Earth will turn to total joy as we embrace our True Spouse, God, our supreme fulfilment.

We will witness how the infinite love of God the Father and God the Son for each other eternally generates God the Holy Spirit. We will fully understand how the Father, Son and Holy Spirit are differentiated yet completely one God in their never-ending flow of giving and receiving divine love.

Everyone in heaven will see the Divine Glory but never totally, for God always and forever transcends us. There will always be more of God to enjoy, for the Lord is an inexhaustible treasure of incorruptible pleasure and goodness.

Book Three
On the Decay and Ruin of Our Love for God

Chapter One
The Onslaught of Distraction and Temptation

Although the Holy Ghost, as a spring of living water, flows up to every part of our heart to spread his graces in it, yet as he will not have them enter without the free consent of our will, he will only pour them out according to his good pleasure and our own disposition and cooperation. 44

And as the sick man who had the potion given into his hand, if he took it not wholly but only partly, would also have the operation thereof in part only, and not wholly, - so when God sends a great a great and mighty inspiration to move us to embrace his holy love, if we consent not according to its whole extent it will but profit us in the same measure. 45

All the saints incessantly, without any intermission, exercise love; while here below God's greatest servants, drawn away and tyrannized over by the necessities of this dying life, are forced to suffer a thousand and a thousand distractions, which often take them off the practice of holy love. 46

As our civilization goes into overdrive with our technological capability doubling every three months, homo sapiens is becoming "homo technocratus." In this increasingly secular milieu, we are constantly exposed to thousands of earthly distractions and temptations, in both our outer and inner worlds.

It is no wonder that depression has reached epidemic proportions: it is difficult not to despair given the unceasing acceleration of loss due to change—the "future shock" which Alvin Toffler predicted back in the 1970s—and that was long before the digital age overtook us!

Another new title for homo sapiens could well be "homo distractus." Distractions lead to previously unheard-of temptations and addictions: to computer games, online gambling and pornography. There are now major industries devoted to helping people stay addicted to these pursuits.

When people abandon God, there is nothing left but ever greater quantities of stimulation which people use to generate some kind of meaning in their lives.

There are the one thousand external distractions and temptations. But they are matched by the one thousand internal distractions and temptations as our moods fluctuate when we identify too closely with external stimulation.

We can constantly swing internally through lust, envy, anger and fear as computer or smart phone social media images dance before our eyes, or as we are downsized at work, or are in conflict with co-workers, spouses or children.

What churches used to call "venial" (minor) sins can weaken our love for God. With ease, we can talk ourselves internally into or out of anything: "I will quit smoking/overeating/drinking tomorrow." As Leonard Cohen sang "I fought the bottle, but I had to do it drunk."

Sins, even the smallest ones, are always devious and insidious. They are usually not as obvious as Saint Peter wrote: "Like a roaring lion your adversary the devil prowls around, looking for someone to devour" (I Peter 5:8).

Our own laziness or lack of energy due to overbusyness can also cause us to lose charity, the love of God which is expressed in service to others: "I will visit my mother in the nursing home some other time.

There is a limited showing of a special movie I want to see tonight."

Temptation causes us to choose the apparently good over the truly good: "Spending half an hour a day in prayer takes too much time away from my family. Prayer can wait."

Or conversely "I know I haven't spent any time with my family in the past month, but I am a minister of God's Word, and my first commitment has to be to the church. I have to put my congregation before my family." Or "I am a farmer, and I have to support my family. My spouse is just too needy, always craves attention, and I can't take the time for that."

Once venial or minor sin weakens our love of God so that we no longer make charity/love of God our first priority, and we no longer make good deeds (the fruit of charity) our main concern, then the lower part of our soul, our senses, rebel against the higher part, our reason, and we engage in "mortal" (serious) sin. We decide not to be charitable to the poor at all.

Here we easily can find and articulate Bible verses to defend our position: "Didn't Jesus say: 'You always have the poor among you?' (Matthew 26:11). Life is hard, it has always been hard, and God helps those who help themselves. Everyone makes their own way and is responsible for their own life. In fact, that homeless person probably enjoys living on the street. That's what he chose, so let's leave him to it. Unlike him, I worked hard for every penny I earned."

Love of God can be lost little by little through repeated minor sins until they lead to serious (mortal) sin, although serious sin can also happen in a flash. We spontaneously decide to shoot our boss who fired us, beat up our lover who is leaving, drive our truck into a crowd of protesters, or tell our spouse that we have to work late, when we are really committing adultery with a sexy co-worker.

In any case, while venial sin weakens our relationship with God, mortal sin severs it. Our relationship to God, our love of God, can be temporarily or permanently cut off. God is always there, but our love of God is not.

CHAPTER TWO
BIBLICAL FIGURES WHO LOST THEIR LOVE OF GOD

There is yet another penitence which is indeed moral, yet religious too, yea in some sort divine, proceeding from the natural knowledge which we have of offending God by sin. For many philosophers understood that to live virtuously was a thing agreeable to the divinity, and that consequently, to live viciously was offensive to him. 47

Whosoever affirms that he sins not, is senseless, and whosoever expects without penitence to redress his sin is mad; for it is our Saviour's exhortation of exhortations: Do penance. 48

It is possible to not just offend God, but to cut ourselves off from God. Not that God is not there, but we are no longer in any kind of harmony with God.

There are several classic examples in the Bible where those who were the greatest lovers of God suddenly engaged in serious mortal sin and at least temporarily cut off their relationship with God.

David, the greatest king of Israel, and the composer of most of the psalms, which are ecstatic love poems to God celebrating God's goodness and glory, fell doubly hard.

He was first overcome by the beauty of a married woman, Bathsheba, when from the royal palace he saw her bathing on the roof of her house at night. He summoned her to the royal court and had an affair with her while her husband was at war.

Then, when he learned she was pregnant with his child, David arranged to have her husband Uriah killed in battle. David had both adultery and murder on his conscience and as such was unfaithful to God, his own wives, Uriah, Bathsheba and as king, to his entire kingdom.

Fortunately, God intervened through the prophet Nathan, who accused David of his sin, and David was heroic and humble enough to turn his heart back to God (2 Samuel 12:13).

The classic Christian example of temporarily turning one's back on God is Peter. He first testifies his great love for God when he swears to Christ that he will die for him. Then after Jesus is arrested, Peter swears three times that he does not know Christ.

Jesus had predicted that a cock would crow if Peter denied him, and when it does crow, Peter realizes his apostasy and goes away shattered (Luke 22:54-62).

Fortunately, after Jesus is resurrected, he gave Peter the opportunity to redeem himself by asking three times if Peter loved him. Chagrined, Peter vowed three times that he does love Jesus, and the relationship is restored. More than restored, for Jesus puts Peter in charge of the church when he says three times to Peter "Feed my flock" (John 21:15-17). Such is the mercy and graciousness of God.

David and Peter lost and regained faith, but the biblical character Judas is the archetype of either the person who had faith and then turned away permanently from God, or the archetype of the one who never had faith in the first place.

It is significant that, at the last supper with Jesus, when Jesus says that one of them will betray him, every other disciple says: "Surely not I, Lord?" but Judas says: "Surely not I, Rabbi?" (Matthew 26:25) indicating that Judas considered Jesus to be just human, not the incarnation of God.

We don't know for sure if Judas had faith, but we do know that he felt remorse and said "I have sinned by betraying innocent blood" and threw into the temple the thirty pieces of silver the chief priests and elders had given him as a payment for betraying Jesus. Then he departed and hanged himself (Matthew 27:3-5).

This is a tragic story, but it drives home the point that even those like Judas, who spent three years in the presence of Jesus, hearing his inspirational teaching firsthand, observing his perfection in everything he did and witnessing his great miracles, could fall away from loving God.

This is a cautionary tale for all of us. If someone who knew Jesus so personally could lose the love of God, how much easier must it be for us to fall away, who never have seen Jesus in the flesh?

CHAPTER THREE
LOSS OF LOVE OF GOD IS OUR CHOICE

In this way then, dearest Theotimus, our free-will is in no way forced or necessitated by grace, but notwithstanding the all-powerful force of God's merciful hand, which touches, surrounds and ties the soul with such a number of inspirations, invitations and attractions, this human will remains perfectly free, enfranchised and exempt from every sort of constraint and necessity. 49

What is as admirable as it is veritable is, that when our will follows the attraction, and consents to the divine movement, she follows as freely as she resists freely when she does resist, though the consent to grace depends much more on grace than on the will, while the resistance to grace depends upon the will only. 50

Theotimus, inspirations prevent us, and even before they are thought of make themselves felt, but after we have felt them it is ours either to consent to them so as to second and follow their attractions, or else to dissent and repulse them. They make themselves felt by us without us, but they do not make us consent without us. 51

As we have already established, everything comes from God, even our desire to know and love God in the first place. God seeks to love God through us. God wants to experience everything—not only the Father, Son and Holy Spirit loving each other—but also everything that falls within the realm of human experience. And the highest human experience is to love God. God therefore wants to love God through us, not just for God's sake, but for our sake as well.

Charity, or love of God, comes not by our will but by God's will. God wants us to love God because God loves us and knows that the best thing for us is to love God back. Thus, if people fall away from charity, as scripture shows can happen, it does not come from God's will. God wants everyone to be saved, that is, to spend eternity loving God with all our hearts and to be eternally ravished by God's love of us.

The only reason therefore that we fall away from loving God is due to our will. We allow ourselves to get distracted by the pleasures or cares of the world's system of competition, materialism, individualism and vanity, or we start to engage in simple, low-level venial sins and it gradually weakens our resolve to love God above all things.

The Holy Spirit warns us over and over again when we start to move away from God, but we are so caught up with distracting surface-level stimulation that we ignore the warnings and spend less and less time pursuing God through scripture, prayer or church.

CHAPTER FOUR
THE DANGER OF IMPERFECT LOVE OF GOD

Certainly, it is good, and this cannot be denied, to repent of our sins in order to avoid the pains of hell and obtain heaven, but he that should make the resolution never to be willing to repent for any other motive, would wilfully shut out the better, which is to repent for the love of God, and would commit a great sin. 52

It is an imperfect repentance, because divine love is not as yet found in it. Ah! do you not see, Theotimus, that all these repentances are made for the sake of our own soul, of its felicity, of its interior beauty, its honour, its dignity, and in a word for love of ourselves, although a lawful, just and well-ordered love. 53

It is possible for our charity, our love of God, to gradually disappear, or even to disappear suddenly, but because we have established certain habitual behaviors such as going to church, meditating, reading scripture and praying, the behaviors continue on for a while longer.

It seems outwardly that the love of God is still there when in fact it is already ebbing away until all that is left is habit. Unfortunately, habit has very little value when it comes to eternal life.

This imperfect love, this going through the motions without any genuine love of God, is dangerous to our spiritual health because it may convince us, or at least lull us into believing, that we have charity when we really do not.

Imperfect love is marked by illicit fears and desires such as show-ing up at church because you fear that if you don't you will go to hell or going to church solely because you desire to go to heaven. There is no real love of God for God alone, only self-centered fear of hell or desire for heaven.

CHAPTER FIVE

WE OVERCOME IMPERFECT LOVE BY RETURNING TO GOD

Fear, and those other motives of repentance of which I spoke, are good for the beginning of Christian wisdom, which consists in penitence; but he who deliberately willed not to attain to love which is the perfection of penitence, would greatly offend him who ordained all to his love, as to the end of all things. 54

Divine inspiration comes to us, and prevents us, moving our wills to sacred love. And if we do not repulse it, it goes with us and keeps near us, to incite us and ever push us further forwards; and if we do not abandon it, it does not abandon us, till such time as it has brought us to the haven of most holy charity, performing for us the three good offices which the great angel Raphael fulfilled for his dear Tobias: for it guides us through all our journey of holy penitence, it preserves us from dangers and from the assaults of the devil, and it consoles, animates, and fortifies us in our difficulties. 55

Our Lord has a continual care to conduct his children, that is such as are in charity; making them walk before him, reaching them his hand in difficulties, and bearing them himself in such travails, as he sees otherwise insupportable to them. 56

Illicit desire is to desire or love any thing, person or life circumstance more than God. Illicit desires beget illicit fears. As Buddhists say, to want something automatically engenders the fear that we won't get it.

If we want to conquer our enemies in war, we automatically fear that we will lose and they will conquer us. If we want a promotion or raise in pay at work, we automatically fear our boss will deny it.

However, because of God there is no need to fear anything or anyone. "The Lord is my light and my salvation; whom shall I fear? The Lord is the stronghold of my life; of whom shall I be afraid?" (Psalm 27: 1).

God totally loves and wants what is best for us. God wants us to be fully alive—our complete mental and physical health and wholeness. This is evidenced in the gospels by Jesus healing all who came to him—the crippled, blind, lepers, epileptics, and the insane. He is constantly casting demons out of those who are possessed and telling people to not be afraid.

Throughout the Bible, the first thing angels say when they appear is "Do not be afraid." As Paul wrote to Timothy "God did not give us a spirit of cowardice, but rather a spirit of power and of love and of self-discipline" (2 Timothy 1:7).

We have nothing to fear because God is totally good, there is absolutely no evil in God. Therefore, God is totally trustworthy. And God wants our total trust. In a way, to fear is an insult to God because the subtext of our fear is the implicit assumption that God is not totally good and therefore cannot be totally trusted to take care of us.

Fear makes absolutely no sense for Christians or anyone who believes in God. God is our True Father and our True Mother and has already made us a part of God's family. We are already living in God's house, we are already saved, so there is nothing to worry, fear or be anxious about.

God is in charge of our life, now and forever. Therefore, our present and our future are glorious. All we need to do is wake up to this fact.

God is constantly protecting our soul and our body through our self and others. When we were young, God protected us through our parents, siblings, friends, doctors, nurses, and teachers.

God has given us five senses to alert us to any danger. We can see or hear any peril coming from afar. Our sense of smell tells us if something is rotten. Our sense of taste tells us if food is edible or not. Touch tells us if something is too hot or too cold.

God works unceasingly within us, trying to motivate us to pursue what is good. The Holy Spirit works in our conscience to tell us what is right and wrong, what enhances life and what destroys it. As God said to the Israelites through Moses "I have set before you life and death, blessings and curses. Choose life so that you and your descendants may live, loving the Lord your God, obeying God, and holding fast to God; for that means life to you" (Deuteronomy 30:19-20).

God also protects us through others. God protects our soul through the preaching we hear at our church, which warns us not to take the wicked way.

God protects us through the laws which the legal system creates—laws governing human rights, and things such as car licensing and housing regulations so we are kept safe from dangerous drivers or unscrupulous builders. God protects us through policies crafted by politicians about health care, unemployment insurance and the economy.

God protects us through others by putting in everyone's heart the desire to protect other people, the implicit knowledge that if we all work together on protecting each other, we will all be safer for it, including each person as an individual.

Of course, all of this intended protection by God can go horribly wrong because God also respects human freedom. Fear, greed and ignorance can get in the way. Politicians and lawyers can create policies and laws that protect the rich and initiate wars and revolutions. Parents, doctors, teachers and we ourselves can make wrong judgements about what is really good for us.

God respects our ability to choose good or evil because God refuses to be a cosmic tyrant and treat us like God's puppets. There cannot be genuine love if there is no possibility of genuine choice, which means the possibility of good or evil.

However, even if hard things happen to us, God will provide all we need to not only survive but to thrive and grow from the experience.

Hardship is how we grow. The obstacle is the path. Suffering can be our best teacher.

And we are never alone. God is always with us, always there for us, always on our side. As de Sales wrote "God will either protect you from suffering or give you unfailing strength to bear it." And if we don't get through it and die, we will spend eternity in God's loving embrace. So, whether we live or die, we belong to God, and all our suffering will contribute to our spiritual growth. As Paul said: "We know that all things work together for good for those who love God" (Romans 8:28).

Sometimes we block our road back to God by over-analysing things. As a wise man once said: "Wisdom is knowing when to stop asking questions." It can help to not overdo questions, to be wise enough at some point to just trust God and obey the command to not be afraid and rest assured that, although unsearchable, God's will is good and just.

As Saint Augustine wrote "Our hearts are restless until they rest in you, O Lord." If we constantly and relentlessly search for God, and always turn back to God, we will find God again.

The rest of *God's Ecstatic Love* will address how we can regain and grow our love for the One who is infinitely more loving and lovable than anything or anyone.

BOOK FOUR

THE TWO MAIN EXERCISES OF SACRED LOVE: COMPLACENCE (RESTING IN GOD'S LOVE) AND BENEVOLENCE (ACTING IN GOD'S LOVE)

CHAPTER ONE

A MUTUALLY REINFORCING CIRCLE OF LOVE

By charity we love God for his own sake, by reason of his most sovereignly amiable goodness. But this friendship is a true friendship, being reciprocal, for God has loved eternally all who have loved him, do, or shall love him temporally.

It is shown and acknowledged mutually, since God cannot be ignorant of the love we bear him, he himself bestowing it upon us, nor can we be ignorant of his love to us, seeing that he has published it abroad, and that we acknowledge all the good we have, to be true effects of his benevolence.

And in fine we have continual communications with him, who never ceases to speak unto our hearts by inspirations, allurements, and sacred motions. 57

Before we go any further, we need to define two of our principal terms.

"Complacence" means resting in God's love; resting in the countless virtues of God: God's humility, patience, peacefulness, kindness and so on. It is a passive reception of and delighting in God. It is hiding our self under God's mighty wings, being at home and at peace in God. "When you sit enthroned under the shadow of Shaddai, you are hidden in the strength of God Most High. God is the hope that holds me, and the stronghold to shelter me, the only God for me, and my great confidence." (Psalm 91:1).

"Benevolence" is an active seeking of God, a pursuing God with all our heart, not passively waiting for the ship of God to come in but rather swimming out to meet it. It is disciplining oneself to constantly think about God and constantly imagine God's never-ending wonderfulness. It is pursuing the Hound of Heaven (the Holy Spirit) who is always pursuing us. It is pouncing on the Hound, rolling on the ground with it and lovingly embracing it.

Complacence in God comes from gently, sweetly and quietly meditating on God's excellence—either in general or on the surpassing excellence of just one aspect of God: unimaginably deep forgiveness, or understanding, compassion, helpfulness, holiness, beauty, justice or wisdom. Each virtue is an abyss we could let ourselves fall into forever.

In complacence we are like a nursing child. A mother's nurturing breasts are God's sign to us that life is not all hard: it is also soft, warm, humane, gentle, comforting and life-giving.

We suck at the breast of God for all we are worth, and God eagerly feeds us for we are God's child. And the more we suck up, the more the mother's milk of God's love flows. As a child grows it needs more and more food, and as we grow in complacence, we want more and more of God's nurturance.

The more we experience complacence, the more we desire God, and the more complacence we find. It is a mutually reinforcing circle of love between us and God. The more we want, the more God gives, and the more God gives, the more we want.

Mary, the mother of Jesus, nurtured Christ at her breast and took complacence in his divinity as he took complacence in her humanity. She loved Jesus with all her heart as only a mother can, and her love was without any blemish or restriction. But she knew that she had to wean him, to let him be a young boy, not a baby, and eventually to become a man who could experience every vicissitude of a fully human life. "And Jesus increased in wisdom and in years, and in divine and human favor" (Luke 2:52).

Similarly, for us there comes a point where we have grown enough that we have to be weaned from the "milk" God initially gives us. We are ready for solid spiritual food (Hebrews 5:11-14). Our love of God has become stronger than any pain or even death. We are strong enough to stand anything. Our loving complacence in Jesus the Christ means that we remain steadfast even when we contemplate his crucifixion. When Mary experienced her son being crucified, because of the depth of her love for him, she co-suffered horribly with him and a sword pierced her soul as well (Luke 2:35). But she stood firm in her faith that it all somehow made sense.

Jesus showed us the unfathomable depths of God's love for us by accepting the brutality of the cross rather than retaliating against humanity. Christ redeemed us by the restorative justice of God, despite our countless sins. And Christ's love for us was fulfilled by his resurrection from death. He broke through the temple veil separating ordinary humans from God. And he broke through the gates of hell to allow everyone to come into heaven, the Holy of Holies.

Out of supreme love for us, Christ's human pain was transformed into divine joy. And he will transform all our suffering in this mortal life into eternal rejoicing in God.

CHAPTER TWO

INCREASING OUR COMPLACENCE AND BENEVOLENCE

True virtue has no limits, it goes ever further; but especially holy charity, which is the virtue of virtues, and which, having an infinite object, would be capable of becoming infinite if it could meet with a heart capable of infinity. 58

The heart which could love God with a love equal to the divine goodness would have a will infinitely good, which cannot be but in God. Charity then in us may be perfected up to the infinite, but exclusively; that is, charity may become more and more, and ever more, excellent, yet never infinite. 59

It is an extreme honour to our souls that they may still grow more and more in the love of their God, as long as they shall live in this failing life. 60

Everything starts with God's benevolence, God's action in the world on our behalf. God created the universe to share with other creatures the infinite love that constantly flows between Father, Son and Spirit. God wanted all creatures to experience something of the absolute wonderfulness of God.

God created the universe out of benevolence, and then God took complacence in the creation. "God saw everything that God had made, and indeed, it was very good…God rested on the seventh day from all the work that God had done" (Genesis 1:31, 2:2).

God loves to just be and contemplate the majesty of the cosmos. In doing so, God provides a model for all of us. God meant for every seventh day to be a holy-day, a holiday, for every person, so we could rest, spend time with loved ones and be renewed with God before working again.

God lacks nothing, God has it all. And so again, why would we love any thing or any person more than God? Anything we love is only an infinitesimal fraction of God, so why not love the Source of all things, otherwise those things will be never-ending distractions from our true calling and purpose, which is to love God madly, deeply and completely.

Even though we can do nothing to increase what God has, we can increase our love for God, our complacence in God, through imagining doing something good for God. We can imagine giving God the hearts and souls of ten thousand lost and broken people and imagine God's delight if we did that.

And we can increase our benevolence, our action for God, by desiring and taking more and more complacence in God, by swooning over God's infinite beauty, kindness and peace. True complacence always leads to true action because we want to do more and more for God.

Another action we could take to increase benevolence would be to renounce all earthly pleasures. In previous times, this was thought to be the best way to focus our attention only on God. However, a much better way would be to use every earthly pleasure to remind us of God.

When we taste chocolate, we can thank God. When we smell incense or roses or lily-of-the-valley, we can worship God for these aromas. When we feel our lover's touch, we can praise God. When we hear birds or bells or Beethoven, we can let our heart thrill because God is talking to us through all these avenues. When we see a marvel such as a giraffe or a child or a gold and mauve sunset over the Rocky Mountains, we can acknowledge God's glory. Earthly pleasures, in and of themselves, are nothing more than a distraction from God. But God can use them all to point us to God.

When people lose connection with God, all they have left is earthly titillations, and so they overload their senses, rushing from one sensation to the next in a desperate attempt to find meaning in their lives. However, meaning has its source in God, so we can go directly to the Source, and love God in and through all the titillation.

The best way to increase our benevolence, our active love of God, is to actively praise God. We can list all the blessings in our life. We can write them down daily, weekly, monthly or yearly. Or every three months we can fill a whole sheet full of the blessings we can remember from the last quarter-year. Then we can praise God for all these blessings.

If we do this powerful exercise of recording all our blessings every three months, we will come to see just how blessed our life is, and just how much there is to praise God for. We may think we cannot fill a page, but if we force ourselves to do so, it will bring up buried memories we would otherwise have forgotten.

We can praise God for all the blessings in our life or for all of God's perfections. We can praise God for God's truth, God's Word the Bible, God's patience with sinners, God's creativity seen everywhere: everything is a prism, a facet of God's face and God's creativity.

We can praise God for our past, particularly for all the hardships that have made us a seasoned and unshakable follower of Christ. We can praise God for God's forgiveness. We can praise God as the Wise One, the Ancient of Days, as our mountain refuge and hiding place, as our Advocate, as our true best friend forever.

Praising God perfects every one of our faculties: our will, reason and emotions. It perfects our will because we all want what is good, and God is the Supreme Good. Listing all our blessings shows us how much God loves us, which encourages us to desire God even more, to detach from any other attachments impeding our benevolence.

Praising God perfects our reason, our rational faculties, because reason is concerned with truth. Reason's basic question is "What is true here?" And God is the Supreme Truth. All truths, both scientific and religious, come from and lead us to God.

The post-modern understanding is that truth is relative to one's historical circumstances. Still, as long as we are seeking *the* truth, Christ could lead us to God through these circumstantial truths.

If we put truth first, we will eventually find the true Christ. If we put culture before truth, we will end up with the Christ of our church or our culture: a Southern Baptist, liberal Protestant or Chinese Pentecostal Christ. In other words, we will find a limited Christ, not the universal Christ.

Since all scientific truth comes from God, believers in God have nothing to fear from science. In fact, scientific theories and discoveries are leading us deeper and deeper into the mystery and glory of God.

Margaret Ferris, a Sister of St. Joseph and a spiritual director, had three master's degrees including one in biology, and she often said that she found God more in the laboratory than in the church.

Praising God also perfects our emotional faculties because praise of God is love of God, and love of God is the queen of all our emotions. Love rules over and calms anger, fear, despair and all other negative emotions. And love leads all the positive emotions: joy, peace, and confidence to their true source and perfection in God, the creator, sustainer and goal of all emotion.

CHAPTER THREE
ENDLESS PRAISE COMPLETES OUR COMPLACENCE AND BENEVOLENCE

We must incessantly demand perseverance, making use of the means which our Saviour has taught us to the obtaining of it: prayer, fasting, alms-deeds, frequenting the sacraments, intercourse with the good, the hearing and reading of holy words. 61

In this conduct which the heavenly sweetness makes of our souls, from their entry into charity until their final perfection, which is not finished but in the hour of death, consists the great gift of perseverance, to which our Saviour attaches the greatest gift of eternal glory, according to his saying: He that shall persevere unto the end shall be saved. 62

In fine, the heavenly King having brought the soul which he loves to the end of this life, he assists her also in her blessed departure, by which he draws her to the marriage-bed of eternal glory, which is the delicious fruit of holy perseverance.

And then, dear Theotimus, this soul, wholly ravished with the love of her well-beloved, putting before her eyes the multitude of favours and succours wherewith she was prevented and helped while she was yet in her pilgrimage, incessantly kisses this sweet helping hand, which conducted, drew, and supported her in the way; and confesses that it is of this divine Saviour that she holds her felicity. 63

Praising God, the essence of complacence in God and benevolence toward God, is always hard while in this earthly life with all its miseries.

Despite all our progress, we have succeeded in creating new psychological illnesses and an epidemic of loneliness. In Canada for example, more people now live alone than with another person. And even if people live together, the former intimacy of partners, family and friends has given way to gazing at screens.

The Internet is a great blessing and a great curse—drawing us together in some ways, fragmenting us in many others. Research shows that, because of the carefully curated images people select for their posts, the main emotion when others look at Facebook or Instagram is envy: "Everyone seems to have a great life except me." Depression and pornography addiction are also new epidemics.

All the media communications systems mean we are constantly fire-hosed with too much information. Being in a hyperdrive of competitive overbusyness has become a badge of honor for many people as a result of corporations convincing us that our only purpose is to produce and consume products.

All these things make the contemplative life of gazing at and praising God more challenging. Praise is something we have to consciously work at and prioritize. It is necessary to set time aside for it, possibly blocking off two half-hour periods a week or when we are running, walking, swimming or in the shower—any time when we can consciously disconnect our self from the all-encompassing business and media grid.

We need to turn our phones and computers off and turn our hearts and minds on to God. Praise/worship is better than anything else we can possibly do, for it floods us with God's graces. But again, it is not something that comes easily or naturally, particularly since we have surrounded ourselves with screens of entertainment instead of the wonders of nature.

On the other hand, praise could come easily because we are surrounded by constant praise: nature praises God all around us. Cedar waxwings, hummingbirds, fireflies, rainbows, the moon shimmering on a lake at night, the Milky Way above us and green dark forests keep us in a continual shower of silent praise just by their very being.

The bounty of nature should make us want to praise God the way the Psalms do:

- "The heavens are telling the glory of God; and the skies proclaim God's handiwork" (Ps 19:1).
- "The meadows clothe themselves with flocks, the valleys deck themselves with grain, they shout and sing together for joy" (Ps 65:13).
- "In God's hand are the depths of the Earth; the heights of the mountains are God's also" (Ps 95: 4).
- "Let the field exult, and everything in it. Then shall all the trees of the forest sing for joy" (Ps 96:12).
- "O Lord, how manifold are your works! In wisdom you have made them all; the Earth is full of your creatures...living things both small and great" (Ps 104:24-25).

As well as nature and scripture, the saints show us how to praise God. A most outstanding example is St Francis of Assisi who called the sun his brother and the moon his sister. Legend has it that birds flocked to him. By his calm presence and sense of God in all things, he praised the divine presence in a wolf that was terrorizing a village, and the wolf became tame and no longer bothered the villagers.

Benevolence, the relentless pursuit of the supreme good, causes us to want to draw all creatures into the praise of God, particularly our fellow human beings. If all of us can exalt God, it makes it easier for each of us individually to do it. We derive energy from the God-praising of others, and it causes us to praise God even more. Then our praise ignites the praise of others still more in a mutually reinforcing circle of praise.

Of course, it is harder to praise God if you are living in an unjust situation. Therefore, Evangelicals, Pentecostals, or Charismatics who want their fellow humans to praise God had better do everything they can to eliminate social injustices and systemic evils so that others, particularly the poor, can more readily praise God. They need to give others practical and real reasons to praise God such as the elimination of inequalities of race, gender, and wealth.

Praising God will be supremely easy in heaven because there will be no distractions—we will be fully aware of God's immediate presence in each and every thing. Hearing angels and archangels sing God's praises with all their hearts will inspire us to levels of praise we presently cannot imagine.

But Jesus praises God more than any angel because only God can praise God adequately. The Father, Son and Holy Spirit praise each other endlessly. The Father endlessly laughs and begets the Son, and the Father and Son laugh together, endlessly begetting the Holy Spirit. This divine laughter, this infinite joy, this constant delight in each other's presence, gave birth to the universe.

In heaven we will see God praising God forever in a never-ending loop of ever-increasing laughter, joy and love. And this will make our complacence and benevolence complete because no greater praise of God would be possible.

BOOK FIVE

CONCERNING THE EXERCISES
OF HOLY LOVE IN PRAYER

CHAPTER ONE

MEDITATION AND CONTEMPLATION
UNITE OUR ACTIONS AND HEARTS TO GOD

We have two principal ways of exercising our love towards God, the one affective, the other effective, or, as St. Bernard calls it, active; by that we affect or love God and what he loves, by this we serve God and do what he ordains; that joins us to God's goodness, this makes us execute his will: the one fills us with complacency, benevolence, yearnings, desires, aspirations and spiritual ardours, causing us to practise the sacred infusions and minglings of our spirit with God's; the other establishes in us the solid resolution, the constancy of heart, and the inviolable obedience requisite to effect the ordinances of the divine will, and to suffer, accept, approve, and embrace, all that comes from his good-pleasure. 64

Of what do we discourse in prayer? What is the subject of our conference? Theotimus, in it we speak of God only: for of what can love discourse and talk but of the well-beloved? And therefore prayer, and mystical theology, are one same thing. It is called theology, because as speculative theology has God for its object, so this also treats only of God. 65

Truly the chief exercise in mystical theology is to speak to God and to hear God speak in the bottom of the heart; and because this discourse passes in most secret aspirations and inspirations, we term it a silent conversing. Eyes speak to eyes, and heart to heart, and none understand what passes save the sacred lovers who speak. 66

In fine, thoughts and study may be upon any subject, but meditation, in our present sense, has reference only to those objects whose consideration tends to make us good and devout. So that meditation is no other thing than an attentive thought, voluntarily reiterated or entertained in the mind, to excite the will to holy and salutary affections and resolutions. 67

There are few who meditate to inflame their heart with holy heavenly love. 68

Such is the devout soul in meditation. She passes from mystery to mystery, not at random, or only to solace herself in viewing the admirable beauty of those divine objects, but deliberately and of set purpose, to find out motives of love or of some heavenly affection. 69

We meditate to gather the love of God, but having gathered it we contemplate God, and are attentive to his goodness, by reason of the sweetness which love makes us find in it. The desire we have to obtain divine love makes us meditate, but love obtained makes us contemplate. 70

In conclusion, Meditation is the mother, and Contemplation the daughter of love. 71

Beyond complacence, that is, our initial attraction to God brought about by our dawning sense of God's beauty, truth and goodness, and beyond benevolence, our enthusiastic pursuit of God, our love for God consists of two more parts.

Complacence is like seeing a beautiful ship in the harbor and dreaming about being on it. Benevolence is not waiting for the ship to come in but swimming out to it, boarding it and becoming part of the crew. Beyond that there is meditative love and contemplative love.

Meditative love involves surrender of our will to God's will, obeying the Captain of the ship and doing whatever God tells us to do. It is effective love, that is, it does not complacently lie or stand there, it takes whatever action is necessary to unite our actions to God's will.

Contemplation is affective love. It is becoming the Captain's best friend and soulmate. Not only is our will united with that of the Captain, our heart is united with God's heart.

In contemplation, we are of one mind and one heart with God in a kind of mind-meld and heart-meld. We know God from within and God knows us from within. God has always known us from within, but we have never known God this way because it is a gift of the Holy Spirit that is only given when we are ready to receive it.

We cannot achieve contemplation, it is a gift, but we can prepare for it. We cannot make it rain, but we can prepare the soil. An effective way to do this is to meditate on scripture, the revelation of God, day and night.

"Happy are those who do not follow the advice of the wicked, or take the path that sinners tread, or sit in the seat of scoffers; but their delight is in the law of the Lord, and on God's law they meditate day and night" (Ps 1:1-2).

Meditating on scripture is not done to increase our knowledge of God's word, it is done to increase our love of God's Word, Jesus, and therefore our love of God. Knowledge pursued without love of God leads to vanity: "Knowledge puffs up, but love builds up" (I Corinthians 8:1).

We can have all the degrees in the world, even a PhD in theology, and still not love God. God is not impressed with all our certificates and degrees; God wants to know where our heart is. Are we on God's side and a genuine member of God's ark, the church, or not?

Quite simply, love and faith go where science cannot: into the inner workings of our heart and God's heart. A doctorate in sub-atomic physics will never get us there. Even theology is just "theo-logos" or "God-talk," it is not "God-love." In theology we are simply talking or thinking about God, which is good and important, but it is far more important to enter into God.

The most uneducated peasant can enter heaven, and the most educated scholar, and even popes, can cut themselves off from God.

Meditation thus goes beyond complacence, dreaming about the ship, and benevolence, boarding it, to what love of God is really all about, obeying the Captain. Everything is easy until we get to obedience, to doing whatever God wants us to do. Not that God will *necessarily* ask us to do things we do not want to do, but that might be the case. If we are willing to obey, we will know, and God will know, that we are really committed to God.

Meditation is the mother whose daughter is contemplation. The mother sets the stage for the daughter to excel, be the Captain's best friend and soulmate, or even marry the Captain.

Meditation invites us into serious love of God, contemplation revels in the love of God and perfects it.

The theology of mystics, mystical theology, is not just talk about God, it is prayer to God that unites us with God: body, mind, heart, soul and will.

CHAPTER TWO
DEEP CONTEMPLATION

Meditation considers in detail, and as it were piece by piece, the objects calculated to move us, but contemplation takes a very simple and collected view of the object which it loves. 72

In meditating, we as it were count the divine perfections which we find in a mystery, but in contemplating we sum up their total. 73

At length, all the universe being accomplished, the divine meditation is changed as it were into contemplation; for viewing all the goodness that was in his works with one only look – he saw, says Moses, all the things that he had made, and they were very good.

The different parts considered severally by manner of meditation were good, but beheld in one only regard all together in form of contemplation, they were found very good. 74

Contemplation has still this excellency that it is made with delight, for it supposes that we have found God and his holy love, that we enjoy it and delight in it, saying: 'I found him whom my soul loveth: I held him, and I will not let him go.' In which it differs from meditation, which almost always is performed with difficulty, labour and reasoning. 75

Now whereas to attain unto contemplation we stand ordinarily in need of hearing the word of God, of having spiritual discourse and conference with others, like the ancient anchorites, of reading, praying, meditating, singing canticles, conceiving good thoughts, - for this reason, holy contemplation being the end and aim of all these exercises, they are all reduced to it. 76

Meditation sees God in parts, contemplation sees the whole, all of God's virtues all at once.

Meditation sees God one virtue at a time. For example, we might mentally reflect on God's beauty or forgiveness or wisdom or peacefulness separately from the other virtues.

Even though we are meditating on just one virtue, it does not mean that we cannot find the virtue, and therefore God, everywhere.

God's beauty is omnipresent: in the Large and Small Magellanic Clouds (which are really small galaxies circling our Milky Way Galaxy) overhead on a moonless night in the southern hemisphere, in photos of swirling Hubble galaxies, star clusters and nebulae. On Earth we can see God's beauty in the humble and craggy faces of Guatemalan peasants and in the vibrant colors of the clothing they weave.

If we crack open a crusty black geode, we can find God's beauty in the purple crystals hidden within. If we crack open a Hell's Angel biker, within we may find the beauty of a man whose heart has been wounded by his father, someone who turns out to be a gentle man who cries tears when the nurse touches him in the emergency ward, because no one has ever touched him tenderly before.

God's beauty is everywhere: in valleys hushed and deep in snow; in the wild mountain thyme that grows around the blooming heather; in the wide eyes of a child; in a chameleon changing colors; in a newly married couple dancing in gown and tuxedo the first dance at their wedding reception. God's beauty overflows its banks everywhere.

Contemplation sees the whole, all the virtues, all at once. This is a mind-blowing, mind-glowing gift of God, a grace, a quick intuition that all God's goodness, truth, justice, compassion, helpfulness, humility, graciousness, holiness, gentleness, omnipotence, consciousness, creativity, freedom, trustworthiness, kindness and so on are all One.

This insight often comes in a nano-second, but the impact lasts a lifetime. It changes everything in an indescribable way. The recipient sees the Truth, and the Truth, which is God's essence, sets them free.

Meditation involves labor and action on our part; contemplation is effortless as it involves action on God's part. Meditation is our mental action in us, contemplation is God's spiritual action in us.

"Lectio Divina," divine reading, contains both meditation and contemplation within it, and can be compared to the process of digestion, in four steps.

First, we obtain the food and put it in our mouth—we read the scriptures twice, once to get the general sense of the passage, and the second time to note key words or phrases. In Latin this is "lectio."

Then we chew the food—we meditate on the words and phrases we have selected—we turn them over and over in our mind, we ask questions: what was the author trying to say? What does this phrase mean? What does it mean to me? How does this apply to my life circumstances? This mental chewing is "meditatio."

Next, we swallow the food and the process of digestion begins in earnest—we pray over our selected words and phrases and over the answers to our questions. For some questions the answer may come to us later, but we can pray for an answer now, and pray when the answer comes. We are asking God to help us understand the scripture verses and their meaning for our psyche and our life. This prayer, this spiritual digestion, is called "oratio." It involves our action, but the results are up to God.

Finally, the food is incorporated into our cells giving them energy and life. We are renewed at the cellular level. This is contemplation or resting in God. Things are really beyond our control and action now. This resting is called "contemplatio."

In deep contemplation, all the soul's faculties of reason, memory and imagination are asleep. Only the will is awake, and all it experiences is deep joy. The will is wide awake, but not active. Deep contemplation happens by the grace of God alone. There is no movement of the intellect, emotions or will. The actions that change our life only happen when deep contemplation is over.

Getting the food into our hand and into our mouth, chewing on the food, digesting the food and incorporating the food into our body represent the whole process of physical digestion. And reading (lectio), meditation (meditatio), prayer (oratio) and contemplation (contemplatio) represent the complete process of spiritual digestion.

We will know our spiritual diet has been fulfilled when we observe behavioral changes in our life and see that our actions produce results, all by God's grace.

CHAPTER THREE
SACRED REPOSE

This repose sometimes goes so deep in its tranquillity, that the whole soul and all its powers fall as it were asleep, and make no movement nor action whatever, except the will alone, and even this does no more than receive the delight and satisfaction which the presence of the beloved affords. 77

However, the soul who in this sweet repose enjoys this delicate sense of the divine presence, though she is not conscious of the enjoyment, yet clearly shows how dear and precious this happiness is unto her, if one offer to deprive her of it or divert her from it; for then the poor soul complains, cries out, yea sometimes weeps. 78

A soul thus recollected in her God would not change her repose for the greatest goods in the world. 79

The well-beloved St. John is ordinarily painted, in the Last Supper, not only lying but even sleeping in his Master's bosom, because he was seated after the fashion of the Easterns (Levantins), so that his head was towards his lover's breast: and as he slept no corporal sleep there, – what likelihood of that? – so I make no question but that, finding himself so near the breasts of the eternal sweetness, he took a profound mystical sleep, like a child of love which locked to its mother's breast sucks while sleeping. 80

So that, to conclude, it is the will alone that softly, and as it were tenderly sucking, draws the milk of his sweet presence; all the rest of the soul quietly reposing with her by the sweetness of the pleasure which she takes. 81

O Eternal God! When by thy sweet presence thou dost cast odoriferous perfumes into our hearts, perfumes more pleasing than delicious wine and honey, all the powers of our soul enter into so delightful a repose and so absolute a rest, that there is no movement save of the will, which, as the spiritual sense of smell remains delightfully engaged in enjoying, without adverting to it, the incomparable good of having its God present. 82

There is a great difference, Theotimus, between being occupied with God who gives us the contentment and being busied with the contentment which God gives us.

The soul, then, to whom God gives holy, loving quiet in prayer, must abstain as far as she is able from looking upon herself or her repose, which to be preserved must not be curiously observed; for he who loves it too much loses it. 83

If we perceive ourselves distracted, through a curiosity to know what we are doing in prayer, we must replace our hearts in the sweet and peaceable attention to God's presence from which we strayed. 84

For in fine the height of love's ecstasy is to have our will not in its own contentment but in God's, or, not to have our contentment in our own will, but in God's. 85

In sacred repose or sacred rest, there is no need of memory, imagination, reasoning or intellect. The purpose of all these faculties is to get us to sacred repose, so we do not need them anymore, or at least until we rejoin the everyday world of "ordinary time."

In everyday life, memory can be used so we do not repeat the same mistakes and so we connect with the Lord more quickly. Imagination can be used to picture being with Jesus, the saints and heaven and to motivate us to pursue God with all our heart. Reason can be used to discern what is the best path to take, what is the greater of two good paths.

This rational discernment can often be accomplished by journaling, that is, listing the pros and cons of the two paths. Then it is important to weigh each pro and con since one pro could outweigh ten cons or vice versa. The key question is always: "Where can I serve God the most?"

Our intellect can be used to draw upon our vast store of knowledge of scripture and other holy writings that can lead us to God.

In sacred repose we don't need any of this now since we have reached, by the grace of God, the goal of all our faculties. In sacred repose, the will, the only faculty still active, simply delights in God, much as a nursing child delights in its mother's breast.

In sacred repose, we focus solely on God, not on our soul, our contentment or on the repose itself. There is absolutely no self-interest in sacred repose. Our contentment, our happiness, our delight is only in God, not in the contentment, happiness, delight or joy in itself.

In fact, as soon as we focus on the delight and not on God, we lose the delight. This is always a deadly trap for meditators. As soon as we start thinking while meditating, "This is going well" or "I am a great meditator" or "I am really diving into God," then poof, the connection is broken and the benefits cease because we are focusing on our self or our delight, not on God.

In sacred repose, our soul essentially becomes liquified and disappears into God. It is like a drop of rain falling into the ocean. Our soul flows into God and God flows into our soul. It is what the apostle Paul wrote: "It is no longer I who live, but it is Christ who lives in me" (Galatians 2:20). The soul is in effect "hidden with Christ in God" (Colossians 3:3). Our soul is still there, we are just not aware of it.

Once this becomes a permanent state, we can reflect on both our soul and on God without losing awareness of either of them. This is our true self, our Godself, Christ-consciousness: the ability to hold God, our soul and our relative temporal self all in our heart, mind and soul at the same time.

Sacred repose helps us to realize that "In my deepest self, I am both human and made in God's image, by God's grace." This is what Christ came to show us: what it is like to be both human and divine at the same time. This was God's plan from the beginning: to take evolution to the next step beyond humanity to the reign of God where all humans realize they are human and divine, by God's grace. Christ is divine by nature, we are divine and divinized by grace.

In sacred repose, if the soul becomes distracted by anything other than God, the soul cries out like a baby when the breast is suddenly removed. If the breast is removed for a long time it is the dark night of the soul. The soul profoundly longs for God because it knows now just how lovable God is, the sum of all desires, what true life and true love are really all about, but now the Beloved is gone and "I sought him whom my soul loves; I sought him but found him not" (Song of Solomon 3:1).

This dark night can go on for years, or even decades as it did with Mother Teresa of Calcutta. Shortly after she began her mission to take care of the poorest of the poor, she felt abandoned by God. God may seem to be gone, but in fact God is not gone. God is in our desire for God, in our profound longing to be restored to God again. Mother Teresa always had this desire even when she felt most abandoned.

Spiritual directors only worry about directees when their desire for God is gone, which means they are not in the dark night but in depression, boredom, ennui or laziness about their spiritual life.

In the dark night, scripture may seem dead, and it may be impossible to pray, but as long as the desire for God is there, we are still spiritually well. God is moving us to base our faith life on will, not emotion. The consolations of the "illumination" phase, when it feels like everything is going well and we are really connecting with God, really loving God, may suddenly be gone, or gradually disappear.

Feelings can come and go, but willing to love God in spite of God being gone (or rather *feeling* like God is gone) is a much more permanent state. Will is much more permanent than feelings, and this is what God, through the dark night, is moving us to.

It is the "Job" stage of the spiritual life. Job willed to be faithful to God, and to trust God, in spite of every consolation being taken away. His health, his children and his great wealth were gone. Yet he still trusted and worshipped God. And we know how the story ended: God restored everything Job had and more.

This is the "union with God" stage of the spiritual journey.

Chapter Four

Sacred Wounds

You see then clearly, Theotimus, that the outflowing of a soul into her God is a true ecstasy, by which the soul quite transcends the limits of her natural form of existence being wholly mingled with, absorbed and engulfed in, her God.

Hence it happens that such as attain to these holy excesses of heavenly love, afterwards, being come to themselves, find nothing on the Earth that can content them, and living in an extreme annihilation of themselves, remain much weakened in all that belongs to the senses, and have perpetually in their hearts the maxim of the Blessed Mother St. Teresa: 'What is not God is to me nothing.' 86

Speaking of heavenly love, there is in the practice of it a kind of wound given by God himself to the soul which he would highly perfect. For he gives her admirable sentiments of and incomparable attractions for his sovereign goodness, as if pressing and soliciting her to love him; and then she forcibly lifts herself up as if to soar higher towards her divine object; but stopping short, because she cannot love as much as she desires: – O God! she feels a pain which has no equal. 87

Seeing the Saviour of our souls wounded to death by love of us, even to the death of the cross, how can we but be wounded for him? 88

Sometimes love wounds us with the mere consideration of the multitude of those who contemn the love of God; so that we faint away for grief for this. 89

There is this admirable in the wounds received from the divine love that their pain is delightful, and all that feel it consent to it, and would not change this pain for all the pleasures of the world. There is no pain in love, or if there is pain, it is well-beloved pain. 90

Truly, Theotimus, when the wounds and strokes of love are frequent and strong they put us into a languor, and into love's well-beloved sickness. Who could ever describe the loving langours of Sts Catherine of Siena and Genoa, or of a St. Angela of Foligno, or St. Christina, or the Blessed Mother St. Teresa, a St. Bernard, a St. Francis. And as for this last, his life was nothing but tears, sighs, plaints, langours, wastings, love-trances.

But in all this, nothing is so wonderful as that admirable communication which the sweet Jesus made him of his loving and precious pains, by the impression of his wounds and stigmata. 91

To conclude, Theotimus, how do you think that a soul which has once tasted divine consolations at all freely, can live in this world so full of miseries, without an almost continual pain and languishing? 92

Sacred love, like human love, can result in wounds to the heart. If we are rejected by the one we love, it is painful. God never rejects us, but God may withdraw from us all of God's consolations in order to move us from operating on the basis of feeling to operating based on will, and this may feel like God's rejection, or at least God's absence. The absence (or seeming absence) of God can be a thousand times more painful than human absence. All of life's meaning evaporates and everything becomes pointless and absurd. The energy of life has been sucked out of us.

Our heart can also be hurt by its own inability to love God as much as God deserves. God as the source, sustenance and goal of all things is infinitely more lovable than anything. God is Being-Itself, the being of all beings, without which nothing would exist. God is all beauty, truth, meaning, joy, wisdom, grace, peace and justice. Therefore, God can never be loved enough. God deserves more love than we can ever give, and our heart knows this.

We live in the Milky Way Galaxy, which is 100,000 light years in diameter. Light travels 6 trillion miles (9 trillion kilometers) in a year.

So even our own galaxy is too mindboggling to comprehend. The latest scientific research indicates that there may be two trillion galaxies, and God is greater than all this, so there is no possible way we can even begin to love the fullness of God. We cannot possibly wrap our heart around all that God is, and because of this our heart may be full of sorrow.

Our heart can also be wounded when it sees Christ wounded and dying an agonizing death for our soul. What has the Master of the Universe done that he should deserve this? How great is human sin that it should want to crucify God? How great is God's love to lay down God's life for us when we are not even a dust mote in the unimaginably vast expanse of the universe?

Then there is the grief our heart feels from knowing that so many people are oblivious to God's love. And their numbers are growing, at least in North America and Europe. So many are desperately walking on a tightrope between life and death, trying to survive, with no knowledge that God's love is all around them and that if they fell, God's loving arms would catch them in eternity.

So, they shamble on through life, silently afraid of everything, living trivial lives of quiet despair when they should be fully and vibrantly alive. When we turn our heart towards God, we start to see our fellow human beings the way God sees them, and we feel the pain God feels when they turn away from God.

The heart that passionately desires to love God feels a quadruple wound from the absence of God, not being able to love God as much as God deserves, seeing Christ wounded and dying because of our sins, and grief that so many people are unaware of, or turn away from, God's love.

Sacred wounds can even have a physical effect. When she watched Jesus slowly die, Mary's heart felt like it was pierced by a sword as Simeon predicted. It is a tragedy to have your child die before you do. It is a far deeper tragedy to see him tortured to death in front of you. And it is another thing again to recall the message of the archangel Gabriel who promised that your son "will be great and will be called the Son of the Most High, and the Lord God will give to him the throne of his ancestor David. He will reign over the house of Jacob forever, and of his kingdom there will be no end" (Luke 1:32-33).

Given this promise, it must have seemed utterly absurd to Mary that the Roman and Jewish authorities should be putting her son to such a humiliating death as a criminal and heretic.

The quadruple sacred wounds of the heart were so painful for the apostle Paul that they made all the beatings, floggings, whippings and stonings he suffered seem like nothing by comparison. Paul's sacred wounds were so deep that they gave him the courage to face any of the relatively trivial pain that humans could inflict upon his physical body.

Other saints like Francis of Assisi and Padre Pio were so intensely focused on the crucifixion of their Lord that they developed the same wounds Jesus suffered on the cross in their own flesh in the form of stigmata.

These sacred wounds make the saint's life in the world, in the midst of the world's miseries, even more miserable. Yet the saint loves these sacred wounds exceedingly more than all the pleasures the world has to offer.

BOOK SIX

THE SOUL'S UNION WITH GOD IS PERFECTED IN PRAYER

CHAPTER ONE

TYPES OF ECSTASY AND RAPTURE

When our spirit, raised above natural light, begins to see the sacred truths of faith, O God! Theotimus, what joy! The soul melts with pleasure, hearing the voice of her heavenly spouse, whom she finds more sweet and delicious than the honey of all human sciences.

God has imprinted upon all created things his traces, trail, or footsteps, so that the knowledge we have of his divine Majesty by creatures seems no other thing than the sight of the feet of God, while in comparison of this, faith is a view of the very face of the divine Majesty. 93

When having arrived in the heavenly Jerusalem, we shall see the great Solomon, the King of Glory, seated upon the throne of his wisdom, manifesting by an incomprehensible brightness the wonders and eternal secrets of his sovereign truth, with such light that our understanding will actually see what it had believed here below – Ah! then, dearest Theotimus, what raptures! What ecstasies! What admiration! What love! What sweetness! No, never (shall we say in this excess of sweetness) never could we have conceived that we should see truths so delightsome. 94

Oh! my dear Theotimus, what pleasure will man's heart take in seeing the face of the Divinity, a face so much desired, yea a face the only desire of our souls? 95

Ideally, there would never be any self-interest in pursuing God. The only motive would be to just be with God. Since God is fully present with us right here and right now all the time, we do not have to seek God externally, we just need to go within and wake up to the fact that God is already there waiting for us with open arms.

God in Christ always takes the initiative in drawing us to God dwelling within us. Even our desire to be with God, to seek God and to go within are due to God's desire for us.

Ecstasy is something we all want, either consciously or subconsciously. The word means "ex-stasis" or "to stand out of yourself." We all want to transcend our petty ego-self. But there are different ways of doing this, and some constitute spiritual devolution, spiritual death, not spiritual evolution and growth.

If we get out of our self by drinking, carousing and leading a wildly promiscuous life, we are pursuing sensual ecstasy rather than spiritual ecstasy. We are becoming a beast or lower than a beast because God has given us a brain with a prefrontal lobe which should know better than the animal brain.

On the other hand, if we go out of ourself in spiritual ecstasy, we become more angelic, we raise ourself above the part of our self that is bodily and animal. If the spiritual ecstasy is temporary, it is called **"transport"** or **"suspension of all faculties."** If it lasts longer it is called **"rapture"**—we are so united with God that our rational faculties are completely suspended until it is over. In summary, there is beastly ecstasy, angelic ecstasy, transport and rapture.

As well, there are different types or degrees of union with God. There is **detectable union with God.** This is the union of the new convert where a noticeable shift of behavior is apparent to all. The person stops their revelry, profanity and debauchery; their speech softens, and they engage in acts of service.

Undetected union with God means that the Holy Spirit is working deep within our soul, drawing us ever nearer into the never-ending abyss that is God.

Union with God of the intellect and will means that our every thought and desire wants to be united with God's thoughts and desires and wants to defend the faith rationally and with all our strength.

Union of all the soul's faculties with God means that our memory, imagination, intuition, feelings and senses all revolve around God, the Source, Sustenance and Goal of our soul.

Union with God by way of memory might take the form of extensively memorizing comforting scripture verses such as "Cast all your anxiety on God because God cares for you" (I Peter 5:7) or "God alone is my rock and salvation, my fortress; I shall not be shaken" (Ps 62:6) or "Trust in the Lord, and do good; so you will live in the land and enjoy security" (Ps 37:3) or "When the cares of my heart are many, your consolations cheer my soul" (Ps 94:19) or "Our soul waits for the Lord; God is our help and shield" (Ps 33:20).

Union with God by way of imagination could happen in the prayer style of Saint Ignatius of Loyola where we imagine ourself right in the center of biblical scenes such as Jesus walking on the raging sea (Matthew 14:22-33). This lets us experience things as the disciples did: with our feelings and senses we now understand their terror and wonder, hear the howling wind and feel the waves rock the boat. This makes scripture study more existentially real.

There are also degrees of union of intellect, emotions and actions with God's intellect, emotions and actions.

Rapture of the intellect means that we totally go beyond earthly truths in the ecstasy of knowing God's Absolute Truth.

Rapture of the emotions means we experience the ecstasy of extreme devotion to God, the ecstasy of the saints in heaven.

Rapture of actions means we experience the ecstasy of extreme deeds done in God's name: we are willing to live in abject poverty with the poor and minister to those dying of an epidemic virus with no thought of our own well-being. We are willing to lay our body on the line in the fight for social justice.

No amount of pain or even torture can deter us from professing the faith. We are more than willing to be a martyr torn apart by lions, or nowadays, shot to death by some right-wing military squad because we fought for justice.

CHAPTER TWO
DISCERNING BETWEEN DIVINE AND DIABOLICAL INSPIRATION

Now one of the best marks of the goodness of all inspirations in general, and particularly of extraordinary ones, is the peace and tranquillity of the heart that receives them: for though indeed the Holy Ghost is violent, yet his violence is gentle, sweet and peaceful. 96

Thus, it is that those servants of God who had the highest and sublimest inspirations were the most mild and peaceable men in the world, as Abraham, Isaac, and Jacob; Moses is styled the meekest of men; David is lauded for his mildness. 97

On the contrary, the evil spirit is turbulent, rough, disturbing; and those who follow infernal suggestions, taking them to be heavenly inspirations, are as a rule easily known, because they are unquiet, headstrong, haughty, ready to undertake or meddle with all affairs, men who under the cloak of zeal turn everything upside down, censure every one, chide every one, find fault with everything; they are persons who will not be directed, will not give in to anyone, will bear nothing, but gratify the passions of self-love under the name of jealousy for God's honour. 98

When considering the types of ecstasy and rapture given in the previous chapter, it is important to discern what is from God and what is not. Remember that, according to scripture, a demon can disguise itself as an angel of light (2 Corinthians 11:14).

The main criteria for this discernment is love. Did the vision, inspiration, ecstasy, transport or rapture, make us a more loving person after it occurred? The experience cannot be discerned in and of itself, but rather by its fruits. It is God's love poured into us that unites us to God; and through us God's love spills over into all the people with whom we come in contact. God's love results in social justice which, to quote the great Protestant theologian Reinhold Niebuhr, is "the proper distribution of love throughout society." If this does not happen, it makes the original experience suspect.

Our intellect is drawn to God's truth. In God all things are mystery, and yet if the intellect is inspired by God, all things make sense on a deeper spiritual, intuitive level. Our will is drawn to God's goodness, since the human will naturally loves what is good. God's truth and goodness are the ultimate magnets drawing our intellect and will.

However, if it is not an underlying love of truth and goodness drawing us, then it is not God doing the drawing. Scientists who love seeking the truth experience God working in them. Psychologists and social workers who love to do good to others also experience God within, whether they acknowledge it or not.

It is possible for the intellect to become separated from love and land in the desert of dry speculation. This happens in the academic world all the time. The dictum of "publish or perish" destroys the joy of learning for many academics. They are no longer pursuing knowledge out of love but out of fear of losing their job and not being able to feed their family. They are not concerned about advancing the truth for other human beings, they are only concerned with themselves and their survival.

The classic examples of knowledge separated from love into speculation were the brutal medical experiments done on Jews by Nazi doctors. "Let's see how long it will take this man to die if we immerse him naked into a bathtub filled with ice? Let's time it and test this out." Or "Let's see if a man can still walk if we remove all the muscles below his knees." The doctors conducted horrifying experiments like these with no pangs of conscience because Jews were considered to be subhuman and the knowledge might help the Nazi troops who have to wade through frigid rivers or who are wounded.

Similarly, our will can become separated from love of goodness into sensuality. Rather than helping others we are drawn or seduced into excitement or stimulation for ourselves. The classic example of this is the multi-billion-dollar pornography epidemic which has spread through the digital revolution. Highly demeaning to women as subhuman sexual objects, it is fueling what some experts call our "rape culture."

Divine versus diabolical inspiration is discernible by its warmth. It comes from God's heart and penetrates the depths of our heart with its warmth and love.

Diabolical inspiration is discernible by its speculative nature. It comes from diabolical minds and penetrates deeply into our mind. Diabolical reasoning leads us astray, deceiving us by mere human reasoning. For example, "There is a lot of suffering in the world, so there must not be a God. God cannot be omniscient, omnipotent and all-loving and also allow evil and suffering."

This reasoning does not consider the possibility of God's conscious self-limitation in order to allow for human freedom and therefore human love. Neither does it take into consideration the awareness faith-filled believers often have of God's presence in the midst of suffering, so they are not destroyed by it.

Mere human reason might also lead us to speculate that "Even if there is a God, I am a good person since I don't kill people or steal, therefore I must be okay with God." This may be true, you may be a conventionally good person, but you may also be missing out on the main purpose of life, that is, "divinization"—being filled to the brim with God. Mere human reasoning may short-change your life.

Divine inspiration on the other hand can produce a supernatural, superhuman life, the life of a saint who sees their own poverty, persecution and suffering as blessings from God because they help us to see through the shallowness and sensual bestiality of much of contemporary life.

In short, just having knowledge and spiritual visions means nothing without love. If our life is not changed for the better, our ecstasy or rapture may come from the "father of lies" (John 8:44). Raptures may convince us that we are spiritually superior to others; we may have had Pentecostal or charismatic experiences and speak with the tongues of angels, but without love all these things are meaningless (I Corinthians 13:1).

Many saints have led superhuman lives without visions or raptures. The supernatural, superhuman life is known by its fruits, for it is where "I have been crucified with Christ; and it is no longer I who live, but it is Christ who lives in me" (Galatians 2: 19-20).

Genuine inspirations, visions, ecstasies and raptures do not involve self-preoccupation with our spiritual superiority, but rather complete focus on God and complete self-forgetfulness in God.

CHAPTER THREE
LOVE IS STRONGER THAN DEATH

Love is strong as death. Death separates the soul of him who dies from the body, and from all things of the world; sacred love separates the soul of the lover from his body and from all the things of the world: nor is there any other difference saving that death does that in effect, which love only does in affection. 99

All the Apostles and almost all the Martyrs died in prayer. 100

St. Francis Xavier, held and kissed the image of the crucifix, and repeated at every kiss these ejaculations of his soul: O Jesus! The God of my heart!" 101

Some sacred lovers so absolutely give themselves over to the exercises of divine love, that this holy fire wastes and consumes their life. 102

When the fervour of holy love is great, it gives so many assaults to the heart, so often wounds it, causes in it so many langours, melts it so habitually, and puts it so frequently into ecstasies and raptures, that by this means, the soul, almost entirely occupied in God, not being able to afford sufficient assistance to nature to effect digestion and nourish itself properly, the animal and vital spirits begin little by little to fail, life is shortened, and death takes place. 103

St. Francis, from the time that he received the holy stigmata of his Master, he had such violent and sharp pains, pangs, convulsions, and illnesses, that he became mere skin and bone, and he seemed rather to be a skeleton, or a picture of death, than a man yet living and breathing. 104

All the elect then, Theotimus, died in the habit of holy love; but fur-

ther, some died even in the exercise of it, others for this love, and others by this same love. But what belongs to this sovereign degree of love is, that some die of love. 105

Before tackling how love of God can kill us, it is important to re-member that God is supremely life-giving. Genesis is about God cre-ating all forms of life, and the rest of the Jewish scriptures say over and over in various ways: "Choose life!" And, as Jesus said: "I came that they may have life and have it abundantly" (John 10:10).

God created things so that life pops up even in the most extreme conditions on Earth: in Antarctic extreme cold and around boiling thermal vents on the bottom of the ocean floor.

God is not only radically pro-life on the grandest scale (to be distinguished from those who are pro-birth but don't care for the mother or child after the birth), God is also death-destroying. God is mediated to us through all human attempts to prevent death through nurses, doctors, social workers, social justice and anti-poverty groups, Mothers Against Drunk Driving (M.A.D.D.) and so many other forms of social action.

While he was alive, Jesus brought back to life several people who were clinically dead, the most dramatic being Lazarus who was four days gone before Jesus raised him. Jesus proclaimed "I am the res-urrection and the life. Those who believe in me, even though they die, will live" (John 11:25). Christians believe that the resurrection of Christ from death conquered death for all of us.

Moreover, God is co-suffering, that is, God suffers with us. And since God knows all the suffering of everyone all the time, God's co-suffering is greater than we can imagine.

Just as a parent suffers when their child is ill, so God, as the su-premely loving Mother and Father of all of us, suffers unimaginably when we suffer. Jesus on the cross is the great sign of God's co-suf-fering.

That is why many Christians wear the symbol of their crucified, co-suffering God on chains around their neck. This practice is meant to help us remember the long-suffering of Jesus. We have become so used to this symbol we often forget how utterly unique it is among the world's religions. Does any other major tradition portray their God as grievously suffering?

How is it then, if God is life-giving, death-destroying and co-suffering, that divine love can end our life on Earth?

First, ecstasy separates the soul from the body and from all worldly concerns. When we are in a state of rapture, our sole focus and concern is on God. As we saw earlier, the intense identification of some saints such as Francis of Assisi with the crucified Jesus can lead to stigmata, the five sacred wounds of Christ experienced in the saint's own hands, feet and side.

Love of the divine can go even further and result in death. A lover of God can become so absorbed in love that they lose all their appetite, forget to eat and starve to death.

Legend has it that, while they did not starve to death, the souls of Mary Magdalene, Clare of Assisi and Teresa of Avila became so separated from their bodies that the silver cord tethering them to earthly life snapped, and they died from love of the Divine.

Another more common way that loving God can lead to death is through martyrdom. How many Christians, because of their love of God, have refused to renounce their faith and in ancient days were ripped apart by lions, impaled with spears, beheaded with swords, burned alive as Roman candles in stadiums, and in our times tortured, raped, and killed in Nazi Germany, Syria, Iraq, El Salvador and other parts of the world? Estimates vary between one and ten million for the number of Christian martyrs in the 20th century, but in academic and church circles it is widely acknowledged in any case that there were more martyrs than in any other century.

In rare cases, love of God can end our life on Earth in a unique way. The Catholic Church in its two-thousand-year history has only two teachings that are considered "infallible:" the immaculate conception of Mary and her bodily assumption into heaven. All the rest of papal teaching, contrary to popular belief, is not infallible (without possibility of error) but "authoritative," that is, to be taken seriously because it is done in conjunction with the Magisterium, the teaching office of the church, the Office of Bishops. Typically, the bishops put a lot of thought, prayer, consultation and research into their teachings, or they would not call them authoritative, but these teachings are not considered infallible. In spite of this, many Catholics think that everything the Pope says or writes is infallible. However, this is not accurate according to official Catholic teaching.

In any case, both Catholics and Protestants should find it easy to believe, as Simeon prophesied in scripture (Luke 2:25-35), that when Jesus died on the cross, a spiritual sword pierced the soul of Mary, so that out of her supreme love for her son, she died, at least emotionally, with him.

It is interesting that her body was never found, leading to the belief in her bodily assumption into heaven. Not finding a grave for Mary is not evidence of her assumption, but when a Catholic saint dies there is often a church built there, as with St. Peter's Basilica in Rome, which marks the place where the apostle Peter died. There has never been a marked grave or a church built over a grave of Mary, one of the most significant people in the history of Christianity. What happened to her, and where did she go? It is a mystery.

We live in an age of science, and from a scientific point of view, the bodily assumption of Mary into heaven becomes truly absurd. Since we now know that heaven is not a place "somewhere beyond the stars," as people believed up until Galileo, what would Mary's assumption mean from a modern scientific view?

Let's make a few assumptions. First of all, let's assume that she was travelling at the speed of light, that is, 186,000 miles (roughly 300,000 kilometres) per second. Secondly, let's assume that heaven is in the center of our Milky Way Galaxy. Earth is about 30,000 light years away from the galaxy's center. So, if Mary was travelling at the speed of light for the past two thousand years, at present she would only be one fifteenth of the way to heaven. She would only eventually arrive in about the year 30,000 CE.

The bodily assumption of Mary into heaven, even given our two ridiculous assumptions, is absurd from a scientific point of view.

However, it makes perfect sense religiously.

The basic differences between science and religion are that science analyzes whereas religion synthesizes, and science has to do with facts whereas religion has to do with meaning. So, science analyzes facts and religion synthesizes meanings.

Reality is mediated to us as much or more by meaning as by facts and data. Money is just bits of paper and metal or now digital bytes, but it is the meaning we ascribe to those things that make them important. Scientists could measure all the dimensions of a room, weigh all the furniture, take the temperature throughout the day, and still have no idea that it was a court of law, church, synagogue, or mosque.

Here is one example of how religion synthesizes (puts together) meanings. During the Exodus from Egypt, Jews put the blood of lambs on their doorposts, so God would pass over their homes in liberating them from Pharaoh. Later, Moses splashed the blood of bulls on the altar and on the people as a sign of the covenant between God and humanity.

In the Christian scriptures, Jesus says on the night of Passover that the wine he wants his followers to drink is his blood, the blood of the new covenant (Luke 22:17-20). The next day, Jesus takes the sins of the world onto himself, shedding his blood on the cross as a sign of his love for all people.

Communion services for the next two thousand years are about sharing in the blood of Jesus to show we are his disciples (I Corinthians 11:23-26). Martyrs took this to the extreme by willingly shedding their own blood as a sign of their faith. And there is the saying that "the blood of the martyrs is the seed of the church." So, we have themes of God's protection, covenant and love as well as our discipleship, martyrdom, and church growth all woven together.

If it was possible, scientists could have done a lab analysis of the chemicals in the blood of the animals and people in each of these situations, and they would have totally missed the depths of meaning in all these blood-connections.

The point is not to throw out reason or science, but simply to say that they only give a limited perspective on life. There are equally important and extremely meaningful ways of approaching the same things that tie everything in reality together. This is what people have always looked for and will continue to look for, and this is what religion specializes in: the unification of meaning.

In short, we need religion if we are going to have not only scientific but deeply meaningful lives.

The point is that love of God may not only result in sacred wounds, it can also end in death by martyrdom or by being swooped up in a chariot of fire as scripture tells us happened with the great prophet Elijah (2 Kings 2:11). Elijah was assumed bodily into heaven. However, Elijah was just a prophet, not the mother of Jesus Christ. If Elijah could be bodily assumed into heaven, surely Mary could be too. In either case, it makes sense in terms of symbolic meaning if not in terms of fact.

Something similar happened to Enoch: "By faith Enoch was taken so that he did not experience death; and 'he was not found, because God had taken him.' For it was attested before he was taken away that 'he had pleased God'" (Hebrews 11:5).

No one knows exactly what happened in actual fact in these three cases with Enoch, Elijah and Mary. They are likely a combination of a certain modicum of history, human imagination, symbolism and divine inspiration. However, the main point is that these happenings, although it is very probable that they were meant by the authors to be metaphorical in nature, are extremely meaningful for many believers.

For all these martyrs, stigmatists and saints, their love of God was stronger than pain, the threat of death, and death itself.

BOOK SEVEN

LIVING IN HARMONY WITH GOD'S WILL

CHAPTER ONE

LOVING GOD BY LOVING GOD'S COMMANDMENTS

The desire which God has to make us observe his commandments is extreme, as the whole of scripture witnesses. 106

Now the love of complacency, holding this divine desire, wills to please God by observing it; the love of benevolence which submits all to God, consequently submits our desires and wills to that will which God has signified to us; and hence springs not only the observance, but also the love of the commandments. 107

The sweetest commandments become bitter when they are imposed by a tyrannical and cruel heart; and they become most amiable when ordained by love. Jacob's service seemed a royalty unto him, because it proceeded from love. O how sweet and how much to be desired is the yoke of the heavenly law, established by so amiable a king! 108

The sacred lover finds such sweetness in the commandments, that nothing so much eases and refreshes him, as the gracious load of the precepts of his God. 109

Thus, then does heavenly love conform us to the will of God, and make us carefully observe his commandments, as being the absolute desire of his divine Majesty whom we will to please. So that this complacency with its sweet and amiable violence, foreruns that necessity of obeying which the law imposes upon us, converting this necessity into the virtue of love, and every difficulty into delight. 110

By complacence, that is, by pondering God's goodness, beauty and glory, we allow our self to be attracted to God's magnificence and rest in God's deep holiness and abundance. In doing so, the life of God absorbs our life, our life absorbs God's life and we are marinated in God.

By benevolence we project our life into God's life. We deeply desire to do everything we can to serve God. We see God's presence in everything and everyone, particularly the poor, take action for social justice and practice restorative justice. It is quite simply true that, if we turn away from compassion for others, we turn away from God the All-Compassionate.

A good mystic always is a good activist, striving to bring about the "Just Society," the reign of God. If the mystic is cloistered, this may involve not leaving the monastery, but praying extra prayers for the poor, writing letters or emails to support activists or writing books about social justice as Thomas Merton did.

God wants all to be saved, but forces no one. This raises an interesting point: what is meant by "salvation?" The short form of salvation is "salve," which means "to heal." Many people today speak of "holiness" as "being whole." Wholeness means that none of our parts are missing, wounded or broken. We are firing on all cylinders; we are completely healed.

So, if salvation means to salve or to heal, and if we are completely healed, we are whole, then "to be saved" means "to be made whole." To be saved means to be fully alive on this Earth, with all our senses, emotions, intellect and spirit fully firing in this life, not in some distant future heaven. To be saved means to be fully alive *now*, and we can only do this if we follow Christ's Great Commandments: "You shall love the Lord your God with all your heart, mind, soul and strength (your will), and you shall love your neighbor as yourself."

These commandments of Jesus contain all the law and the prophets. The rest of the Bible is just an introduction to, and commentary on, these two commands.

God desires that everyone be saved, that is, fully healed, fully whole and fully alive in this life and the next. Now, we cannot do this if we are full of fear or self-centered desire. True benevolence is to love God, not out of fear of hell, or desire for heaven, but to love God as God, in and of God's self.

God in God's self is infinitely more loving and lovable than anything or anyone because God is all good and all good comes from God. If anyone has a good intention, it came from God. The intention might be to build a new hospital in a poor area, or to clean up corruption in a government, institution, corporation or church.

All good intentions come from God because God comes to us through people, not from above or outside them. God is a God of incarnation. If anyone does a good deed or takes good action, that good deed or action is from God and is God at work in the world. God is constantly intervening in worldly affairs through us.

God is more lovable than anything. Some people love the truth above all things, but God is Truth, the source of all scientific and religious truth. Religious people have no need to fear scientific truth, because it all comes from God. The truth in all disciplines—math, physics, botany, archaeology, history, architecture, medicine and so on leads us and points us to God.

Truths like Einstein's famous equation $E=MC2$ (energy equals matter times the speed of light squared) were not created by Einstein, they were already there, resting in God, waiting to be discovered. Like our souls, these truths were "hidden with Christ in God" (Colossians 3:3).

God is more beautiful than anything, the source of all beauty, not just on Earth but on billions of planets. There is beauty in the universe that the human eye will never see. Can we imagine being on a planet in the glowing bulge at the center of our Milky Way Galaxy? The bulge glows because there is a concentration of billions of suns there. There would never be a dark night sky as we know it. No matter what direction we looked, the sky would be full of billions of stars of all colors.

God is not only the source of all beauty, God is the ultimate artist because God does not create works of art with paint, God creates them with reality. God is constantly creating beautiful sunrises and sunsets; spring, summer, autumn, and winter scenes; mountains and valleys; rainbows; wildflowers; strange and wild creatures of the sea, land and air. And God's painting with reality changes from moment-to-moment.

People often say: "Life is not fair," but in general this is not true. We ought to love God because God is fair and just and has created a fair and just world. Indeed, how could you love a God who deliberately chose to create an unjust and unfair world? Such a God would not be loving at all but rather a monster.

Addressing the Israelites, God says "Yet you say, 'The way of the Lord is unfair.' Hear now, O house of Israel: Is my way unfair? Is it not your ways that are unfair?" (Ezekiel 18:25). Often, when people experience unfairness in life, they blame God. However, the unfairness comes from human actions not God. We are to blame not God.

God is more lovable and loving than anything because God is more just than anyone. God has designed life to be fair, contrary to many peoples' opinions. God has created the law of "return" or "consequences" (in eastern religions this is called the law of karma), which Jesus refers to over and over without explicitly naming it. Instead he says: "Do not judge so that you may not be judged" (Matthew 7:1) and "Forgive, and you will be forgiven; give and it will be given to you...for the measure you give will be the measure you get back" (Luke 6:37-38).

The law of return basically means that what we do has consequences that will come back to us sooner or later. If we work hard, we will normally prosper and do well in school and in life. That is the general rule underlying everything and operating all the time. If we exercise and eat healthily, we will generally be in better shape than those who don't. If we put our heart and mind into raising good children, they will normally become good citizens and will take care of us in our old age.

If these things don't happen—if we work hard and do not get promoted or rewarded; we take care of ourselves and get cancer anyway; we try to raise good children and they turn out bad—these would be exceptions to the general rule of return that God created and that we will find in every major world religion.

God is just because God inspires and motivates us to strive for justice. Through us God has created all of humanity's police and justice systems in the world. If people commit crimes, the police usually apprehend them sooner or later.

However, most justice systems in the world continue to be punitive not restorative. In other words, they punish the criminal, but they don't restore the community that has been violated. God's way would be to have the perpetrator and victim meet, fully hear each other's story, and forgiveness, reconciliation and restoration of the victim's former life would take place, if possible, as well as restoration of the perpetrator to the community. This restorative justice flows from fundamental Christian principles of repentance and rehabilitation.

God's notion of justice is not retributive but distributive. As previously noted, true justice is "the proper distribution of love throughout society."

There is such a thing as systemic injustice—laws and economic systems that are set up by the rich to favor the rich over the poor—so that the rich get richer and the poor get poorer. This is not God's way at all. God wants the fair and just distribution of wealth so that as Paul wrote "The one who had much did not have too much, and the one who had little did not have too little" (2 Corinthians 8:15).

God does not want one or five percent of the world's population to hold 50% or 90% of the wealth. It is not God's intention that the eight richest men in the world hold as much wealth as the bottom 50%.

Some of the wealthy elite, such as Bill Gates, are using their brains and great wealth to save the lives of millions of people through developing inoculation programs and proper sanitation in poor countries. This is the beginning of a proper distribution of love throughout those societies.

God commands us to love God with all our heart and to love others as we love our true self because we become what we love. If we love God, we become more like God. We are transformed and begin to mirror God, that is, we show forth the image of God, our true nature. If we love others, we become more holy or saint-like, and if we love our true self, we become more whole and integrated, just as our true self is whole and integrated.

The true self integrates the false self and the body into our spiritual life. It is aware of the ego and all our earthly desires and therefore is able to consciously manage them rather than being controlled by repressed (and therefore unconscious) motives.

Thomas Aquinas wrote "The things we love and why we love them tell us who we are." If we love base things, we become baser and more animalistic. If we love holy things, we become more holy.

Complacence, that is, marinating our soul in God's unfailing love and presence, leads us to benevolence, the active pursuit of God and God's will. God's will is that we obey the Ten Commandments, and in particular for Christians, that we obey Christ's Commandments to love God with all our heart and to love others as we love ourselves.

But what does this love look like? It is all in the Beatitudes taught by Jesus, which should be for Christians what the Ten Commandments are for Jews. The Sermon on the Mount is the greatest preaching/teaching of Jesus and it is delivered on a mountain just as the Ten Commandments were. In the Sermon, Jesus lays out his whole glorious vision of how the world should be. And the Beatitudes are the summary of the Sermon.

Jesus said in the Beatitudes that love is meek (gentle), humble, pure in heart, thirsting for restorative justice, peacemaking, mourning (over sin, that is, repenting or turning away from sin) and merciful (Matthew 5:3-12). It is a vision of a nonviolent world.

Similarly, the apostle Paul outlined his vision of love in I Corinthians 13:4-8: love is patient, kind, never jealous, bragging, arrogant, self-seeking or vengeful. Love rejoices in the truth, bears all things, believes all things (has faith), hopes all things, endures all things. Love never fails. Love creates a peaceful and just world.

Love of God and love of others go together. Loving God results in loving others and has a direct impact on all our relationships on Earth. Love of God makes us kind, gentle, pure, just, merciful, peaceful and willing to persevere and endure all kinds of suffering for others.

When we realize just how great God's Commandments and Beatitudes are; how they are a blueprint for a totally fulfilling spiritual life
for both individuals and communities; and how they tell us exactly
what God wants for us, we begin to love the Commandments and
Beatitudes as the verbal incarnation of God's Word, and they draw
us into God's will.

We are never forced to do God's will, we are only *drawn* into it,
because the Spirit works by freedom not force. If we are *driven* to do
something, it is the ego, the false self, or evil forces at work in us. But
if we are drawn into doing God's will, we know it is from the Spirit
and from our true self, which is like a homing device for God's will.
Our true self is our internal GPS, that is, "God's Positioning System."

We obey God's will out of both complacence, which draws us into
God's will, and out of benevolence, the gentle or passionate motivation from the Holy Spirit to do God's will. If we resist the subtle or
strong drawing or prompting of the Holy Spirit, we end up condemn-
ing ourselves. God condemns no one.

We are "saved" or "made whole" by loving and fully living into
the Ten Commandments, the Great Commandments of Jesus and his
Beatitudes. If we do that, we will be fully alive in this life and surely,
if we are fully alive in this life, we will also be fully alive in the life to
come.

Chapter Two
Loving God by Loving God's Counsels

There is a difference between commanding and recommending: in commanding we use authority to oblige, but in recommending we use friendliness to induce and incite: a commandment imposes necessity, counsel and recommendation induce to what is of greater utility: commandments correspond to obedience, counsels to credence: we follow counsel with intention to please, and commandments lest we should displease. 111

A counsel is indeed given for the benefit of the person who receives it, to the end that he may become perfect: "If thou wilt be perfect," said our Saviour, "go sell all that thou hast, give it to the poor, and come, follow me." 112

Nor does God desire that everyone should observe all the counsels, but such only as are suitable, according to the diversity of persons, times, occasions, strengths, as charity requires: for she it is who, as queen of all the virtues, of all the commandments, of all the counsels, and, in short, of all Christian laws and works, gives to all of them their rank, order, season and worth.

If your assistance is truly necessary to your father or mother to enable them to live, it is no time then to practice the counsel of retiring into a monastery. 113

Charity not only forbids fathers of families to sell all and give it to the poor, but also commands them honestly to gather together what is requisite for the support and education of wife, children and servants. 114

We are to take our orders from charity how to exercise counsels. 115

Some charity dyes with the fine violet of mortification, others with the yellow of marriage-cares, variously employing the counsels, for the perfection of the souls who are so happy as to live under her conduct. 116

When our love is exceeding great towards God's will, we are not content to do only the Divine will which is signified unto us by the commandments, but we also put ourselves under the obedience of the counsels, which are only given to us for a more perfect observing of the commandments. 117

Our Saviour when he was in this world declared his will in some cases by way of commandment, and in many others he only signified it by way of desire: for he did highly commend chastity, poverty, obedience and perfect resignation, the abnegation of one's own will, widowhood, fasting, and continual prayer. 118

And why shall not we then in return be so zealous in following God's holy will, as to do not only what he orders, but also what we know he likes and wishes. Noble souls need no other spur to the undertaking of a design than to know that their beloved desires it. 119

It is a horrible irreverence towards him who with so much love and sweetness invites us to perfection to say: I will not be holy or perfect, nor have any larger portion of thy benevolence, nor follow the counsels which thou givest me to make progress in perfection. 120

We shall sufficiently testify our love for all the counsels, when we devoutly observe such as are suitable to our calling. 121

Now we may with ease practise some of them, though not all of them together; for God has given many, in order that everyone may observe some of them, and not a day passes without our having some opportunity of doing so. 122

Is it inexpedient for you, on account of your rank, to preserve perfect charity? Keep it at least, as much as you may without violating charity. Let him who cannot do all, at least do some part. 123

In counsels there are various degrees of perfection. To lend to such poor people as are not in extreme want is the first degree of the counsel of alms-deeds; to give it to them is a degree higher; higher still to give it all; but the highest is to give oneself, dedicating our person to their service. 124

The Sermon on the Mount is full of God's counsels starting with the Beatitudes and continuing on. It is important to understand that there is a big difference between a command and a counsel.

A command imposes the will of the commander: "Do this or you will die, be flogged or court-marshalled." A counsel on the other hand is an invitation to growth. "Do this and you will be living a life of integrity and fulfilling your true self."

Resisting or disobeying a command equals damnation or something like it. Resisting or disobeying a counsel simply means you lead a less praiseworthy and integrated life.

The only thing Jesus *commands* us to do are the absolutely essential requirements for this life and the afterlife: to love God with all our heart and to love others as we love our true self. All else in the scriptures is commentary on these two commands. Jesus does not command us to obey these commands for his sake but for our sake because he knows these commands are the absolutely best thing for us.

Of course, when we face God in the afterlife, we will find that none of us, even the official Catholic saints, has obeyed Christ's commands absolutely. All of us are somewhere along the continuum of loving God, others and our true self.

No one is going to be damned by God; all of us will be saved except for those who absolutely turn away from love and damn themselves. But the question is: would anyone do this, that is, damn themselves to eternal misery or even eternal torture? And if they did, it would be because they are so broken internally. As such, God will have mercy on them anyway, pursuing them until they are willing to give in and accept God. God wants no one to die or be cut off from God's divine life.

The whole Sermon on the Mount is not *prescriptive*, that is, a list of things we *must do* to get to heaven. Rather it is *descriptive* of what a totally free life would look like. The Christian life is not about getting into heaven but rather living the way God intended us to live in this life, aligned with God's truth and thus participating in God's life, love and spirit. If we do that, we will surely get into heaven anyway.

Heaven should not be our primary concern but rather living optimally in this life by following the counsels of Jesus to the best of our ability out of gratitude for God's great love of us rather than out of fear that, if we don't do all these counsels perfectly, we won't get into heaven.

Here are some of the counsels of Jesus in the Sermon:

"Let your light shine before others, so that they may see your good works and give glory to your Father in heaven" (Matthew 5:16).

"If anyone wants to sue you and take your coat, give your cloak as well" (Matthew 5:40).

"Give to everyone who begs from you, and do not refuse anyone who wants to borrow from you" (Matthew 5:42).

"When you give alms (donate money), do not let your left hand know what your right hand is doing, so that your alms may be done in secret" (Matthew 6: 3,4).

"Do not worry about your life, what you will eat or what you will drink, or about your body, what you will wear...Strive first for the kingdom of God and God's righteousness, and all these things will be given to you as well" (Matthew 6: 25,33).

We are called by Jesus to *love* all his counsels, because to not love them would be to not love spiritual perfection, which is the will of the Holy Spirit for us. But we are not called to *follow* all of them. We are called to follow the counsels *according to our circumstances*.

For example, if we are married with dependents, selling all we have would be an abrogation of our original calling to be married, be a father or mother and provide for our children's well-being. Disobeying God in this way would be folly.

Francis de Sales and other spiritual masters recommend that, if we cannot in good conscience do all of the counsels, at least do some of them. If we cannot sell all we have because we are a family woman or family man, a mother or father, we can still fast, pray and give alms in secret. We can still turn the other cheek, seek first the reign/kingdom/queendom/kindom of God and keep our marriage bed pure.

We can still be "chaste," that is, "sexually integrated," whether we are married or not.

Spiritual masters also recommend that if we can't do all of an individual counsel, at least do part of it. If we can't sell all we have, at least sell/give up some of it. Live simply, and give what our family doesn't need to Goodwill, the St. Vincent de Paul Society or some other charity that takes care of the poor.

There are different *degrees* in which we can engage in hospitality and welcoming the stranger. We could share our spare change with the person standing on the traffic island holding a sign that says: "Please help, I am residentially challenged." Or, instead of giving this person who is homeless money which they might spend on drugs or alcohol, we could give them an apple or granola bar, or invite them to lunch and buy them a whole meal, or invite them to our home for a meal and shower, or invite them to stay a night at our home, or invite them to stay with us until they find a job.

People who are homeless often cannot find a job or even receive welfare support because they have no fixed address. We could not only share our wealth and our food and our home with them. We could share our life with them, let them get to know us, and we could really get to know who they are too. This would be the most valuable gift we could give them, the gift of love and respect.

People who are homeless are often isolated, lonely and have internalized society's rejection of them so that they are full of self-loathing. This is when they need the tender touch of God's love and human love the most.

For people in religious orders, there are the counsels of poverty, chastity and obedience. However, lay people can also embrace the spiritual essence of these counsels. If we are a single parent, we may not be able to exist free of possessions, but we could at least embrace the value of poverty and see the good in it.

Poverty, if approached in the right spirit, can help us detach from the folly of thinking that possessions are all-important. It can remind us that relationships are the key to happiness: harmonious relationships with God, our self, friends, family and the planet are essential for our well-being. Poverty is so much more ecologically friendly than constant and unlimited consumption of Earth's resources.

If we are a married person, we may not be able to be nonsexual or celibate and never have sexual intercourse, but we can still embrace the essence of chastity, that is, to value sexuality as a great and sacred gift of God and an ongoing opportunity to be a physical sacrament, a visible sign of God's invisible love, to our spouse. God created sexuality not just for procreation so that the human race might continue, but also so that both men and women, who are made in the image of God, might give themselves body, mind, heart and soul in love to each other.

As well as the procreative dimension, there is the unitive dimension of sexuality. According to Pope John Paul II's theology of the body, the goal is to become one—body, mind, heart and soul—with our partner. God's love is mediated to us through our partner. And our love of God is mediated to God through our body and our partner's body. Sexuality is where we and God can physically make love to each other through our partner.

Given all of this, the way we treat our partner is the way we treat God. Our spouse is the closest we get to God-in-the-flesh because we are both made in the image of God, and nobody else in our whole life is going to be that totally intimate with us, body and mind and heart and soul, as our spouse.

So, we should treat each other with great dignity and respect. We should treat sexuality with great dignity and respect. God is also passionate, creative, fun-loving and playful. So, if our lovemaking is passionate, creative, fun-loving and playful, it is all good. We are imitating God.

The religious value of obedience can also be followed by lay people. However, it is more important to obey God, the gospel and our conscience than to obey church authority. As much as possible lay people should obey church authority, but if the priests or bishops are in bed with the military or the rich, or if they are in bed with children or adolescents, then laity are called to be prophets and speak out.

Throughout history, military leaders have often requested that priests bless their armies before going off to war. However, this is a violation of the values of Jesus who traditionally had as one of his titles that he is the "Prince of Peace" (Isaiah 9:6).

Bishops have sometimes kowtowed to the wishes of the rich and powerful who wanted the church to not speak out about social injustices. And sexual scandals involving church leaders will always need to be addressed if they continue to occur.

As Jesus said: "The scribes and Pharisees sit on Moses' seat; therefore, do whatever they teach you and follow it; but do not do as they do, for they do not practice what they teach" (Matthew 23:2,3). On the other hand, many clergy do practice what they preach and teach. Constant discernment is necessary for both clergy and lay people as to what appropriate behavior is in any situation.

The root of "authority" is "author." To author something is to bring it out or to initiate it. Authority is something that comes from within, from the Holy Spirit acting within us. Only clergy or laity who humble themselves will be trusted by others and given the authority that comes from within them. True authority in the Christian life comes not from one's office in the church as deacon, priest or bishop, but from living the gospel and therefore winning the hearts of the rest of the faithful so that they give their internal assent to our leadership and freely obey us.

It is leaders who genuinely love and follow Jesus the Christ who gain the admiration and respect of the masses. This is why popes like Pope Francis, are so popular—they demonstrate love of God and neighbor in everything they do. People from every nation and world leaders listen to them and let them be their authority and see them as the conscience of the world because they practice what they preach.

True spiritual leaders lead by example not just by word. They do not just exhort us to love the commands and counsels of Jesus, they show us how to do it by living the teachings in their own life.

CHAPTER THREE
LOVING GOD BY LOVING GOD'S INSPIRATIONS

Without inspiration our souls would lead an idle, sluggish and fruitless life, but on receiving the divine rays of inspiration we are sensible of a light mingled with a quickening heat, which illuminates our understanding, and which excites and animates our will, giving it the strength to will and effect the good which is necessary for eternal salvation. 125

God's vital breath is called inspiration, because by it the divine goodness breathes upon us and inspires us with the desires and intentions of his heart. 126

Oh how happy are they who keep their hearts open to holy inspirations! For these are never wanting to any, in so far as they are necessary for living well and devoutly, according to each one's condition of life, or for fulfilling holily the duties of his profession. 127

The souls which are not contented with doing what the heavenly beloved requires at their hands by his commandments and counsels, but also promptly comply with sacred inspirations, are they whom the Eternal Father has destined to be the spouse of his well-beloved son. 128

Very often, says the glorious St. Bernard, the devil deludes us, and to draw us from the effecting of one good he proposes unto us some other good, that seems better; and after we have started this, he, in order to divert us from effecting it, presents a third. 129

He that is in a good way, let him step out and get on. It happens sometimes that we forsake the good to seek the better, and that having forsaken the one we find not the other; better is the possession of a small treasure found, than the expectation of a greater which is to find. The

145

inspiration which moves us to quit a real good which we enjoy in order to gain a better in the future, is to be suspected. 130

We are to behave ourselves in those inspirations which are only extraordinary in the sense that they move us to practice ordinary Christian exercises with an extraordinary fervour and perfection. But there are other inspirations which are called extraordinary, not only because they make the soul pass the bounds of ordinary actions, but also because they move it to actions contrary to the common laws, rules and customs of the most holy Church, and therefore are more admirable than imitable. 131

St. Paul the first hermit, St. Anthony, St. Mary of Egypt, did not bury themselves in those vast desert wildernesses – deprived of hearing Mass, of Communion, of Confession, and deprived, young as they were, of all direction and assistance – without a strong inspiration. 132

St. Francis, St. Dominic and the other Fathers of Religious Orders were called to the service of souls by an extraordinary inspiration, but they did so much the more humbly and heartily submit themselves to the sacred Hierarchy of the Church. 133

In conclusion, the three best and most sacred marks of lawful inspirations, are perseverance, against inconstancy and levity; peace and gentleness of heart, against disquiet and solicitude; humble obedience, against obstinacy and extravagance. 134

We can love God, as we have seen so far, by obeying God's commandments and by following God's counsels to the best of our ability. We can also love God by being wide open to God's many inspirations.

There are multiple ways God can inspire us: through the wonders of God's creatures, through the wisdom of scripture, through hearing about or meeting saints (even if it is only in our imagination) and through our dreams.

There are so many creatures that can increase our love of God through admiring God's endless creativity. Think of the exotic multi-colored plumage and complex mating dances of thousands of different species of rainforest birds. Or the male Emperor penguins of the Antarctic, who keep their female mate's one huge annual egg warm not by building a nest but by balancing the egg on top of their feet and covering it with their warm belly fat throughout the howling winters. There are strange creatures of the deep oceans: manta rays, jellyfish, and the octopus. God's imagination knows no boundaries.

We can love God by opening our soul to all the inspiring verses in holy scripture:

"Guard the good treasure entrusted to you, with the help of the Holy Spirit living in you" (2 Timothy 1:14).

"Now to the One who by the power at work within us is able to accomplish abundantly far more than all we can ask or imagine, to him be glory in the church and in Christ Jesus to all generations, forever and ever" (Ephesians 3:20-21).

"We know that all things work together for good for those who love God, who are called according to God's purpose" (Romans 8:28).

"For everyone who asks receives, and everyone who searches finds, and for everyone who knocks, the door will be opened" (Matthew 7:8).

"My child, give me your heart, and let your eyes observe my ways" (Proverbs 23:26).

"The spirit of God has made me, and the breath of the Almighty gives me life" (Job 33:4).

"May the God of hope fill you with all joy and peace in believing, so that you may abound in hope by the power of the Holy Spirit" (Romans 15:13).

"Above all, clothe yourselves with love, which binds everything together in perfect harmony" (Colossians 3:14).

"Do not be afraid, little flock, for it is your Father's good pleasure to give you the kingdom" (Luke 12:32).

"What does the Lord require of you but to do justice, and to love kindness, and to walk humbly with your God?" (Micah 6:8).

The inspiration of scripture is endless.

There are also many sung and unsung saints who can inspire us to love God more. To give but one example, Pierre Toussaint was a slave in Haiti. His owner taught him to read and write and took him to New York City in 1787. When the owner died, the owner's wife gave Pierre his freedom. This owner and his wife are unsung saints in themselves.

Pierre had become a hairdresser to the wealthy and with his money he purchased the freedom of many Haitian slaves, and helped refugees find jobs in New York and cared for them when they were sick. He provided financial support for the Oblate Sisters of Providence (a religious order of black women) and started the first Catholic school for black children in New York City. He also started an orphanage for abandoned children.

Pierre inspires us to be godlike through charitable works for the poor. He is considered one of the pioneers of Catholic charitable work in the United States. He died in 1853 at age 87 and is buried behind the main altar of St. Patrick's Cathedral in New York City.

God can also inspire us through dreams. Some people guide their whole life based on their dreams. A man I know found that his dreams were repeatedly full of archetypal symbols: golden keys, deep dark passageways, vestments, ancient books, monks, gurus, martial arts masters, and disembodied voices telling him what to do. And if he started to go the wrong way, a large growling and barking black dog would always show up warning him to reconsider his path. He took all of this as guidance from the Holy Spirit and it helped him discern his calling and inspired him to love God and others through congregational ministry.

There are three marks within a person that the inspiration is truly from God. The first one is vocational perseverance in spite of difficulties. As a Catholic parish priest once said: "If you are doing anything that is spiritually significant, there is going to be spiritual opposition. The devil will try to knock you off your original course either by temptations to sin or laziness, or to drop what you are doing to follow seemingly holier tasks."

The second mark of authentic inspiration is inner peace and joy. Evil forces will sow doubt about the project working out, doubt about our ability to rise to the occasion and meet the demands being placed on us, doubt about the sincerity and commitment of other people involved.

Restlessness may arise within us, as well as bitterness and contention in the people with whom we are working. These are all normal reactions if we are doing something worthwhile. Still, if it *is* spiritually significant, beneath all the surface angst and turmoil, there will be a deep well of abiding peace and joy because our innermost heart and intuition, the places where the Holy Spirit dwells, tells us that we are on the right track.

The third mark of true inspiration is a willingness to listen to and obey our superiors. If we are not willing to do this, it is a sure sign that our ego is in charge. Listening to honest criticism requires humility, and if humility, the queen of all the virtues, is lacking, we can be sure that self-centered pride, the queen of all the vices, is on her royal throne.

Naturally, we need to discern whether the obedience our superiors are demanding is really in line with the will of God or not. Peter and John were hauled up before the Sanhedrin and ordered to stop telling others about Jesus. Their response was to say that they would obey God not the council of high priests and elders. The Sanhedrin had them flogged, but they went on their way, telling others about the good news of Jesus and rejoicing that they had been deemed worthy to suffer for the cause (Acts 5:40-42).

True inspiration can also be discerned by the fact that it normally creates various virtues in those who receive it: patience, kindness, perseverance, wisdom, courage and so on.

Inspiration may also lead people to extraordinary, heroic virtue that seems insane to the relativistic postmodern mind. This is where we enter the realm of the historic saints: people willing to be burnt alive, shot full of arrows, or drawn and quartered for their faith.

Maximilian Kolbe volunteered to be hung by the Nazis in place of a man who had a young family. Francis of Assisi licked the sores of lepers. Simeon Stylites spent his whole life on an elevated platform praying without ceasing. When, as holy men and women sometimes do, he was attracting large crowds of pilgrims who wanted to be near him, his bishop ordered him to come down. Simeon immediately obeyed his superior. But the bishop was a wise man and ordered him to go back up on his fifty-foot high pedestal, explaining to Simeon that, as part of his role as bishop, he had to test Simeon to see if being up there was a true calling and inspiration from God.

The lives of the saints are meant to be admired but not necessarily imitated. We have to discern what God is calling us to do, given our particular circumstances. We cannot spend all our time praying in our closet, our cell, or upon a fifty-foot high platform if we have children to raise or a school, city or country to govern.

Sometimes inspiration calls us to go beyond ordinary church laws. For example, rather than attending their local church, the desert fathers and mothers left the confines of their dioceses to eventually form monasteries in the desert. And they did not wait for their bishop's approval to do so. It just evolved that way as they tried to escape the noisy chaos of the cities, and others started to join them. They were also trying to recapture the true spirituality of the gospel in the face of a church that had become too Romanized, too authoritarian and too concerned with politics, law, power and control.

Like Martin Luther, the desert mothers and fathers were trying to reform the Roman Catholic Church, not demolish it. True prophets and reformers always love God through loving God's church and want to obey church authorities as much as possible. However, their commitment is first of all to love God, and if their personal conscience tells them the church authorities have lost sight of the true calling of the gospel, that is, love of God with our whole heart and love of our neighbor as our self, they follow the calling to love and protest what the authorities are doing. This was the basis of the conflict Jesus constantly had with the Jewish high priests.

God's love is better than life (Psalm 63:3). Nothing, even our own life, is more lovable than God, and this sometimes involves following God's commandments, counsels and inspirations all the way to the cross.

Of course, God also freely leads us to happiness, joy and fearlessness in the new life God has given us in the resurrection. To be a follower of Jesus is also to take up the abundant life he promised us.

There will indeed be crosses in every person's life, but Jesus said,

"In the world you face persecution. But take courage, I have conquered the world" (John 16:33).

BOOK EIGHT

SURRENDERING TO GOD'S WILL

CHAPTER ONE

LOVING GOD BY LOVING WHATEVER GOD ALLOWS

Painful things cannot indeed be loved when considered in themselves, but viewed in their source, that is, in the Divine Will and Providence which ordains them, they are supremely delightful. 135

Look at tribulations in themselves, and they are dreadful; behold them in the will of God, and they are love and delights. 136

The truly loving heart loves God's good-pleasure not in consolations only but in afflictions also; yea, it loves it better upon the cross in pains and difficulties, because the principal effect of love is to make the lover suffer for the thing beloved. 137

To love God's will in consolations is a good love when it is indeed God's will that is loved, and not the consolations which is the form it takes: however, this is a love without contradiction, repugnance and effort: for who would not love so worthy a will in so agreeable a form?

To love the will of God in his commandments, counsels, and inspirations is a second degree of love, and much more perfect, for it leads us to the renouncing and quitting of our own will, and makes us abstain from and forbear some pleasures, though not all. To love sufferings and afflictions for the love of God is the supreme point of most holy charity, for there is nothing therein to receive our affections save the will of God only. 138

St. Catherine of Siena, having from our Saviour her choice of a crown of gold or a crown of thorns, chose this later, as better suiting with love; a desire of suffering says the Blessed Angela of Foligno, is an infallible mark of love: and the great Apostle cries out that he glories only in the cross, in infirmity, in persecution. 139

There are three degrees of the love of God.

The first degree is to respond seriously to God's commands, counsels and inspirations.

The second degree is to treat with indifference whatever God sends us, whether it is consolation or desolation or riches or poverty. "Indifference" relates to the Buddhist ideal of "nonattachment." The idea here is that we love God no matter what God gives us—we love God beyond our own likes and dislikes—our life is not about us, it is about God.

Another step beyond this is the third degree, that is, carrying our cross out of love. This far outweighs the first and second degrees. We are now not just indifferent to our hardships; we welcome and love them. We relish our suffering because it participates in the suffering Jesus underwent on the cross for the life of the world.

Paul wrote: "Join with me in suffering for the gospel, relying on the power of God" (2 Timothy 1:8) and "We endure anything rather than put an obstacle in the way of the gospel of Christ" (I Corinthians 9:12). And Jesus himself said "Those who lose their life for my sake, and for the sake of the gospel, will save it" (Mark 8:35).

At this point we have absolute trust that, whatever crosses God has allowed us to bear, God has meant it for our good and for the sake of others, whether it is some kind of personal loss, illness or disability, or working as a personal support worker in a nursing home feeding, clothing and cleaning the bodies of elderly residents who have dementia or Alzheimer's disease.

A Christian man touched many of the staff in a local hospital by the way he patiently and faithfully endured many painful operations, always praying for and thanking the staff and loving them. Their lives were also touched by the community of believers who surrounded him with prayers and love.

He was not cured of his many medical problems and eventually died, but he healed the staff of their separation from God by his loving trust in whatever God allowed to happen to him. There is a big difference between curing and healing. The staff did not cure the patient physically, but the patient healed the staff spiritually.

The only question for the true disciple is not "Why has this good or bad thing happened to me? What did I do to deserve this?" but rather "Will I embrace with trust and love whatever God has allowed, whether it is health or sickness, pleasure or suffering?" It no longer matters what happens to us, what matters is our attitude to it.

Jesus showed his greatest love for us and gave us the greatest example of unconditional trust by willingly going to the cross that God the Father had allowed. He knew that beating, whipping and an extremely painful and ugly crucifixion lay before him, but he prayed "My Father, if it is possible, let this cup pass from me; yet not what I want but what you want" (Matthew 26:39). He embraced it all with love.

God is equally kind to us whether God allows consolation or desolation to happen to us because God knows everything about us and knows exactly what we need in each moment to grow spiritually. If we are depressed, God will allow consolation to help us get out of it. If we are too sure of ourselves, too proud of our spiritual growth, God will allow desolation in order to create greater humility in us.

Most believers discover that, after they have been on fire from having discovered the Bible for the first time, or after having a "born-again" or mystical experience, eventually the petals fall off the rose, and their spiritual life takes a nose-dive into desolation. But if they get back to slowly plodding along on their spiritual path, putting one foot in front of the other, they will eventually recover, and desolations and consolations will regularly come and go.

What is important is to be attached only to God rather than to our feelings about God or about the spiritual state we are in.

Riches and marriage and disobedience could attach us to God more, and be spiritually superior to poverty, chastity and obedience (the traditional surface hallmarks of holiness) depending on our attitude to what God has called us to.

Generous use of our wealth, setting an example for others of marital love and faithfulness when the relationship is rough, and being a prophet railing against unloving church practices, are superior to a person who has taken religious vows who constantly complains about poverty, fantasizes about sex, and grudgingly obeys church authorities.

Of course, poverty, chastity and obedience, if authentically embraced, will liberate a person much more from temptations to abuse wealth and sexuality and to rebel against church authority just for the sake of it.

In this third degree of loving God, that is, loving God by loving whatever God allows, carrying our own cross out of love of God, it is important to remind our self that both God's justice and God's mercy come out of God's goodness. God is purely good and nonviolent and therefore can be totally trusted. God is never wrathful, although references to God's wrath in the Old Testament, and even some sayings of Jesus in the New Testament, may have caused us to think otherwise.

For example, in Matthew 25 Jesus invites the sheep (those who did God's will) into the reign of God and says the goats (those who neglected God's will) will be cast into eternal punishment. God's justice and wrath, at least in the Christian scriptures, the New Testament, is always a metaphor for the earthly consequences of our own sin. We are not punished by God for our sins—our sins punish us.

Virtue is its own reward; sin is its own punishment. God is always slow to anger and quick to forgiveness, but God has set up the universe in such a way that the consequence of living a dissolute, drunken, angry, immoral, narcissistic life is that we will experience our own self-created hell on Earth.

But even as we experience the consequences of our own sin, God will be with us, accompanying us in our pain. The cross of Christ is the symbol that God is always with us, even in the worst pains of the hell we have created. If we are at all open to it, God allows us to taste God's mercy, the antidote to the bitterness of our hell and the way out of hell.

The "eternal" punishment lasts only as long as we resist God's mercy. Theoretically, it could be eternal if we resisted eternally. But all people, it is to be hoped, will eventually surrender to the mercy that is always offered by God, and eventually "All will be well, and all manner of things will be well" as Julian of Norwich wrote.

We could be bitter and estrange our self from God in this life because of some suffering we had endured. We know God does not want or cause suffering, but suffering is an inevitable part of being a creature with a body. Being embodied is the source not only of our suffering, but also of our pleasure. Therefore, God has allowed not only infinite ways of suffering but also infinite ways of pleasure on Earth.

We could be led away from God as easily by pleasure (perhaps even more easily!) than by suffering. Or we could be willing to submit to whatever God allows us to go through: pleasure or suffering, health or illness, long life or short. Through absolute unconditional trust that God is working in us no matter what happens, we can, with God's help, turn whatever happens into pure gold.

We should therefore love and rejoice in trials and tribulations because they are allowed by God. Saint Paul had the choice of dying and being with Christ in heaven or continuing his fruitful but painful earthly ministry. He chose to continue on Earth because he felt it was more God's will. God allowed him to suffer greatly, but Paul rejoiced in it all because God allowed it.

The cross of Christ is the great symbol that God allows all people, even the incarnate Son of God, to suffer. And the cross is also the great symbol of how suffering can be redeemed by our acceptance of it; the great symbol that God accompanies us in our suffering, and suffers when we suffer; and it is the great symbol of Christ's invitation to us to suffer for the gospel with him: "If any want to become my followers, let them deny themselves and take up their cross and follow me" (Matthew 16:24).

CHAPTER TWO
LOVING GOD BY SUBMITTING TO GOD'S WILL

Now of all the efforts of perfect love, that which is made by acquiescence of spirit in spiritual tribulations, is doubtless the purest and noblest. 140

Indifference goes beyond resignation: for it loves nothing except for the love of God's will; insomuch that nothing can stir the indifferent heart, in the presence of the will of God. 141

What matter whether God's will be presented to us in tribulation or in consolation, since I seek nothing in either of them except God's will, which is so much the better seen when there is no other beauty present save that of this most holy, eternal, good-pleasure. 142

The indifferent heart is as a ball of wax in the hands of its God, receiving with equal readiness all the impressions of the Divine pleasure; it is a heart without choice, equally disposed for everything, having no other object of its will than the will of its God, and placing its affection not upon the things that God wills, but upon the will of God who wills them. Wherefore, when God's will is in various things, it chooses, at any cost, that in which it appears most. 143

God's will is found in the service of the poor and of the rich, but yet somewhat more in serving the poor; the indifferent heart will choose that side. God's will lies in moderation amid consolations, and in patience amid tribulations: the indifferent heart prefers the latter, as having more of God's will in it. 144

Isaac's life and death are indifferent to Abraham in the presence of God's will. When God gives him the order to sacrifice his son he does not grow sad, when God dispenses with the order given he does not rejoice, all is one to this great heart, so that God's will be fulfilled. 145

We must love God for God alone, not for God's consolations to us. If we love the consolations of God more than the God of consolations, it is nothing other than self-love.

There are many classic examples in scripture of heroic, archetypal characters who simply did whatever they believed God wanted, even though God's will appeared to be totally irrational at the time.

God tells Abraham that he will be the father of many nations and his descendants will be as numerous as the stars or the grains of sand on all the beaches of the world. But Abraham is in his nineties and he and his wife Sarah have not been able to conceive any children throughout their long lives together. Then the Angel of the Lord appears and says that within a year Sarah will give birth. She laughs because she is well beyond menopause and it seems so absurd to even think such a thing.

However, before long she is pregnant and gives birth to a son in her old age. Abraham and Sarah are utterly in love with this precious gift from God, their little boy Isaac. But then God asks Abraham to offer Isaac up to God as a burnt sacrifice.

This request is beyond absurd, but Abraham's faith is unconditional, and so he prepares to sacrifice Isaac. Just when he is about to plunge a knife into Isaac's heart, the angel of the Lord tells him to stop. Isaac is spared, Abraham's lineage continues, and he does become the father of many nations as God promised. He is also the father of three great religions: Judaism, Christianity and Islam. Abraham's unreserved trust in God is rewarded with innumerable descendants.

Similarly, Job accepted both consolation and desolation from the Lord. Job had it all: a strong faith, great wealth, many children. Then the devil bet God that Job's faith in God depended on all these blessings. To paraphrase Job 1:12, God said to Satan: "I know my servant Job and he will never desert me. And to prove it, you have my permission to do whatever you want with Job."

Job immediately loses all his wealth, his children are killed, and his health totally deteriorates—he is covered in painful boils and cannot sleep. His friends all accuse him of sinning and this, in their judgement, is why these multiple disasters have fallen upon him. However, Job cannot think of anything he has done wrong. Then his wife, his former lifelong supporter, encourages him to curse God and die.

The whole situation, as with Abraham, is absurd. Job knows in his heart of hearts that he has done nothing to deserve this horrible fate. His "friends" continue to grill him for days on end, but Job continues to protest his innocence and refuses to curse God.

Finally, God gets impatient with seeing his faithful servant suffer, reveals God's glory to Job and his friends, and tells Job that God's ways completely transcend human ways and human rationality. God cannot be put in the box of human reason.

Then God restores all of Job's fortunes, giving him twice as much as he had before: more children, wealth and health and he lives to a ripe old age (Job 42:1-17).

This tragedy and restoration for Job is a foreshadowing of Christ's death and resurrection. With Jesus, things become infinitely more absurd than with Abraham or Job: the religious authorities decide to kill God. And the pain and the submission required of Jesus becomes even more personal and profound.

Abraham grudgingly goes along with what he thinks God's will is, his son is spared, and Abraham suffers no physical pain. Job may be confused, but he accepts both consolation and desolation from God. He rails against the physical pain and against his friends and is vindicated in the end. Jesus is not only led to give up his health but also his life. He willingly goes, is brutally flogged, crucified, publicly humiliated and rejected as a heretic by the religious authorities. And whereas Abraham and Job were merely human, Jesus knows he is the Messiah and God incarnate. He knows how utterly absurd the situation is, but he forgives his torturers and murderers, and asks God the Father to forgive them "for they do not know what they are doing" (Luke 23:34).

The reward is far greater for Jesus than for Abraham or Job because in the resurrection Jesus becomes not only the father of nations, or the father of a new earthly family, but the God and father of eternal life for all who trust in him down through the ages. He becomes the Saviour of the world.

In his willingness to go to crucifixion Jesus gives all of us the perfect model of complete love of God by unmitigated submission to God's will, whatever it is and however absurd it seems at the time. We must always be willing to say: "Not what I want Lord, but what you want." We must do our part, whatever we think God's will is.

If we suffer, not because of God's will, but because of our laziness or disobedience, we can expect the consequences of our sin. Scripture says numerous times that what we sow we reap. This works both negatively and positively. The law of return/consequence/karma is universal. As Jesus said "give, and it will be given to you. A good measure, pressed down, shaken together, running over" (Luke 6:38). In other words, if you are generous, you will get more than you deserve.

God and life are not only fair, they are superabundant. The laborers who only worked at the last hour of the day received as much as those who had slaved all day (Matthew 20:1-16). This may seem unfair to the day-long workers, but those workers received what they had agreed to receive. The party thrown for the prodigal son may seem unfair to the faithful and hardworking older son, but it is meant to demonstrate God's superabundant fairness.

Which of us has done anything great enough to deserve eternal life with God? How hard does a couple have to work to get pregnant and receive the great gift of children? They don't have to spend every waking hour knitting their child together in the womb. For most couples all they have to do is love each other and have a good time in bed. This is a sign of God's super-fairness. And it is a sign of God's superabundance that the best things in life are free: the love of spouses, sex, children, family, friends, the air we breathe, the beauty of nature and so on.

For life to be fair, and more than fair, all we have to do is nurture virtues such as kindness, honesty, wisdom, patience, compassion, humility and forgiveness. If we cultivate these things, we will normally reap many benefits. For "all who humble themselves will be exalted" (Matthew 23:12). As a religion professor said "To become rich in our society is easy. All you need to do as a businessperson is be honest. Give your clients an honest and good deal. People will flock to you."

Of course, life is full of hard things: an elderly couple killed by a drunk driver; a business partner who absconds with the company's funds; the deserving person who gets passed over for a promotion; the mother of two children under five years old who develops brain cancer and dies at age thirty-two.

Life is full of suffering and unfairness, but foundationally it is still fair, and not only the law of return/consequence/karma but also God's super-abundant graciousness still applies. The mother and elderly couple are with God in paradise forever. Thieves and adulterers are usually eventually caught and given a chance to repent, receive God's grace and start a new life. The unpromoted deserving person will usually eventually find more meaningful work where people appreciate her, or gain wisdom that life is about more than work.

As Helen Keller (who was blind and deaf) articulated "Yes, life is full of suffering, but it also full of the overcoming of suffering."

Those who love God love God's will, whatever it is. God may not protect our body, but our soul is always "hidden in Christ with God" (Colossians 3:3). God is the Ground of Being and our soul is like a perennial bulb hidden in that ground. The bulb puts out shoots and flowers every year, and every year our life is filled with events, good or bad, that come and go like shoots and flowers. But the bulb and our soul remain, year after year. Our body may suffer and die, but when it is rejoined with the soul in the afterlife, it is resurrected as an indestructible spiritual body.

Lovers of God love God by submitting to God's will whatever it is because God is thoroughly good, there is no evil in God; God can be absolutely trusted without reserve.

CHAPTER THREE
LOVING GOD BY TRUSTING GOD ALONE

The great Apostle proclaims to us a general Indifference; to show ourselves the true servants of God, in much patience, in tribulation, in necessities, in distresses, in stripes, in prisons, in seditions, in labours, in watchings, in fastings, in chastity, in knowledge, in long-suffering, in sweetness, in the Holy Ghost, in charity unfeigned, in the word of truth, in the power of God. 146

God oftentimes to exercise us in this holy Indifference, inspires us with very high designs, which yet he will not have accomplished and as then we are boldly, courageously and constantly to commence and to pursue the work as far as we can, so are we sweetly and quietly to acquiesce in such result of our enterprise as it pleases God to send us. St. Louis by inspiration passed the sea to conquer the Holy Land; the event answered not his expectation, he sweetly acquiesces. 147

Oh how blessed are such souls, bold and strong in the undertakings God proposes to them, and withal tractable and facile in giving them over when God so disposes! 148

We are commanded to have great care in what appertains to God's glory and to our charge, but we are not bound to, or responsible for, the event, because it is not in our power. 149

God has ordained that we should employ our whole endeavours to obtain holy virtues, let us then forget nothing which might help our good success in this pious enterprise. But after we have planted and watered, let us know for certain that it is God who must give increase. 150

It belongs to us diligently to cultivate our heart, and therefore we must faithfully attend to it, but as for the beauty of the crop or harvest, let us leave the care thereof to our Lord and Master. 151

He who prays fervently knows not whether he prays or not, for he is not thinking of the prayer which he makes but of God to whom he makes it. 152

Look at this man who prays, apparently, with such great devotion, and is so ardent in the practice of heavenly love. But stay a little, and you will discover whether it be God indeed whom he loves. Alas! As soon as the delight and satisfaction which he took in love departs, and dryness comes, he will stop short, and only casually pray. If it had been God indeed whom he loved, why should he cease loving him, since God is ever God? It was therefore the consolations of God that he loved, not the God of consolation. 153

O how happy is the heart that loves God without pretence of any other pleasure than what it takes in pleasing God! 154

We are oppressed with a thousand fears, and frightened with a thousand false alarms which the enemy raises round about our heart; suggesting that perhaps we are not in grace with our master, and that our love is fruitless, yea, that it is false and vain, since it brings forth no comfort. 155

O God! my dear Theotimus, now it is that we are to show an invincible courage towards our Saviour, serving him purely for the love of his will, not only without pleasure, but amid this deluge of sorrows, horrors, distresses and assaults, as did his glorious Mother and St. John upon the day of his Passion. 156

When therefore all fails us, when our troubles have come to their extremity, this word, this disposition, this rendering up of our soul into our Saviour's hands, can never fail us. The Son commended his spirit to his Father in this his last and incomparable anguish, and we, when the convulsions of spiritual pains shall bereave us of all other sort of solace and means of resistance, let us commend our spirit into the hands of this eternal Son who is our true Father, and bowing the head of our acquiescence in his good pleasure, let us make over our whole will unto him. 157

What becomes of man's will when it is entirely delivered up to God's good pleasure? It does not altogether perish, yet is it so lost and dispersed in the will of God that it appears not, and has no other will than the will of God. 158

Yes, Theotimus, the same God who made us desire virtues in our beginning, and who makes us practise them on all occurrences, he it is that takes from us the affection to virtues and all spiritual exercises, that with more tranquillity, purity and simplicity, we should care for nothing but the divine Majesty's good pleasure. 159

Love is as strong as death, to make us quit all, it is magnificent as the Resurrection, to adorn us with honour and glory. 160

True love of God consists in loving God for God alone, not for what God does for us either internally or externally. God may bless us with external wealth or God may bless us with poverty, that is, a simple uncomplicated life. We are called to love God anyway, whether we are rich or poor.

In both cases there are temptations to not love God. If we are wealthy, there will be a temptation to put our trust in our money rather than in God. But as Christ said, "No one can serve two masters…You cannot serve God and wealth" (Matthew 6:24).

If we are living in poverty, there will be a temptation to either be materialistic or doubt God's love for us. We could become so obsessed with getting enough money to pay the bills and get our next meal that all our focus is on that and we have no time for God. We could make money our primary concern, our idol and false god.

On the other hand, our poverty might tempt us to believe that God has forgotten us and does not care about us. Jesus himself felt this way on the cross: "My God, my God, why have you forsaken me?" (Matthew 27:46). Jesus in his humanity understood what it felt like to be abandoned by God. At the end though, rather than separation, Jesus experienced completion, fulfilment and deliverance when he cried out "It is finished" (John 19:30).

Neither poverty nor riches are good or bad in and of themselves. It depends on what we do with them. As Proverbs has it: "Give me neither poverty nor riches; feed me with the food that I need or I shall be full and deny you, and say, 'Who is the Lord?' or I shall be poor, and steal, and profane the name of my God" (Proverbs 30:8-9).

Just as we need to learn to love God for God alone, not for what God does for us externally, so we need to love God solely for God, not for what God does for us internally. The major task spiritually is to unconditionally love God in all things, whether external or internal.

God is still far more lovable than anything or anyone, whether we are in a state of consolation or desolation. Again, there are temptations in either case.

If we are in a state of consolation, the temptation will be to love the consolation rather than God. The feeling of consolation can be such a blessed high that it can be addicting. The famous statue of Teresa of Avila in a state of ecstasy has a facial expression similar to that of a person having an orgasm or of a drug addict high on heroin. In sexual climax, drug highs or mystical ecstasy, the brain may release similarly addictive chemicals.

The person in spiritual climax loses all sense of time and wants to stay there forever. Normal day-to-day existence loses its appeal and they cannot wait to get spiritually high again. But God is to be found in the struggles of everyday reality, perhaps even more than in the highs.

In the gospel story of the transfiguration of Jesus, Peter wants to build dwelling places for Moses, Elijah and Jesus so they could stay there longer, but Jesus led the disciples back down the mountain (Matthew 17:1-9). There is a constant interplay in the life of Jesus between withdrawing for extended prayer and then plunging back into the marketplace.

At the other end of the spectrum from consolations, internal desolations can make us feel existentially separated from God even though essentially this is not the case. The temptation in this case is to believe the feelings. Again, this is Jesus on the cross, feeling not only externally abandoned, but internally as well. He fully knew every human feeling, high and low.

Whether in external wealth or poverty or internal consolation or desolation, the focus of genuine mystics is always on God, not on themselves or their external or internal circumstances.

Even when it comes to virtue, we should love virtue for God's sake, not for the sake of the rewards virtue brings us. Virtues like discipline and wisdom can keep us employed, fed, healthy and safe. But still we ought to love virtue or righteousness because it is God's will for us.

God wants us to be righteous, therefore we should want it too, for no other reason than God wants it. God wants us to be righteous because God loves us and unrighteousness and sin destroy us. We should love God back by being virtuous/righteous since God knows what is best for us and God is the Righteous One. God is Righteousness-Itself.

In order to live solely for God, we must be completely stripped of self-interest and die to our small self. The only way our higher, bigger, truer self can be born is if we give up our ego's identification with temporal, relative things.

To live out of our higher self we have to realize that our soul transcends being Canadian, American, German, Catholic, Muslim, Buddhist, gay, straight, female or male, conservative or liberal. All those labels are going to pass away. Our soul is bigger than anything earthly.

Our will must be whatever God's will is. The only way we can do this is if we keep our focus on God in even the worst circumstances. This requires faith and unconditional trust of God, which may seem naïve given all the chaos, random shootings, disease and accidents in modern society, but this kind of trust will give us "the peace of God, which surpasses all understanding" (Philippians 4:7).

This peace will create a spiritual energy field or aura around us that others will subconsciously pick up. Because we are radically trusting God, others will trust us, feel safe around us and want to be near us.

Blessings will flow to us. People will trust our word and even trust us with their money because they sense that money means nothing to us. To us "the ordinances of the Lord are true and righteous altogether. More to be desired are they than gold, even much fine gold" (Psalm 19: 9-10).

God is our absolutely loving and sovereign eternal protector and provider. So, if some disaster happens to us—an illness, accident, loss of a loved one or even a war, God did not want that or will it, but God allowed it and will be with us through it, doing everything God can to help us survive, hoping that we use it for our spiritual growth. As the psalmist says, "Though an army encamp against me, my heart shall not fear; though war rise up against me, yet I will be confident" (Psalm 27:3).

As long as we trust God's will we are spiritually safe and will discover the reasons why our suffering and trust are justified. We may have to dig deeply or wait a long time, but the truth will be revealed to us eventually. In the meantime, God will give us unfailing strength to cope with and get through the suffering. And if we keep our focus on eternal life with God, this life and its woes will seem like a fleeting daydream.

The peace that surpasses all understanding comes from being wholly surrendered to God's will, whether in good or evil, pleasure or pain. It is the Holy Spirit that can accomplish that surrender in us. All we can do is pray for it. Complete surrender to God is a gift of the Holy Spirit. Jesus said "Peace I leave with you; my peace I give to you. I do not give to you as the world gives. Do not let your hearts be troubled, and do not let them be afraid" (John 14:27).

So, we are called to sing God's praises when we are in pain, just as Paul and Silas did. After they were given a severe beating with rods, they were chained up in an innermost jail cell. Most of us cannot imagine what it must be like to be beaten with rods, but still they sang spiritual songs to God. Around midnight an earthquake shook the jail to its foundations, their chains were broken, and the jail doors opened. The jailer thought everyone had escaped and was going to kill himself (as the Roman authorities would somehow blame him and torture him to death). However, Paul reassured him they were not gone. Paul preached the gospel to the jailer and his family, and they were all converted (Acts 16: 22-34).

God allowed Paul's pain for the sake of the jailer and his family. The jailer would likely not have heard the gospel any other way. If we trust God no matter what, our example of faith in the midst of very hard times may make others want what we have and result in their conversion. If God allows us to suffer, it may not be just for our own spiritual growth, but also for the spiritual growth and conversion of others.

It is important to keep trusting God and crying out to the Lord even if we feel like no one is listening. Sometimes our prayers may seem to bounce off the ceiling back to us, but this is due to our projections onto God. We imagine God is not hearing or answering. God is always there, always present and always hears our cries, but for God's own purposes, God may not answer right away. Perhaps the timing is not right, or the prayer is not appropriate in that, if God fulfilled it, it would be to our detriment.

Even if our faith, hope and love seem to be stripped away and we feel empty, we are called to try to praise God anyway. The purest faith happens when we are in a state of "kenosis," that is, emptiness.

Many of the greatest saints have experienced a dark night of the soul when God seemed completely absent. In our own time, St. Teresa of Kolkata (Calcutta) experienced God's abandonment for forty years. Yet Mother Teresa soldiered on, fulfilling her ministry to the poorest of the poor, since this is what she knew God had called her to.

The fact that the great saints continue on when every consolation is gone is the greatest testament to the depth of their soul, their love of God, their faith, and to the power of the Holy Spirit working in them. They are the great exemplars to all of us of loving God solely for God alone.

BOOK NINE
LOVING GOD ABOVE ALL ELSE

CHAPTER ONE
LOVING GOD ABOVE ALL PERFECTS ALL THINGS

Man is the perfection of the universe; the spirit is the perfection of man; love, that of the spirit; and charity, that of love. Wherefore the love of God is the end, the perfection and the excellence of the universe. In this, Theotimus, consists the greatness and the primacy of the commandment of divine love, which the Saviour calls the first and greatest commandment. 161

From the sacred tree of this commandment grow all the counsels, exhortations, inspirations, and the other commandments, as its flowers, and eternal life as its fruit; and all that does not tend to eternal love tends to eternal death. Grand Commandment, the perfect fulfilment of which lasts through eternal life, yea, is no other thing but eternal life! 162

In heaven, we shall indeed have a heart quite free from passions, a soul purified from all distractions, a spirit liberated from contradictions, and powers exempt from opposition, and therefore we shall love God with a perpetual and never interrupted affection. 163

We love God for his sovereign infinite goodness, as God, and because he is God. Now one drop of his love is worth more, has more power, and deserves more esteem, than all the other loves that can ever enter into the hearts of men or amongst the choirs of angels. For while this love lives, it reigns and bears the sceptre over all the affections, making God to be preferred in its will before all things, indifferently, universally, and without reserve. 164

Above all these souls, there is yet one most only one, who is the queen of queens, the most loving, the most lovely, and the most beloved, of all the friends of the divine beloved, who not only loves God above all things and in all things, but also loves only God in all things, so that she loves not many things, but only one thing, which is God himself. 165

But leaving this peerless queen in her matchless eminence, - there have yet been other souls who have been in such estate of pure love that in comparison with others they might take the rank of queens, of only doves, of perfect friends of the spouse. 166

What must have been the feelings of that great lover, who sighed all the night: "My God is to me all things?" Such were St. Augustine, St. Bernard, and the two St. Catherines, of Siena and of Genoa, and many others, in imitation of whom everyone may aspire to this divine degree of love. 167

And this is what God requires of us – that among all our loves his be the dearest, holding the first place in our hearts; the warmest, occupying our whole soul; our whole spirit; and this strongest, exercising all our strength and vigour. And inasmuch as by this we choose and elect God for the sovereign object of our soul, it is a love of sovereign election, or an election of sovereign love. 168

Sovereign honour is due to sovereign excellence, and sovereign love to sovereign goodness. The love of God is a love without peer, because the goodness of God is a peerless goodness. 169

When a heart loves God in respect of his infinite goodness, with however little a portion of this excellent love, it will prefer God's will before all things, and in all the occasions that present themselves it will forsake everything, to preserve itself in grace with the sovereign goodness, and nothing will divert it from this. 170

How great an extent then, O my dear Theotimus, ought the force of this sacred love of God above all things to have? It must surpass all affections, vanquish all difficulties, and prefer the honour of God's goodwill before all things; yea I say, before all things absolutely, without any exception or reservation. 171

To make an act of true charity, it must proceed from an entire, general, and universal love, which extends to all the divine commandments, and if we fail in any one commandment, love ceases to be entire and universal, and the heart wherein it is cannot be called truly loving, nor, consequently, truly good. 172

The universe comes from and is heading toward Divine Love. The human race has been in the making for 13.7 billion years, so we are the perfection so far of the evolutionary process from the Big Bang onwards: the creation of giant stars, then galaxies, the Milky Way galaxy, our sun created in a star forming region of our galaxy, the creation of a proto-planet ring of debris around our sun, the conglomeration of debris within the ring to form our mother, Earth, the evolution of life on Earth.

Life on Earth headed towards beings of greater and greater consciousness which culminated in the most conscious creature: the human being. Then the formation of primitive nature worship and the spread of more sophisticated religions around the world: Judaism, Hinduism, Buddhism, Christianity, Islam, all aiming for the spiritual perfection of humans.

The most loving human beings, holy men and women, the saints and mystics within these great religions bring the spirituality of these traditions to perfection. And those most filled with Divine Love are the greatest exemplars and founders of these traditions: Abraham, Moses, Krishna, Buddha, Mohammed and Jesus. Christians believe that God is most fully revealed in Jesus the Christ, but there is no doubt that God has been active in all other holy people in varying degrees.

The best part of humans is their spirit, the best part of spirit is love, and the best part of love is Divine Love. The greatest commandment in the Bible: to love God with all your heart, mind, soul and will is the perfection of all Jewish and Christian scriptures. The rest of scripture is, again, simply commentary on this one Great Command. It sums up all other commands, counsels and inspirations since they all depend on this one commandment.

This Great Command, if we follow it, perfects our lives because it gives us eternal life, even while we live on Earth. This Command is given to us on Earth, it is not given in heaven, because it is easy to love God in heaven.

It is easy to love God when we are constantly in the presence of, and are saturated with, God's infinite glory, wisdom, understanding, peace, joy and compassion. Nothing is easier than to love God in heaven because God's love of us is constantly before us, and not only before us but in our heart and bursting to get out and love God even more. We and God are constantly loving God. The Father, Son and Holy Spirit are constantly loving each other in and through us.

It is also easy to love God on Earth if we have "eyes to see and ears to hear" as Jesus said (Matthew 13:9-17). If we sit still and meditate for fifteen or twenty minutes twice a day on all the ways God has loved us throughout our life, we will be amazed to find that God's love is constantly all around us, we just have not noticed it until now.

God constantly loved us in our mother's womb before we were born, and when we were a child God loved us through our parents, siblings, uncles and aunts, grandparents, pets, friends and teachers. God has fed and clothed us since we were born.

God has constantly loved us through our senses: pleasurable sights, sounds, tastes, smells and touch. God has been loving us through our seeing sunsets, waterfalls, mountains and valleys; through our hearing romantic love songs, jazz, blues, classical music and the songs of birds; through our smelling fresh-baked bread, incense and flowers; through our tasting chocolate, ice cream, pecan pie, lasagna, beer, lemonade, steaks and liqueurs; through our sense of touch in massages, caresses, kisses, hugs and sex.

God has particularly loved us when we were ill, poor, struggling and broken. God never abandons us no matter what.

God has loved us within our heart, intellect, intuition and soul by leading us from within into the right paths, paths of virtue and righteousness for God's sake and our sake, paths that avoid unnecessary suffering and bring joy to us and others, paths of peace, prosperity and love.

It is easy to love God while we are on this earthly plane if we have eyes and ears to see and hear God's love all around us. However, there are numerous distractions and, again, that is why Christ *commands* us to love God.

When we consider trying to keep our spouse happy, our children happy, pay down the mortgage, keep our boss happy, have a career, do or find meaningful work, stay in shape, travel, do housework, stay on top of home maintenance and repairs, keep our mind alive and active through taking courses or at least reading, help with the crises of friends and relatives, take care of our pets and aging parents, help out in some volunteer role, and all the while we are being fire-hosed with information and advertising from television, radio, magazines, newspapers, Facebook, Twitter, Instagram, Pinterest, Linked In and other social media that tell us why our life is not good enough the way it is, no wonder our life is fragmented and scattered.

Unless we prioritize God, prayer, scripture study and attending our religious community over all these distractions, we will put the things that are absolutely essential for our spiritual survival on the backburner and give priority to the fire alarms that are everything else in our life.

The urgent will overwhelm the important over and over. The biggest challenge for everyone in contemporary life is to put our priorities in the right order and then stick to them through thick and thin.

We can grow in our love of God while on Earth, but only if we put the kindom/kingdom/queendom/reign of God first in our life. Of course, it is good to love our spouse, children and our work as long as we love God more than all these other priorities.

In fact, we can love God in and through our spouse, children, work, friends, relatives and others.

Thanks to God's initiative within him, Jacob loved God with divine love, and he loved God through loving Rachel with a God-given spousal love. Jacob loved Rachel so much that he worked seven years for Laban, Rachel's father, so that Laban would give him Rachel as his wife.

But Laban tricked Jacob into marrying Leah, his older daughter, and then Jacob had to agree to work for another seven years if he wanted Rachel too. This was probably all the law of return/consequence/karma in operation because Jacob had tricked his own brother Esau out of his birthright. In any case, Jacob agreed to Laban's new terms because he knew Rachel was the soulmate that God had chosen for him (Genesis 29:15-30). So, out of commitment to God's will, Jacob kept working for Laban until he received Rachel as his bride.

If we don't love God more than the other things we love, it is easy for those other things to take over our life, so we have no time for God. These things will get in the way, distract us, and demand to be prioritized over less important things (like God!).

As C. S. Lewis put it, the devil has two main strategies for turning us away from God. The first is to make us believe we are so unlovable that God could not possibly love us. The second is to keep us so busy that we do not have time for God or prayer.

The modern self-esteem and human potential movements have convinced us that we are lovable and that loving our self is essential to our mental health and success in life, but they have also convinced us that we don't need God, we are so great we can do it all our self. While this counters one of the tactics of the devil in that it tells us that we are lovable, it plays into a third strategy of the devil, that is, to convince us that the goal of life is self-fulfilment not divinization.

Divinization, being completely united with God in love, is only possible through the initiative and grace of God. Ironically, and contrary to what humanists believe, we cannot be fully human, we cannot fulfill our purpose as human beings, without God.

In the western world however, we are not so likely to believe we are unlovable as we are to get so caught up in busy-ness (business) that we have no time for God. The whole capitalist system is based on the idea that resources are scarce and therefore we have to out-compete the other seven billion people on the planet or we will not get our fair share. If we do not compete, we will live in poverty or even starve to death. It is our buying into the myth of scarcity and the consequent hyper-competitiveness that causes us to not have time for God.

Since the corporate world won its bid years ago to keep stores open on Sundays, so that consumers could consume corporate products seven days a week instead of six, there has been a steady erosion of "shabbat," the sabbath, or any time for God.

In the past, Sundays were an ideal time for church, family, friends and relaxation. It was a time for taking naps or making love with our spouse in the afternoon or sitting on the porch and watching the corn grow or the chipmunks or grandchildren play in the yard, or for taking long walks in the woods, or time for extra prayer or studying scripture and other spiritual books. It was a time to just "be" and remember that life is more than work.

Now, with smartphones, people are at work or potentially at work 24/7 which adds up to a 168-hour work week! Our boss or coworkers now can be in our face at any time—when we are on holidays, lying in the bathtub or even having sex.

This is the opposite of the silence and solitude necessary for soul-health. Our soul craves time to catch up with our body and our emotions. Not only that, but if we do not take time to recharge, we will probably be less productive the other six days of the week. So, not taking Sabbath-time is actually counterproductive.

Taking time out for God, even if it is only one morning or even one church-hour a week in order to put our life back into perspective, has now become a major Christian discipline. Time for God must be a conscious, intentional choice: a command that not only Christ gives us but that we give our self. Otherwise, we cannot prevent what used to be called "backsliding," the back-burnering of our spiritual life and our love of God.

God has all the time in the world for us and is always patiently waiting for us to show up. Should we not make time for the One who is more loving and lovable than anything?

Novices in the spiritual life begin to love God, but their former unrighteousness, their former sin, has not yet been completely washed away by years of spiritual practices. Their sin still clings to them. They have escaped the spider's web, but sticky, gossamer threads still cling to them.

The threads, the stains on their soul from former sins, are still there. They may still love some things—their home, work, spouse, or children more than God. To love things and people is not evil, but to love them more than God is a sin. These things can distract us from God, take priority over God, and eventually turn us away from God.

The classic illustration of this is the story of the rich young man. He asks Jesus "Teacher, what good deed must I do to have eternal life?" Jesus tells him to follow the Ten Commandments. The man, a religious Jew, replies "I have kept all these; what do I still lack?" Jesus then says, "If you wish to be perfect, go, sell your possessions, and give the money to the poor, and you will have treasure in heaven; then come, follow me." At this the young man "went away grieving, for he had many possessions."

Jesus turns to his disciples and says, "It is easier for a camel to go through the eye of a needle than for someone who is rich to enter the kingdom of God." His disciples are amazed at this because up until then they believed that wealth was a sign of God's blessing. They ask, "Then who can be saved?" Jesus replies "For mortals it is impossible, but for God all things are possible" (Matthew 19:16-26).

The moral of the story is: love God before all things. The book of Proverbs and the book of Psalms say over and over that God's commandments, God's word, "is more precious than gold, even much fine gold." God's holy scriptures and Jesus the Christ give us the wisdom to see how ephemeral riches are, that we all end up in the grave and have to give all our wealth to others who may lose or squander it.

"Adepts," that is "seasoned veterans in the spiritual life," love God before all other things, particularly their own ego, their false self, which is always behind the love of things other than God. If we love anything more than God, it is because our ego does not want to admit that God exists.

God is the death of the ego because God is the only thing bigger than our ego. God is the only thing more important to the true self than the false self. The false self, the ego, wants us to focus on it alone. But when we discover God, we discover our true self, and the false self, the ego, dies, although not totally. The ego is something the true self always has to be consciously aware of and keep in check.

There are still higher forms of loving God than just loving God before all things. Loving God before all things simply means that we make God our absolute number one priority. We value God and place God before all things. However, a higher form of loving God is to love God in all things and all things in God.

God is in all things, so, while loving God *before* all these things, we also love God *in* all these things. We highly value all these things, not more than God, but because we see God in them all. Everything is a facet of the face of God, and we keep seeing new aspects of God by contemplating all these things. We learn more and more about God and fall deeper and deeper in love with God by contemplating all God's faces. Just as a lover cannot get enough of contemplating his or her beloved's face, so the devout cannot get enough of seeing God's infinite faces.

God is not only in all things, all things are in God and derive their very being, life and beauty from God their Source. They derive all their biology, physiology and complexity from God. Through studying them, lovers of God learn even more about God's beauty, intelligence, creativity, strength and wisdom.

All things reveal not only God's infinite faces but also God's infinite depths and complexity. Anyone who has worked on a graduate degree knows that the more we know, the more we realize we don't know. Expanded knowledge of God's creatures through science should result in expanded awe and humility in the admirers and lovers of God. There is no end to this expanded awe and humility. They are as infinite as God is infinite.

If we love God first and we love God in all things, then the false self, the proud ego, is forced to give up its pride in itself more and more and to surrender into the loving hands and arms of the God-Who-Is-Love. God is in all things, and all things are in God. That is all the true self knows, and all it needs to know.

Beyond loving God in all things and all things in God, there is pure love of God alone. We no longer love all things because they are in God, we love only God in those things. Love of other things begins to disappear.

We no longer love the consolations God has sent us in the past. These consolations are temporal and ephemeral, they come and go, but now we have established our relationship with God not on feelings, but on our daily decision, our commitment, our will to love God. Willing to love God, and only God, gives us a much more stable foundation to our relationship with God than mere feelings.

If we love *only* God, we still strive to build God's reign of justice and peace on Earth, we still care for the poor, marginalized, the shunned and rejected. But we don't set all our hopes on God's reign on Earth because it may not happen. It depends on the free choice of human beings aided by God's grace, but we may choose to destroy Earth.

If we humans are capable of slaughtering about one hundred million people in the twentieth century, we are capable of wiping out all seven billion of us in the twenty-first century.

Russia has already ramped up its nuclear weapons and the United States is planning to spend over a trillion (a thousand billion!) dollars on updating its nuclear capabilities.

God will not stop nuclear proliferation or even the use of nuclear weapons because God is wholly and irrevocably committed to allowing human freedom without which there could be no love. God's commitment to love means that God will allow extreme hatred. God therefore allows nations to hate and destroy each other as happened in the Second World War and continued in the many local wars (Vietnam, Iraq, Afghanistan) throughout the world to this day.

The pure lover of God alone therefore sets her or his sights and love not on God's reign but only on God's self. God's reign is still extremely important, and lovers of God do everything in their power to bring it about. But again, it may not happen. God alone will survive an all-out nuclear war. The reign of God may come, and the reign of God may go, only God is eternal, the only fully permanent foundation of the lover's life and love.

Scripture says that if we love God and participate in God's present and coming reign, a new heaven and a new Earth will happen (Revelation 21:1). God will not be defeated as long as we live the gospel. Therefore, God probably *will* bring about God's kingdom/queendom/kindom as in John's Revelation vision. In any case, even if we destroy everything as we know it, we *can* hope that God will eventually make all things new again and God will reign.

The lover of God alone also does not love heaven. Heaven is the ultimate consolation, but the pure lover of God does not dwell on heaven or concern her or his self with it. God's lovers love only God, not God's consolations, no matter how small or great the consolations are. They know that, if they love God, they are already in heaven even while they are on Earth. They have no need to concern themselves with heaven because if they love God alone, heaven is assured.

Many saints have loved only God. The greatest saints in the early church, Paul and Augustine, learned to love God alone after they recovered from being serious sinners earlier in their lives. Paul described himself as the greatest sinner of all before his conversion on the road to Damascus (Acts 9:1-19) because he so harshly persecuted the budding fellowship of Christians, arresting them, putting them in chains, locking them in prisons and even overseeing Christians being stoned to death as in the case of Stephen (Acts 8:1).

Saint Augustine was also highly aware of all his sins before his conversion, and thoroughly analyzes them in his *Confessions*. Like Paul, Augustine probably wrestled with at least venial (minor) sins all his life, even after his conversion, which is perhaps why his writings are so powerful—he knew firsthand the lingering power and temptation of sin. It takes a great sinner to have a great conversion and to learn to love only God.

CHAPTER TWO
WE MUST LOVE GOD ABOVE OUR SELF

Love of God precedes all love of ourselves, even according to the natural inclination of our will. 173

The blessed are carried away and necessitated, though not forced, to love God whose sovereign beauty they clearly see. 174

But in this mortal life, Theotimus, we are not necessitated to love him so sovereignly, because we see him not clearly. In heaven, where we shall see him face to face, we shall love him heart to heart. 175

Though we have this holy natural inclination to love the divinity above all things, yet we have not the strength to put it in execution, unless the same divinity infuse its most holy charity supernaturally into our hearts. 176

Let us love him more than ourselves who is to us more than all and more than ourselves. Amen, so it is. 177

Why do we love ourselves in charity? Surely because we are the image and likeness of God; and whereas all men are endowed with the same dignity, we love them as ourselves, that is, as being holy and living images of the divinity. 178

To love our neighbor in charity is to love God in man, or man in God; it is to hold God alone dear for his own sake and the creature for the love of him. 179

The love of God not only oftentimes commands the love of our neighbor, but itself produces this love and pours it into man's heart, as its resemblance and image: for even as man is the image of God, so the sacred love of man towards man, is the true image of the heavenly love of man towards God. 180

The supreme love of the divine goodness of the heavenly Father consists in the perfection of the love of our brothers and companions. 181

We are commanded to love God more than the thousands of things that distract us. We can love God in our spouse, children, parents or best friend, but you cannot love them more than the God who transcends them all. Other people, spouses, children (or congregations if we are a minister or priest) can distract us from loving God.

Spiritual directors often hear clergy tell them they are too busy to pray. They consider their sermon preparation to be prayer, and it is, but they are doing it for two external purposes: to motivate their congregation and to keep their own employment.

Authentic prayer is about having a personal one-to-one relationship with the Lord with no external purpose. It is about "wasting time with the Lord" as a wise woman said. Having personal quality time with the Lord as our first priority will naturally spill over into service to people inside and outside the church. But service without a healthy prayer foundation is a perfect recipe for burnout or cynicism.

As tempting as quality time with our spouse, playing with our children, being with friends, watching movies, reading classic novels, participating in or watching sports, enjoying hobbies or getting satisfaction from our work can be, we need to make our time with God the priority that transcends all other priorities simply because God transcends and grounds everything.

Love of God brooks no equals because as human beings we are built to love the good and God is not only the absolute good, God is infinitely good and therefore to be loved completely. God has planted our deep longing for absolute goodness, for God, in the depths of our soul. Even agnostics and atheists long for greater goodness and for the absolute good. This instinctual longing is hardwired into us all by God.

A certain priest, Jeremiah we will call him, became obsessed with his enemy, who we will call Bartholomew. Bartholomew was a retired priest and the former pastor of Jeremiah's church, and had served the congregation for twenty-five years. Most people loved him, but the Elders and quite a few congregants agreed that when Bartholomew retired, they would look for some fresh young blood to pump into the church. Things had gotten rather stale under old Bartholomew.

When Bartholomew retired, the Elders threw a big party for him, everyone came out, Bartholomew was lauded, and the Elders announced that they had hired a dynamic young pastor named Jeremiah to replace Bartholomew. Everyone went home happy and satisfied.

However, Bartholomew, rather than attending a different church after he retired, continued attending St. Jerome's Parish out of curiosity to see how things would develop under the new pastor. Jeremiah, who was fresh out of seminary, where everyone loved him for his brilliance, began changing things right away.

The hard pews were taken out and replaced with individual chairs that could be moved around into small circles or one big circle around the altar. Hymn books were replaced with screens connected to computers. Taize chanting began in the service, and liturgical dance. Most disturbing of all to many in the elderly congregation, Jeremiah started preaching fiery sermons about social and restorative justice.

Bartholomew quickly decided that Jeremiah was an inappropriate fit for the congregation and started to gather like-minded people around him. But the Elders and half of the congregation loved the changes and backed Jeremiah.

Things escalated and started to get ugly, as these things do, and soon there was talk about splitting the church. No one could seem to humble themselves and listen to the other side.

However, Bartholomew, as an experienced pastor, knew how to bend a congregation to his will, and eventually got more people on his side and the congregation fired Jeremiah.

Jeremiah on his part relished being a martyr for social justice, and when he left he took a substantial portion of the congregation with him and they formed a new church.

Jeremiah loved hating his enemy Bartholomew more than he

loved God's will, that is, listening to and being reconciled to those who oppose him.

And Bartholomew loved his power and control of the congregation more than he loved God's will of letting new, creative ideas in and revitalizing the church.

Both of them were guilty of idolatry, that is, loving something (in Jeremiah's case new ideas, and in Bartholomew's case the old way of doing things) more than God. Even educated, talented and deeply religious clergy can become seduced into loving things, even seemingly good and godly things, more than God.

We must love God in all ways possible: through care of the dear neighbor, which means making a preferential option for the poor, for those least able to defend themselves. All love of God is meaningless if it is not accompanied by charity, that is, actual social justice action that carries all the way down to the most defenceless creature, that is, the child in the womb. We are called to defend every human life all the way from conception to natural death.

We are called to love God in all ways, but what most of us love in all ways are trivialities: status, money, power, and pleasure above all. Status, money and power would be meaningless if they did not bring us pleasure.

We are commanded to love God with all our faculties—with all our heart, mind, soul and strength (will) and to love others as we love our true self. Still, because in this life we can only love darkly, we cannot see God directly (I Corinthians 13:12), even the great commandments of Christ which sum up the rest of scripture, are really *invitations* to love God completely. God does not force us to love God because forced love is not true love. Christ makes his invitations into commands simply to stress the gravity of his requests.

Everything, even eternal life with God, depends on us obeying these invitations, but no force is involved. We have to follow them out of our own free will. Still, even if we do not love God utterly and completely with all our heart, mind, soul and will, we must love God more than we love our self, for God is the Creator, Sustainer, and Goal of our life. And we must make the *effort* to love God totally.

God recognizes that in this life we are wrapped around with the sin and corruption of others right from birth. So, God does not expect us to love God totally. God does not demand complete success in this most critical skill of loving God completely, but God does hope and long for our effort in that direction. Again, God does not long for this for God's sake but for our sake, because God loves us, and loving God is the best thing we can do for ourselves.

God does not expect perfection in our love of God. Even Peter, the one Christ chose to lead his church, failed miserably and loved his own self before Christ, denying three times that he knew Christ in order to save himself, just as Christ had predicted he would. But Peter repented of his sin and proved also that he was a worthy religious leader who could own his own sin and shadow.

Jesus said that the first Great Commandment is to love God, "And a second is like it: 'You shall love your neighbor as yourself.' On these two commandments hang all the law and the prophets" (Matthew 22:39-40). Loving God and loving others are inseparable. We cannot love the God we cannot see if we cannot love the spouse, children, sibling, extended family members, friends, neighbors and enemies we can see.

The way we treat those closest to us is the way we treat God. This particularly applies to the way we treat our spouse if we are married, but it should extend all the way out to loving our enemies. Loving our enemies is the "Magna Carta," the Great Charter, of Christian non-violence, peacemaking and justice.

Love of God should automatically result in love of neighbor, that is, love of other people. Our neighbor, rich or poor, friendly or hostile, gay or straight, abled or disabled, colored or white, male or female, Muslim or Christian, is made in the image of God, just as we are. We can love our neighbor as the face of God, one of the billions of facets that show forth God's infinite faces. We can love the God who lives in our neighbor and shines forth through them.

It is impossible to love God if we hate the most precious thing in God's sight, that is, God's children, which is all of us. And we could extend this to the natural world and all its creatures as well. We cannot say we love God if we despise God's Creation that God's daughters and sons depend on for their survival.

If Christians and Muslims, who together make up at least a third of human beings, worked together on environmental issues, they could have a far greater impact in reversing climate change than governments who are lobbied by oil companies. The world's major religions, if they cooperated, could literally save the world and all its creatures.

Pope Francis, in his powerful encyclical "Laudato Si" (Latin for "Praised Be") has already taken the initiative on this. The title comes from the lines of St. Francis of Assisi's famous poem/hymn/religious utterance *The Canticle of Creation* which begins "Praised be you, my Lord, for all your Creation."

It is now up to imams, sheikhs, patriarchs, gurus, rabbis, indigenous chiefs, and all other key religious leaders to join in the chorus and teach their followers to make care of the environment, love of our great common home, Mother Earth, their number one priority in loving God. How can we love the God who we cannot see if we do not love Mother Earth who is everywhere we can see?

However, we cannot love God through loving our mother, Earth, if we love our self more than we love God or the planet. Bringing climate change under control is primarily a spiritual problem because it involves self-sacrifice—loving God and God's Creation more than we love our self.

Chapter Three
True and False Zeal for God

"Do not lag in zeal, be ardent in spirit, serve the Lord."
(Romans 12:11)

When love therefore is fervent and is come to that height that it would take away, remove and divert, what is opposite to the thing beloved, it is termed zeal. So that, to describe it properly, zeal is no other thing than love in its ardour, or rather the ardour that is in love. And therefore, such as the love is, such is the zeal, which is its ardour. If the love be good its zeal is good, if the love be bad its zeal is bad. 182

When therefore we ardently love worldly and temporal things, beauty, honours, riches, rank – this zeal, that is the ardour of tis love, ends ordinarily in envy. 183

Jealousy proceeds from love, envy comes from the defect of love. Jealousy never happens but in matter of love, but envy is extended to all kinds of goods – honours, favours, beauty. 184

However, God's jealousy of us is not truly a jealousy of cupidity, but of sovereign friendship: for it is not in his interest that we should love him, but ours. Our love is useless to him, but to us a great gain; and if it be preferable to him, it is because it is profitable to us: for being the sovereign good, he takes pleasure in communicating himself by love, without any kind of profit that can return to him thereby. 185

Perfect love, namely, love which has gone as far as zeal, cannot suffer any mediation, interposition, or mingling of any other thing, not even of God's gifts, yea, up to this extreme, that it permits not even the love of heaven, except with intention to love more perfectly therein the goodness of him who gives it. 186

Now as zeal is an inflamed ardour, or an ardent inflaming of love, it requires to be wisely and prudently practised; otherwise, under the cloak of it, one would transgress the limits of moderation or discretion, and it would be easy to pass from zeal into anger, and from a just affection to an unjust passion. 187

Wherein consists the zeal or the jealousy which we ought to have for the divine goodness? Theotimus, its office is, first, to hate, fly, hinder, detest, reject, combat and overthrow, if one can, all that is opposed to God; that is, to his will, to his glory and the sanctification of his name. 188

The zeal which consumed our Saviour's heart, made him cast out and instantly take vengeance on the irreverence and profanation which those buyers and sellers committed in the temple. 189

In human jealousy we are afraid lest the thing beloved be possessed by some other, but our zeal for God makes us on the contrary fear lest we should not be entirely enough possessed by him. Human jealousy makes us fear not to be loved enough, Christian jealousy troubles us with the fear of not loving enough. 190

As zeal is an ardour and vehemence of love it stands in need of guidance; otherwise it would exceed the limits of moderation and discretion. 191

Anger or hardihood once aroused, and unable to contain itself within the limits of reason, carries away the heart into disorder, so that zeal is thus practised indiscreetly and inordinately; which makes it bad and blameworthy. 192

Self-love often deceives us and leads us away, gratifying its own passions under the name of zeal. Zeal has once made use of anger, and now anger in its turn uses the name of zeal, in order to keep its shameful disorder covered under this. 193

There are persons who think one cannot be very zealous unless one is very angry, thinking that unless they spoil all they can manage nothing, whereas on the contrary true zeal most rarely makes use of anger. 194

It is true, indeed, my friend Theotimus, that Moses, Phineas, Elias, Mathathias and many great servants of God made use of anger in the *exercise of their zeal, on many remarkable occasions, yet note also, I pray you, that those were great souls, who could well handle their passions and regulate their anger. 195*

St. John and St. James, who would have imitated Phineas and Elias in making fire descend from heaven upon men, were reprehended by our Lord, who gave them to know that his spirit and his zeal were sweet, mild, and gracious, making use of indignation or wrath but very rarely, when there was no longer hope of doing good any other way. 196

Zeal may be practiced in three ways. First in performing great actions of justice to repel evil. Secondly, one may use zeal by doing actions of great virtue in order to give good example, by suggesting remedies for evils, and exhorting men to apply them, by effecting the good that is opposite to the evil which we desire to banish. This belongs to everyone, and yet few will do it. Finally, the most excellent use of zeal lies in suffering and enduring much to hinder or divert evil. 197

True zeal is the child of charity as being its ardour; wherefore, like to charity, it is patient, is kind, envieth not, dealeth not perversely, seeketh not her own, is not provoked to anger, rejoiceth in the truth. 198

Zeal in like manner has ardours which are extreme, but constant, solid, sweet, industrious, equally agreeable and untiring; whereas on the contrary, false zeal is turbulent, troubled, insolent, arrogant, choleric, transient, equally impetuous and inconstant. 199

When contemplating the Lord, it is important to distinguish between jealousy and envy. The Hebrew scriptures say in several places that God is a *jealous* God. For example: "You shall worship no other god, because the Lord, whose name is Jealous, is a jealous God" (Exodus 34:14).

Richard Dawkins, Christopher Hitchens, Sam Harris, Daniel Dennett and other "New Atheists," have used passages like this to discredit the scriptures and make their point that the God of the Bible is narcissistic and petty.

In responding to their critique it must first of all be said that human language fails miserably when it compares God's transcendent feelings to human ones, and secondly it is necessary to remind our self that jealousy happens when someone we love and who loves us gives their love to someone else. Jealousy originates in love given and received.

Envy on the other hand, comes from not having any love, wishing we had it and envying those who do have it. So, God is a jealous God because God loves us, has given us all God's love, and is dismayed when, after giving God our love, we suddenly turn away. God is jealous *for us*—God wants us to love God more than anything else, again, not for God's sake, but for our sake because God knows that loving God is by far the best thing for us.

And again, what could be as big a blessing for human beings compared to loving God? Loving money, sex, power, or knowledge more than God has resulted in the human race getting into trouble collectively and individually over and over. Loving false gods we have created in our mind, based on our culture's values, always fails because these images of God are always idols, shallow attempts to capture in human terms the True God who transcends all our cultures and all our values.

Loving our spouse, children and friends has something of the eternal in it, but they or we will pass away. Loving our work serves us well yet should be limited or we will become a workaholic with no work-life balance. Loving Mother Earth is now more important than ever, but she is limited and cannot return our love the way humans can.

It is not that love of these things is bad in itself. Love of money, sex, power, knowledge, spouses, children, friends, work and Mother Earth, if used appropriately by including God's ethics and without usurping God's absolutely primary role, can be very fulfilling and invigorating. However, none of these compare to the blessings that come with zeal, the ardent and unreserved love of God.

There is beginning love of God, the love of novices. Then there is moderate love of God, the love of proficients. Proficients are skilled at the love of God, but not as skilled as adepts. Adepts are highly skilled, totally proficient, well-versed in the love of God. The love of

God practiced by adepts is strong love of God, commonly called zeal.

Zeal has three basic tenets.

First, zealots hate anything opposed to God. They will brook no other love. They cannot stand fools who say there is no God. They hate all the flim-flam and shallowness of modern culture, the senseless pursuit of things that don't last, whether it is wealth, sports victories, possessions or pleasure. They hate the chasing after wind, the nonsense of endless sensory titillation in a meaningless existence without God. They strongly oppose the rational obfuscations of atheists' arguments against God. But, although zealots speak the truth, they do so with love.

Secondly, zealots long for other souls to love God. Those who strongly love God know the endless blessings that God showers upon them. God's store of treasures and delights knows no limits, and zealots want others to experience the utter joy, wonder and awesomeness of this. Zealots spend long hours praying for the souls of others and thinking of ways to reach out to them. They do all this not for themselves but solely for the other person. Out of pure altruistic love, they want others to experience the authentic liberation and joy they have found. There is no ego, no small self, involved in their zealous love.

Thirdly, the strong lover of God, the zealot, fears not loving God enough. They want nothing more than to totally love God and are very aware of their own weaknesses, shadows and sin. They know they are living in a world rife with temptations and distractions. They have seen the promised land, the second Garden of Eden that is, total union with God, and they are afraid that past traumas and wounds will limit their ability to respond to the divine call, the invitation to dine at the Lord's never-ending banquet.

True zealots know that their zealotry has to be kept in check. They know they need to produce the spiritual fruit of self-control. Otherwise, the fire burning in their hearts can burn them and others. Like a well-tended fire, zeal has to be contained or, rather than warming the whole house, it will burn it to the ground.

False zealots fail to contain their zeal and allow it to become chronic anger against those who do not love God as the zealot does.

Even in churches, false zealotry can set one believer against another. Many clergy have experienced a parishioner who gets in their face and insists that the minister or priest's sermons should be ramming Christ down the throats of the congregation or the clergy should be ramming Christ into their own life more.

The false zealot becomes self-righteous like the Pharisee thanking God that he is not like the tax collector who he sees as a sinner. False zeal never looks at its own shortcomings. It becomes enraged with the seven deadly sins of others without recognizing its own anger, spiritual pride and lack of humility. The problems and pain in the heart of the false zealot are all projected onto others so that the zealot never has to look at herself or himself. In false zeal, the ego comes before God. In true zeal, there is no ego, no selfishness.

False zealotry can even become violent: "If the infidels will not convert, I will wrap myself in a suicide vest and blow them up. And I will go straight to heaven because of this self-sacrificing act of love for God. I love God more than my own life. In death I will be considered a martyr and a hero for God."

Islam is not the only source of false zealots. Christianity has produced its own share of unhealthy zealots in crusades, inquisitions, and religious wars in Europe between Catholics and Protestants. And Buddhists in Sri Lanka have been involved in a civil war for decades.

True zeal by contrast is always tempered with charity for all. The true zealot recognizes that God may call all of us to the fierce love of God characteristic of a zealot, but not everyone is capable of responding with their whole being in the same way.

A person's parents may not have been very devout or may have been rigidly religious because of a twisted view of God as a tyrant. There may not have been a lot of love flowing in a person's family of origin. A man or woman may never have experienced a healthy love of God or may have been a victim of bullying, rape or other traumas that impede their ability to trust and love other human beings. So, the love of God has no natural human love to build upon.

The true zealot, while strongly loving God, is also humble and contrite and strongly loves the fallible, imperfect human beings that

God loves. True zeal for God always involves both loving God with all our heart and loving others as we love our true self, since Christ commanded both loves.

There are three types of zeal or ardent love of God: acts of justice to repel evil, acts of virtue to counter evil and acts of sacrifice to prevent evil.

Zeal in the form of acts of justice to repel evil manifests itself in lovers of God who work hard to create systemic justice that repels the evil of corrupt governments and the evil of rich people lobbying governments to set up laws that favor those who are already well off. Acts of justice create the Just Society or the Beloved Community (formerly called the Kingdom of God)—communities free of systemic evil, societies where everyone has enough health care and education, where, as St. Paul wrote "The one who had did not have too much, and the one who had little did not have too little" (2 Corinthians 8:15).

Zeal in the form of justice addresses the big picture, whereas zeal for acts of virtue to counter evil happen in lovers of God on a more personal level. These acts involve standing up for the truth when the truth is not in the popular zeitgeist of the time.

For example, it may not be popular to accept refugees from Mexico or Islamic countries, but the lover of God sees everyone as children of the one God. Virtues like inclusiveness, empathy, understanding, wisdom, peacemaking and forgiveness are keys in birthing the Beloved Community and countering the evils of exclusion, aggression, rage and hatred.

Lovers of God recognize that outward behaviors are the symptoms of an underlying cause, that is, our inner attitudes. True mysticism, that is, the experience of the overflowing love of God for us and our love for God, always results in outward behavior that sets up conditions of peace and structures of justice so that the Beloved Community can thrive. True mysticism results in communities that counter evil.

Zealous lovers of God also engage in acts of sacrifice to prevent evil. For example, they are willing to sacrifice any excesses, any extra but unnecessary pleasures they may have engaged in before, in order to prevent climate change. They are more than willing to live simply so that others may simply live. They are determined to give up the convenience of cars if bicycles will suffice. They are willing to sacrifice their love of beef steaks if tofu steaks are more environmentally friendly. They are happy to sacrifice their time and energy to educate the poor and help them find jobs, in order to prevent the dual evils of ignorance and unemployment.

True zealots will go out of their way and endure any inconvenience if it means everyone will be treated fairly as children of God. They will march for women's rights, oppose unjust gun laws, engage in acts of civil disobedience and stand firm with Black or Indigenous protesters even though this may mean being attacked by police dogs, sprayed with mace or pepper spray, clubbed, forced to inhale tear gas or be shot with rubber-covered bullets.

Moses, Elijah and Paul knew how to channel their zeal for God into constructive anger. When Moses descended the mountain and found the people worshipping a golden calf, he smashed the tablets God had given him and forced the people to grind down the gold into dust and put it in water, so they had to drink and defecate their idol.

Elijah used his zeal for God to challenge the prophets of Baal to a duel. He challenged them to get their god Baal to immolate the sacrifices on the altar. Whoever lost the duel would be killed. Zealous lovers of God are willing to risk losing everything and even be killed for God. In order to show the Israelites the True God, Elijah angrily mocked the four hundred Baal prophets as they tried everything from dancing to gashing themselves with swords in order to get Baal to win the duel. Then Elijah calmly prayed and brought down fire from heaven to immolate the sacrifices on the altar (I Kings 18:20-40).

Paul used anger constructively when he opposed Peter, the leader of the apostles, because Peter started to withdraw from taking the message to the Gentiles (Galatians 2:11-14). If it wasn't for Paul's zealous love of God manifested as anger, Christianity might have remained confined to a small band of converted Jews. Authentic zeal keeps the flow of love going and ever-growing.

Although Jesus was more zealous for God than anyone, he rarely displayed anger. The most dramatic example was when he cleared the moneychangers out of the Temple and shouted out that God's house was to be a place of prayer, not business transactions.

True zeal is simply the ardor of charity. It is strong love of God. And like charity, true zeal is patient and kind and forgiving of others. The true zealot keeps their zeal in check so that it does not become chronic anger or violence. True zeal is not arrogant or unjust. If it ever unleashes as anger, it is only when the situation justifies it. The anger of Moses, Elijah, Paul and Jesus were all examples of just or warranted anger. Like God, true zeal is rich in mercy, slow to anger and abounding in steadfast love.

To sum up, in false zeal, the ego comes before God. In true zeal there is no ego, no self-centeredness. One is willing to die for God.

CHAPTER FOUR

IMITATION OF THE TWELVE MARKS OF CHRIST'S MOST EXCELLENT LOVE

Having spoken at large of the sacred acts of divine love, I present to you, that you may more easily and holily preserve the memory of them, with a collection or abridgement of them. 200

Christ loved us with a love of Complacency, for his delights were to be with the children of men and to draw man to himself, making himself man. He loved us with a love of Benevolence, bestowing his own divinity upon man, so that man was God. He united himself unto us by an incomprehensible Union. 201

He flowed out into us, and as it were melted his greatness, to bring it to the form and figure of our littleness, whence he is styled a source of living water, dew and rain of heaven. 202

He had a thousand thousand Langours of love; for whence could those divine words proceed: I have a baptism wherewith I am to be baptized: and how am I straightened until it be accomplished? 203

Finally, Theotimus, this divine lover died amongst the flames and ardours of love, by reason of the infinite charity which he had towards us, and by the force and virtue of love: that is he died in love, by love, for love, and of love. 204

O God! Theotimus, what burning coals are cast upon all our hearts to inflame us to the exercise of holy love towards our all-good Saviour, seeing he has so lovingly practised them towards us who are so evil! This charity then of Jesus Christ presseth us! 205

De Sales lists twelve marks of Jesus the Christ's most excellent love that God calls us to adopt and imitate in loving God and loving others.

Complacence. Jesus delighted in the Father: "I thank you, Father, Lord of heaven and Earth, because you have hidden these things from the wise and the intelligent and have revealed them to infants" (Matthew 11:25). And Jesus delighted in his fellow humans: "You are the salt of the Earth…you are the light of the world" (Matthew 5:13-14); "Do not be afraid, you are of more value than many sparrows" (Matthew 10:31).

We are called to delight in the love of God all around us: God's love in our friends; our work; in the gloriousness of the planet with its seasons, flowers and landscapes; in the miracle of being human and being alive. We could take complacence in our self, others and the diversity of peoples: Zulus, Dutch, Scots, Filipinos, Inuit. We could relish the diversity of countries: Yemen, Chile, Vietnam, Croatia, Afghanistan.

Benevolence. Jesus the Christ was on fire for his God-given and God-centered mission: to build the Beloved Community on Earth and the Communion of Saints in heaven. His whole life was centered on helping everyone, the essence of benevolence. We could be on fire for the same reason: to help God build communities in which all are loved and taken care of, where no one had too much or too little (2 Corinthians 8:15). We could be benevolent towards God by helping and serving others.

Conjunction. Jesus loved God and loved us by always joining himself to God and to us. He always returned to solitude with God after expending all his energy in serving us. He regularly set aside time from giving his all outwards in ministry to go away by himself, sometimes praying all night long. This is a good model for ministers and priests in particular: Jesus recharged his batteries through solitary prayer on a regular basis (not that clergy should pray all night, but they should recognize when they need recharging—a good spiritual director can help them discern this).

The Cosmic Christ, the Son of God, the Second Person of the Trinity emptied himself out and conjoined himself totally to us in becoming human. He went further by being born lower than most people: in a stable not a home or safe place like a hospital. And he died lower than the vast majority of us: nailed to a tree.

We could conjoin ourselves to Christ, the Father and the Holy Spirit by praying without ceasing, constantly studying and trying to understand God's Word, the Bible, and through taking holy retreats where we are silent with the Lord. And we can conjoin ourselves with the Lord and others by engaging in charity and justice: "Just as you did it to one of the least of these who are members of my family, you did it to me" (Matthew 25:40).

Serving those who are homeless at hospitality centers (soup kitchens often run by nuns or parishes) teaches people one overarching lesson. When they first start passing out food and drinks, volunteers normally have instantaneous judgmental thoughts running through their minds. They may not like these thoughts and try not to think them, but the thoughts persist, nonetheless.

People who are homeless will often be extraordinarily wrecked compared to the average citizen. They often look totally unemployable with shabby clothes; missing teeth; paranoid or glazed or drugged or broken looks on their faces; many tattoos on their necks, faces and hands; starved or limping bodies. New volunteers try to be humble and graciously serve the homeless but still the judgmental thoughts, the "I am superior" thoughts, keep spontaneously coming.

What eventually quells these thoughts for most people are two things, and they are both based on seeing things in new perspectives. One is sitting at the table with the homeless and listening to their stories: the poverty; the broken homes; the verbal, physical and sexual abuse by alcoholic or drug-addicted or mentally ill or criminal parents (who came from similarly broken homes); the bullying, mocking and ostracism by schoolmates; the physical or mental disabilities and illnesses; the learning disabilities that prevented them from advancing in school.

It changes the perspective of helpers when they develop a relationship with people who are homeless and recognize their shared humanity. When helpers learn that every person who is homeless has a story, it is easy to feel compassion for them rather than treating them as a "thing" to be pitied.

The other thing that cures judgmentalism is the realization that the way we are looking at people who are homeless is the way God looks at us. In fact, we are probably infinitely more poor, blind and naked in God's sight than these people who are homeless are in our sight. And on the positive side, God sees our goodness and the goodness of people who are homeless more than our and their brokenness. God sees the depths of brokenness and heights of glory of all people and we need to learn to do the same.

There is an infinite gap, not in distance but in greatness, between who and what God is, and who and what human beings are. In spite of Hinduism saying "Tvat Tvam Asi"—"Thou art that," and the Unity and New Thought churches claiming that your consciousness and God's consciousness are one, and Thomas Merton and Richard Rohr writing that when you discover your true self you discover God, God and your true self are not one.

Rohr recognizes this when he notes that "You and God are not two, yet not one." This is a great paradox that only the contemplative mind can fathom, since it is beyond rationalism and logic. Rohr is not a strict non-dualist or monist (there is only one thing—God), and I am sure neither was Merton. They, and perhaps the Unity/New Thought churches, are panentheists. They believe that God is in and permeates everything and yet God also transcends everything. There is an infinite gap—again, not in distance but in greatness—between God and everything else, including humans.

What can we compare God to, in terms of God's lovability? Our spouse, parents, siblings, best friend, our dog? God is Lord and Master of all galaxies. God has all the wisdom of all religions on planet Earth. God knows everything about everything. God has all creativity, mercy, truth, righteousness and love. God deserves to be loved above all things because God is infinitely greater than all things.

This is why reminding our self who and what God is and who and what we are allows us to serve with humility the broken people who are homeless. God is infinitely beyond both them and us. There is an infinitely greater gap between God and us than there is between us and any person who is homeless. From God's perspective, God sees just how broken we are.

In fact, is it not a sign of our brokenness if we think we are superior in God's eyes to any of our human sisters and brothers? It is so inexpressibly amazing that God Almighty would want to conjoin with mere humans!

Pouring. To continue with the twelve marks of Christ's most excellent love, Christ poured his divinity into a human body. Christ reserved nothing of himself in becoming human. He gave us his all.

The Cosmic Christ maintained his cosmic divinity as the Son with the Father and the Holy Spirit just as, like a roaring waterfall, he poured all that divinity into Jesus of Nazareth.

In the imitation of Christ, we could pour all we have into serving others. In fact, the way life and love and the universe works is that, the more we sow, the more we reap: "The one who sows sparingly will also reap sparingly, and the one who sows bountifully will also reap bountifully" (2 Corinthians 9:6). The more love we give, the more love we have.

Emptying. Even when the human side of Jesus felt exhausted, he continued to give. There are gospel stories of Jesus and his disciples being so busy with ministry that they had no time to eat. When he says to his disciples "Let's withdraw and rest," they get in a boat to go to the other shore, but when they get there, they find that the people have run along the shore and arrived before them.

Seeing them, Jesus has compassion, and in spite of his utter exhaustion, he ministers to them. He emptied himself until God the Father created a break in the action for him or it became dark. This explains why Jesus prayed all night—it was the only time he could be free of demands placed on him by others.

We can also empty ourselves out for others. There is of course a danger here—the danger of burnout. We are human not God incarnate. It requires a lot of discernment to figure out if it is the God within who is *drawing* us onward when we feel we are running on empty, or it is our ego, our pride, *driving* us to believe we can keep going when to do so would be to burn out and be no good to anyone?

This is where a good spiritual director can be very helpful. She or he can aid us in discerning the type of thoughts that cause us to cross the line between authentic emptying and burnout. Is our pride causing us to be presumptuous, that is, to presume God will save us from burnout?

It is instructive here to remember how Satan tempted Jesus to presumption after taking him to the pinnacle of the temple: "If you are the Son of God, throw yourself down, for it is written: 'God will command his angels concerning you,' and 'On their hands they will bear you up.'" Jesus responded: "It is written 'Do not put the Lord your God to the test'" (Matthew 4: 5-7). Jesus knew when he was being tempted to pride, and we must carefully discern this too.

Dilection. The Son of God and the Father take mutual delight in each other and the fruit of this love is the Holy Spirit. The Spirit, Father and Son delight in each other's greatness, mystery, creativity and love.

"Father," "Son," and "Holy Spirit" are placeholder names for mysteries too great to imagine. The "Father" is the depths of God, the depths of love; the "Son" is the humanity and brotherly love of God; the "Spirit" is the dynamic soul-force of God in the world, the sacred love-force that animates all things. All these qualities are interchangeable among all of them.

"Dilection" means "delight" or "savoring." The Father, Son and Spirit savor and delight in each other, and they all taste, savor and delight in human beings as the perfection of the universe they have created.

As Shakespeare wrote "What a piece of work is a human being!" How do all our internal systems complement and interact with each other so perfectly: nervous system, digestive system, endocrine system, reproductive system, lymphatic system, circulatory system, respiratory system? As Psalm 139:14 says we are "fearfully and wonderfully made."

How is it that we can see and hear things that are miles away? How is it that touch, taste and smell are inexplicable to someone who has never experienced them? How is it that we have seven chakras or energy centers that become more spiritual as they move up our body? How is it that a woman and man fall in love and produce a third being, a baby, from their love?

The Father, Son and Spirit delight in each individual person regardless of age, ability, gender, race, religion, sexual orientation, culture and everything else that defines us. And they call us to do the same. We are called to delight in God in whom there are "pleasures forever" (Psalm 16:11). And we are called to delight in each and every person. Each person has so much to teach us. Each person is a deep well of emotion, experience and knowledge.

Contemplation. Christ's most excellent love means that the Cosmic Christ is a contemplative lover. He sees the whole universe at once and every creature within it. The Cosmic Christ is one with the kangaroo, squid and nightingale. We are invited to contemplate, wonder at and learn from every one of God's magnificent creations: the lilac bush, centipede and amethyst. There is always more to love and ponder. The love of God knows no end.

Loving Rest. Christ loves us in his loving rest. The Cosmic Christ was at perfect peace in Mary's womb and she was at perfect peace knowing the Christ-child was growing within her. The miracles of human growth in the womb are another cause for contemplation, and Mary spent all her time at it. She was in such deep love with her baby boy even before he was born.

The Cosmic Christ is everywhere and so never moves. The Cosmic Christ rests in love all the time and rests in us all the time. The Cosmic Christ is always loving us from within with absolute love. If we are wise, we let this absolute love rise up in us a little bit at a time so it doesn't overwhelm us, and we constantly work on letting more of Christ's love into our heart every day until we grow "to maturity, to the measure of the full stature of Christ" (Ephesians 4:13).

As Teresa of Avila wrote: "Christ has no feet except our feet, no hands except our hands, and no eyes except our eyes." Subsequently, we let Christ love others through us a little more each day. Christ is always at loving rest in us and in the person we are loving, hence it is really God in us loving God in them, and God in them loving God in us.

Why does God love God through us? Why doesn't God just love God directly? God does love God directly in the Trinity. The Father, Son and Spirit all love each other with unimpeded love. However, when they love one another through us as well, it enriches and grows God's love, delight and contemplation. Each one of us humans loves God a little differently, so God wants to experience God's love in every possible way. We all have a new facet or a new color to add to God's multi-faceted, multi-colored love!

Tenderness. Jesus the Christ loves us tenderly. His tenderness was shown in the way he treated children. Every mother in ancient Israel, like all mothers of all times and places, wanted their children to be blessed by a holy man. But Jesus' disciples tried to keep children away from him as they thought the Master had more important things to focus on. Women, and children in particular, had no status in ancient days. Nevertheless, Jesus scolded his disciples and said, "Let the children come to me." Then he blessed them and sent them on their way.

The times when he chastised his disciples also reflect the importance he placed on children. When the disciples were arguing over who was the greatest among them, as some men are inclined to do, Jesus stood a child in their midst and said "Unless you change and become like children, you will never enter the kingdom of heaven" (Matthew 18:3).

Another time he said that if you lead a child astray "it would be better for you if a great millstone were fastened around your neck and you were drowned in the depth of the sea" (Matthew 18:6).

Now, we are all children of God. Whether we acknowledge God or not, God acknowledges us and wants us to be with God in paradise forever. Accordingly, God has tender feelings toward every human being. Jesus tenderly touched lepers when no one else wanted even to be near them. He tenderly healed blind Bartimaeus who shouted "Jesus, Son of David, have mercy on me!" (Mark 10:47).

The tenderness of Jesus is also shown in the times when he wept: over Jerusalem because he knew the Romans would soon destroy it (which they did in 70 CE); and when his friend Lazarus died. God weeps when any of us, God's children, die.

Similarly, the Cosmic Christ calls all of us to love others tenderly, particularly those who are most disadvantaged. The "preferential option for the poor" adopted by the Second Vatican Council in the 1960s is a clarion call for all of us to give tender loving care to all people but especially those disabled by poverty, illness or circumstances.

Zeal. The tenth mark of Christ's most excellent love is that he is zealous for us. His love was not merely strong, it was filled with zeal. In modern terminology, we could say his love was "fanatical." And, like any true fanatic, Jesus was willing to die for what he loved. His love was zealous unto death, even a brutal death on a cross.

If it was necessary for him to be beaten, whipped and nailed to a tree for us, he was willing to do it. This point does not need to be belabored as much has been said about it by Christian preachers and writers who ascribe to a theology of substitutionary atonement.

Languors of Love. Jesus Christ's most excellent love was also marked by languor—a combination of desire for us and sorrow about us.

When he was among us, Jesus the Christ was sorrowful that so many turned away from him. Many stopped following him when he said that we must eat his body and drink his blood, or we would have no life within us. In fact, so many turned away that he asked his disciples if they were going to leave him too? Fortunately, Peter said "Lord, to whom can we go? You have the words of eternal life" (John 6:51-68).

The Cosmic Christ must also feel sorrow over our modern lifestyles that turn away from the gospel of love: atheism, sexual abuse, sexual trafficking of innocent children, pornography, racism, consumerism, abortion, high divorce rates, corrupt and lying politicians, terrorism, constant wars, the threat of nuclear war, the destruction of our beautiful planet, so many people who are impoverished, homeless and refugees, so many young people who can't find work or buy a home, the elite and banks and corporations hoarding vast sums of money for themselves, and on and on.

The Cosmic Christ would not experience cosmic sorrow if he did not also experience cosmic desire for us, a desire that transcends words and human understanding. God, according to scripture, "chose us in Christ before the foundation of the world" (Ephesians 1:4).

We now know that the foundation of the world, the Big Bang, occurred 13.7 billion years ago. Each one of us is made of stardust from the explosions of gigantic stars billions of years ago. Subsequently, each of us is 13.7 billion years old and has 4.5 billion years of evolution on Earth packed into every cell of our body. As St. Francis de Sales wrote so prophetically over four hundred years ago, "humans are the perfection of the universe."

The Cosmic Christ has been waiting and longing for an incomprehensibly long time for each perfect human being to show up, and then so often we mess things up so badly! Christ's disappointment and sorrow is as equally unfathomable as his ongoing, committed, never-giving-up, unconditional love for us. It is the combination of infinite love and infinite sorrow that causes Christ's languors of love. As the hymn "When I Survey the Wondrous Cross" puts it:

See from his head, his hands, his feet,
Sorrow and love flow mingled down!
Did e'er such love and sorrow meet,
Or thorns compose so rich a crown?

Sacrifice. The most excellent mark of Christ's most excellent love is, of course, his sacrifice, his total immolation of himself for us.

No wonder he cried out "My God, my God, why have you forsaken me?" (Matthew 27:46). He had been mercilessly flogged by strong Roman soldiers until there were deep lacerations all over his body. He was crowned with thorns which dug into his flesh like needles. He was repeatedly punched in the face and had his beard pulled out. He fell several times face down on the pavement while struggling to carry a heavy cross through the streets of Jerusalem while people jeered at him and the Romans continued to whip him. He had spikes driven through his hands and feet. He was publicly disgraced even further by being hoisted up on the cross completely naked for all to see. The religious leaders mocked him as a heretic while he writhed impaled in the blazing sun. All of his closest disciples and all of his followers, except for a few women, deserted him in his darkest hour.

Jesus of Nazareth died an extremely painful and ugly death. And he did it all out of love for us. He chose it freely. As scripture says, when Peter protested after Jesus told his disciples he was going to Jerusalem to suffer and die, Jesus reproved Peter (or rather Satan speaking through Peter) for trying to dissuade him. Then he "set his face like flint" toward Jerusalem (Luke 9:51).

Jesus could have called upon a legion of angels to rescue him at this point. He could have asked his many followers to fight the Romans with swords and knives and clubs. He could have refused to go to Jerusalem in the first place. But he freely chose to follow God's will wherever it led him, even into the jaws of the dragon. In doing so he gave us an extreme example of unconditional trust in God.

Jesus remembered the verses in Isaiah that said the Messiah would be "crushed with pain" and take the sins of all of us upon himself (Isaiah 53:5-10). This is the truly unimaginable part of the crucifixion of Christ. He took the sin and evil of every rapist, torturer and murderer on himself. He took all our wounds and suffering, all physical diseases and mental illnesses, all our betrayals, lust, greed, lies, adultery, drunkenness, addictions, jealousy, hatred, pride, deceit, fear, revenge and backstabbing on himself.

And in doing so he freed us from our sins, from death, the devil's clutches and hell. "No one has greater love than this, to lay down one's life for one's friends" (John 15:13).

By his most excellent and unimaginable Love, Jesus became the Universal Savior of us all.

Book Ten

Love is the Ultimate Virtue

Chapter One

Love of God
The Supreme Virtue

Virtues which are found in the friends of God, though they be only moral and natural in themselves, are yet ennobled, and raised to the dignity of being holy works, by reason of the excellence of the heart which produces them. It is one of the properties of friendship to make the friend and all that is good and honest in him dear to us: friendship pours out its grace upon all the actions of him who is loved. 206

All the virtuous actions of a heart at friends with God are dedicated to God, for the heart that has given itself, how has it not given all that depends on itself? 207

Oh the sovereign goodness of this great God, which so favours its lovers that it cherishes their least little actions, so long as they have the slightest degree of goodness, and excellently ennobles them, giving them the title and quality of holy! 208

"Add charity to a man," says St. Augustine, "and everything profits; take charity from him, and what remains profits him no longer." And: "To them that love God all things work together unto good," says the Apostle. 209

Some virtues which by reason of their natural alliance and correspondence with charity are also much more capable of receiving the precious influence of sacred love, and consequently the communication of the dignity and worth of it. Such are faith and hope, which, together with charity, have an immediate reference to God; and religion, and penitence, and devotion, which are employed to the honour of his Divine Majesty. 210

Charity then, is a virtue beyond comparison, which not only adorns the heart in which it is, but by its mere presence also blesses and sanctifies all the virtues which it meets there. 211

Wherefore, Theotimus, of all virtuous actions we ought most carefully to practise those of religion and reverence towards divine things, those of faith, of hope and of the most holy fear of God, taking occasion often to speak of heavenly things, thinking of and sighing after eternity, frequenting churches and sacred services, reading spiritual books, observing the ceremonies of the Christian religion. 212

Love is the master of the heart, and consequently of all the works of the other virtues done by its consent. 213

The virtuous actions of the children of God all belong to charity; some of them because she produces them of her own nature; others because she sanctifies them by her quickening presence; and finally others, by the authority and command which she exercises over the other virtues, whence she makes them spring. 214

Patience is not patient enough, nor faith faithful enough, nor hope confident enough, nor mildness sweet enough, unless love animate and quicken them. 215

Charity, the love of God, has the supreme place in the soul over any of the other virtues. Love of God influences, strengthens and motivates all the other virtues. Charity makes use of all the virtues, but it builds on these and goes beyond them. Christ taught this: it is not good enough to love those who love you since even non-believers do this. We must love our enemies. This is the essence of Christian non-violence.

It is not enough to engage in the hospitality and kindness that even non-believers show to their family and friends. "Pray for those who persecute you, so that you may be children of your Father in heaven; for he makes his sun rise on the evil and on the good and sends rain on the righteous and the unrighteous" (Matthew 5:44-45).

God is kind to those who reject him. Therefore, be merciful as God is merciful.

It is important to remember that, just as natural virtues like hard work and honesty normally reap natural/temporal/earthly rewards like steady employment, so supernatural virtues receive eternal rewards.

There is a hierarchy of virtues. Some virtues are closer to holy love than others. For example, the three supernatural or theological virtues are faith, hope and love. Faith, or trust in God, is higher than any of the cardinal virtues, that is, justice, fortitude, temperance and prudence.

Engaging in justice without any trust in God will help us build a safe and secular kingdom on Earth, but it will not build the kingdom of God. Prudence, that is, being cautious, is always wise and will help us avoid a lot of suffering in our earthly life, but it does not give us the hope in God that we will one day be in eternal bliss with all the saints praising God in the heavenly kingdom forever.

Some virtues facilitate holy love more than others. Some virtues may be holier than others. For example, voluntarily choosing to be poor may be holier than the proper use of wealth. The proper use of wealth would be using our wealth to serve others, that is, wise stewardship of our resources. We would use our wealth to take care of those closest to us, our family, first of all, but charity should go beyond the home and far out into the community.

Proper use of wealth would be to join our wealth with that of others, philanthropists and governments, to provide low-cost housing, schools, medicine and dentistry to the poor locally and across the world. It would take care of those who are developmentally delayed, disabled and elderly. All of this flows out of one's love of God.

Voluntarily choosing poverty may be holier than proper use of wealth simply because proper use of wealth does not necessarily involve giving up any of our own personal privileges. It may be more effective in getting things done in the world, but it will probably not involve any sacrifice of our personal comfort or status. Voluntary poverty focuses us more on God and the spiritual life. It clears out the physical and mental debris that comes with having a lot of possessions. There is more personal self-sacrifice than simply managing money properly.

Similarly, voluntary virginity may be holier than marital chastity. In western culture, to say you are a virgin may stop the conversation or bring stares of disbelief. "Marital chastity" does not mean abstaining from sexual intercourse when we are married, it means sexual integration within marriage. It means keeping free from affairs, pornography and anything else that would degrade our sexual commitment to our spouse. We can be chaste within marriage and still enjoy great amounts of God-ordained sexual pleasure.

However, to give all that up and choose voluntary virginity so that we can more fully focus on the Lord involves much more self-sacrifice than marital chastity. If we are not part of a larger community, it can result in a lot of loneliness. However, whether we are part of a community or not, voluntary virginity can free us up to completely immerse our self in the things of God. Our attention is not divided between God and our spouse (I Corinthians 7:32-34). We can fully commit to God's missionary, evangelistic work in the world, whatever that looks like in our situation.

In any case, charity, the love of God, inflames, strengthens and motivates all the other virtues. Charity is the virtue underlying and supporting all virtue. For example, humility does not mean self-devaluation, it means standing before the Lord in full awareness of all our weaknesses, shortcomings, limitations, failures, temptations, sins and mortality and knowing how much we are loved by God in spite of (or because of!) all that. But we would not take that humble stance in the first place if we did not know God and want to please God and know that arrogance and self-righteousness are displeasing to God.

Similarly, we would not engage in the virtue of perseverance if we did not love God. As soon as the going got rough in serving the Lord, we would immediately give up if we did not have a deeper desire to do God's will. And this deep desire, this longing for God, is planted in us by God. It is God desiring God through us. It all comes from and goes to God. We are mere players or observers in God's pageant.

God is playing through us. All the virtues come from and go to the Sacred Life Force loving the Sacred Life Force, a never-ending cosmic water wheel of giving and receiving Love.

As St. Paul wrote, virtue without charity is useless. We could have all knowledge, and faith to move mountains, give up our body to be tortured or burned, but if we do not have love, all this is futile. All virtue, no matter how heroic, is meaningless without love (I Corinthians 13:1-3).

Atheists, agnostics and secular humanists can be virtuous as well. Because God is everywhere and lives in everyone whether they acknowledge God or not, atheists can be kind, patient, peaceful, humble and persevering. God is not limited to the church or to any one religion. God is constantly there for all people. It may be the case that non-believers are walking toward the sun except they are doing it while wearing a blindfold. The big difference is that believers have taken the blindfold off and nonbelievers have no idea of all the riches of God they are missing!

And it is not as if church-going believers never sin. It is not the case that everyone in church is a saint and everyone outside church is a sinner. Evil forces such as lust and greed are always lurking in the shadows, waiting to take both believers and non-believers down. The only advantage to being a believer is that we are more aware of this. The awareness of evil spirits, and also the help and love of God, can make believers less susceptible to temptation. The more the believer shores up her or his heart with the love of God, the less likely they will stumble and fall.

Prayer and attending church also helps greatly in all of this and makes us more likely to keep growing in the supernatural virtues of faith, hope and love. It is virtually impossible to be a Christian if we do not belong to the Body of Christ, the Beloved Community in one form or another.

This does not necessarily mean attending formal Sunday church services every week. It might be a mid-week prayer or meditation or spiritual book-reading group during the day or evening. It might be a church-affiliated seniors, youth, or Alcoholics Anonymous group.

The point is that we need the support of others if we are going to sustain our Christian faith. Without this support there are too many distractions, temptations, and subtle wiles of the devil out there that we can easily get sucked into.

In North America and Europe, we are not persecuted for our faith, we are seduced by our culture of competition, materialism and consumerism. Our support group might be our family (the domestic church), or friends who are believers. Christianity is meant to be a communal, counter-cultural gathering place under the banner of the Cosmic Christ's unconditional divine Love.

As far as prayer goes, it can be the other main support and facilitator in developing the virtues that find their fulfillment in loving God. It helps to have a balance between intercession for ourself and others, wrestling with scripture in meditation, sitting in silent contemplation, and also a balance between individual, small group and formal ecclesial prayer with the larger institutional Body of Christ. The more time we spend in the Lord's presence, and the more varied the ways of praying we engage in, the more our love of God and God's love of us can flow to, in, through and as us.

CHAPTER TWO

LOVE OF GOD PERFECTS AND UNITES ALL THE VIRTUES

*In conclusion, virtues cannot have their true integrity and suffi-
ciency unless they be all together, as all philosophy and divinity assure
us. What prudence, I pray you, Theotimus, can an intemperate, unjust
and cowardly man have, since he makes choices of vice and forsakes
virtue? And how can one be just without being prudent, strong, and
temperate? 216*

*Charity purifies the soul from all sins, and then adorns and embel-
lishes it with a most delightful beauty; and finally spreads its waters
over all the faculties and operations thereof, to give the understanding
a celestial prudence, the will a holy justice, the concupiscible appetite a
sacred temperance, and the irascible appetite a devout fortitude, to the
end that man's whole heart may tend to the supernatural honesty and
felicity which consist in union with God. 217*

*God has sown in our hearts the seeds of all the virtues, which, how-
ever, are so covered with our imperfections and weakness that they do
not appear, or appear very slightly, till the vital heat of holy love comes
to quicken and resuscitate them, producing by them the actions of all
virtues. 218*

*Temperance is a love which gives itself entirely unto God. Fortitude
is a love which willingly supports all things for God's sake. Justice is a
love which serves God only, and therefore disposes justly of all that is
subject to man. Prudence is a love that makes choice of things proper to*

unite itself unto God, and rejects such things as are contrary to it. 219

He therefore that has charity has his soul invested with a fair wedding garment, which, as that of Joseph, is wrought with the variety of all the virtues; or rather he has a perfection which contains the virtue of all perfections and the perfection of all virtues. 220

Charity is then the bond of perfection, since in it all the perfections of the soul are contained and assembled, and since without it, not only can one not have the whole array of virtues, but one cannot even have the perfection of any virtue. Without the cement and mortar which fasten the stones and walls, the whole edifice goes to rack. 221

Faith, hope, fear and repentance ordinarily go before charity into the soul to prepare her lodging; and upon her arrival, they with all the train of virtues obey and wait upon her, and she with her presence animates, adorns and quickens them all. 222

The perfection of divine love is so sovereign that it perfects all the virtues, and can receive no perfection from them, no not from obedience itself, which is the one most able to give perfection to the rest. 223

We may all utter this true saying, in imitation of the holy apostle: "Without charity I am nothing, nothing profiteth me." And that of St. Augustine: "Put charity in a heart and everything profits, take charity away and nothing profits." 224

The works then of a sinner, while he is deprived of holy love, are not profitable to eternal life, and therefore they are called dead works; on the contrary the good works of the just man are said to be living, inasmuch as divine love animates and quickens them with its life. 225

Love, Theotimus, is the standard in the army of virtues: they ought all to range themselves by it; it is the only flag under which our Saviour, who is true General of the army, makes them fight. Let us therefore reduce all the virtues to the obedience of charity: let us love particular virtues, but principally because they are agreeable to God; let us excellently love the more excellent virtues, not because they are excellent, but because God loves them more excellently. Thus will holy love give life to all the virtues, making all of them full of love, lovable, and lovable above all things. 226

All virtues: kindness, patience, peace, thoughtfulness, forgiveness, are created by the Holy Spirit flowing to, in, through and as us in order to bring more and more lovers of God into the Life Divine.

Charity, that is, love of God, creates the four cardinal virtues of prudence, justice, temperance and fortitude which then flow into and through the will, intellect, emotions and desires.

Charity not only perfects all the virtues, it unites them. One cardinal virtue without another does not work. For example, fortitude (courage) without prudence (caution) will simply create destruction. There was a teenage boy in the news years ago who, to prove his bravery to his friends, climbed to the top of the Golden Gate Bridge in San Francisco. Then he jumped off, thinking he would dive into the water and survive. He was brave, but not cautious, and he died.

All the cardinal virtues work together, and we have to have them all together or nothing of significance happens. Pursuing justice without temperance (moderation) would result in burn out. Justice without fortitude means we would never do anything—we would be afraid to speak truth to the unjust powers that be.

Fighting for justice without prudence, love and forgiveness would mean we angrily, arrogantly and brutally abuse those we are fighting against, thus replacing their injustice with ours. As Gandhi and Martin Luther King said, when we strive for justice, we need to have a converted heart of compassion for wrongdoers or we will just substitute our own pack of wolves for theirs.

It is charity, our love of God, and God's love of us, that underlies and therefore unites all the virtues. No virtue can exist without the foundational virtue of charity. Virtue without charity is lifeless. As St. Paul wrote, any action, no matter how heroic, if it is done without love, is dead.

If we are virtuous for the wrong reasons—out of pride, vanity, for human praise, or for the rewards that virtue brings, then the virtue will not produce fruit in the long run. People will see that our virtue is self-centered, meant to serve us and not others, and they will turn against us and our false virtue.

The only legitimate reason to be virtuous is love of God. Charity perfects, protects and unites all the virtues. Our love of God, born out of God's love of us, is the king and queen of all virtues.

It is important to put things in their proper order. To put any virtue above love of God would be idolatry. It would mean we loved something more than God. Fasting, prayer, almsgiving and even martyrdom are all empty without love of God.

Virtue without charity, with no love of God—our Source, Sustenance and Goal—possibly could benefit someone in this life, but it would do them no good when it comes to eternal life with God. Accepting God's love and loving God in return is the only *assured* way to participate in the afterlife with God.

Yet God is merciful and all-knowing and will weigh each person's individual case. Atheists, agnostics and secular humanists may find the creeds hard to understand or believe in our scientific age, may have been turned off by the hypocrisy of believers, or may never have been taught the gospel. They may also implicitly love God if they love others, work for social justice and care for God's creation.

Since God is a God of unfathomable mercy and grace, perhaps even atheists may be in heaven, to their great shock and surprise!

Book Eleven

The Seven Gifts of the Holy Spirit and the Twelve Fruits of the Love of God

Chapter One

The Seven Gifts of the Holy Spirit

Charity will be another Jacob's ladder to us, consisting of the seven gifts of the Holy Ghost, as of so many sacred steps, by which angelic men will ascend from earth to heaven, to be united to the heart of God Almighty, and by which they will descend from heaven to earth, to take their neighbour by the hand and lead him to heaven. 227

For, as we mount the first step, Fear makes us forsake evil; on the second, Piety excites us to will to do good; upon the third, Knowledge makes us discern the good we are able to do, and the evil we are to fly; upon the fourth, by Fortitude we take courage against all the difficulties which occur in our enterprise; upon the fifth, by Counsel we make choice of suitable means; upon the sixth, we unite our understanding to God to behold and penetrate the features of his infinite beauty; and upon the seventh, we join our wills to God, to taste and experience the sweetness of his incomprehensible goodness; for upon the top of this ladder, God bending towards us, gives us the kiss of love, and makes us taste the sacred breasts of his sweetness, better than wine. 228

Love of God is similar to Jacob's ladder except in this case it is not angels per se that ascend to God and descend to Earth but rather angelic human beings. This ladder has seven steps which are the seven gifts of the Holy Spirit.

Scripture states that fear of the Lord is the beginning of wisdom (Proverbs 9:10). Most people understand that "fear" in this case does not mean psychological fear but "absolute respect."

Absolute respect for God is the beginning of wisdom. This makes absolute sense. As Jesus said to his disciples, "Don't fear those who kill the body but cannot kill the soul; rather fear the one who can destroy both body and soul in hell" (Matthew 10:28). God is the only one we need fear. However, Jesus assures them right after he says this that there is nothing at all to fear because God the Father loves them so much that "even the hairs of your head are all counted" (Matthew 10:30).

This first rung of the ladder, absolute respect for God, gets us started on our spiritual journey and motivates us to give up evil ways. We cannot absolutely respect God and love evil at the same time because God hates evil.

There is no evil or shadow in God. God is pure goodness. And since we naturally love the good, we naturally will love God even though, if we are an atheist, we will not be aware that it is God who we love.

The second step on the ladder is piety, a word not often used in the 21st century but which can mean simple reverence, religiosity, devotion, godliness, faithfulness or holiness. Piety means a life of purity, penance and humility, obedience to God out of respect, the way a daughter or son quietly respects and obeys her or his parents.

Piety arouses in us the desire to do good. This is a positive step beyond just avoiding evil. This is actively seeking the good, whatever that may look like. We do good in order to please God and to avoid the "consequences of our own sin"—what was previously thought of as "the wrath of God." There is no wrath of God, only the consequences we bring upon ourselves by our own sin. Piety means we seek God constantly and see God in all things.

The third rung is "science" or knowledge. Knowledge tells us what the good is that we must seek and engage in, and the evil that we must flee from. Thus, each rung builds on, includes and transcends the previous one.

The fourth gift of the Holy Spirit is fortitude. Fortitude gives us the courage to withstand all the obstacles and difficulties we will inevitably face as we flee evil and pursue the good.

When people are in crowds, a kind of "mob mentality" can take over and a sense of right and wrong can disappear. This is how lynchings occurred in the past and how bullying takes place today. Bullying can take place on many levels, all the way from playgrounds to national politics. One person or group can use their power to intimidate another person or group.

Usually mob mentality is based on fear of the "other." Rather than welcoming persecuted and terrified refugees who are fleeing for their life and the life of their family, the mob, in the form of the state, can bar them from entering the country and send them back into deadly situations.

It takes courage to speak out against an angry mob and say that what they are doing is wrong. Fortitude gives us the strength to be unpopular and follow our conscience, the still small voice of God within us.

Counsel, the fifth step up the ladder of charity, helps us choose the means proper to advancing in the love of God. The Beloved Community, the church, the community of faith can be a source of good counsel through its practices, teachings and traditions. The People of God have the Holy Spirit working in them and can help us when we are faced with challenging decisions.

The services of a good spiritual director can be particularly invaluable. The director can help us discern what God the Father wants us to do, what Jesus the Son has shown us to do, and what the Spirit is prompting us from within to do.

A spiritual director may lead us through the steps of Ignatian discernment. First, she or he will help us narrow down our options to two choices. Then we will be asked about any consolations (joy, peace, love) or desolations (fear, despair, anger) we feel about the two options. If we have no consolations or desolations, we will go from the heart to the head level and make a list of the pros and cons of the two options. Then we weigh each of the pros and cons, keeping in mind "where can I serve God the most?"

If we cannot decide, we go from the head to the gut level—what are our own gut instincts telling us about each option? All the while as we are doing this, we pray about the two options and look for signs from God. However, we have to be careful with signs.

There is a story about a farmer who wanted his son to take over the farm, but the son wanted to preach the gospel. They were out in the field one day when the son said, "Look father, those clouds are forming a 'p' and a 'c'—that means God wants me to preach Christ!" However, the father replied, "No, no, what they are telling you to do is plant corn!" The point is that we can read into "signs" whatever we want to see in them. A good spiritual director will help us to objectively look at things.

Our spiritual director will also recommend that we consult the legitimate authorities in our life (our spouse, parents, deacon, minister, priest or bishop) as well as trusted friends. What do they think is the more suitable of the two options given their knowledge of who we are?

Once we have discerned all this with our spiritual director and made our decision, we should not give up if we run into obstacles. Anything really worth doing is usually not easy.

The sixth step when ascending is the Holy Spirit's gift of understanding. We understand what we can about God while at the same time being aware that God transcends our mortal mind and is ultimately ineffable. The closer we get to God on the ladder of ascendance, the more ineffable and the more beautiful God will be. The more we love God's beauty, the less we will be able to put it into words.

The final and seventh rung on the ladder is the gift of wisdom. We join our will to God's will in order to savor the sweetness of God's incomprehensible goodness. Whereas fear of the Lord is the beginning of wisdom, wisdom itself is the ultimate goal. Once we have stepped onto the rung of wisdom, we recognize our own absolute weakness, brokenness, mortality, poverty and sinfulness compared to God.

On the rung of wisdom, we realize that human beings are infinitely capable of self-deception, that while we think we are good and achieving it all, the fact of the matter, as Jesus said, is that "No one is good but God alone" (Luke 18:19). It is only God who is doing good through us. Subsequently, we wake up to God's absolute goodness, truth and beauty and our absolute finitude. As even the great medieval philosopher and theologian Thomas Aquinas said after being given a revelation of God's greatness: "All my work is straw and should be burned."

When we have reached wisdom, we turn around and start descending, start returning to Earth in order to lead our neighbor to God. The seven gifts of the Holy Spirit help us to descend Jacob's ladder so we can eventually lead our neighbor back to God with us. Then they can descend from God and bring other neighbors, neighbors who we do not know, back up to God with them. So, there is a constant flow of saints and angels ascending and descending on Jacob's ladder, Jesus Christ, who is the bridge/ladder between heaven and Earth.

On step seven, the top rung of the descent, we fill our soul with wisdom, that is, with God's supreme charity, which results in the most ardent zeal for the good of others. We are so full of the Spirit that our face is glowing like the face of Moses when he came down from Mount Sinai with the tablets of the Ten Commandments, and the people of God had to put a veil over his face it was so blindingly bright (Exodus 34: 29-35).

Being full of God's charity means that we are ready to love and accept anyone, no matter how despicable they are, as long as they have repented of their evil ways. Generals who ordered the torture of political prisoners are welcome. Priests who sadistically whipped little children with bullwhips as they sexually assaulted them are welcome. All who repent, no matter how disgusting their former lives were, are welcome at the table of God's supreme and unconditional charity, where they can be transformed into the image of Christ.

On rung six of the descent we are given the Holy Spirit's gift of understanding. We receive incomparable light that penetrates all our thoughts with God's most excellent beauty and goodness. God is the source of all goodness, truth and beauty. God *is* all goodness, truth and beauty.

God is absolutely pure and good and so can be absolutely trusted and loved like no other. God will never, never harm us. God does not want, cause or relish suffering. God wants to give us a thousand pleasures, not suffering. And that is what God wants us to share with others: God's goodness, truth, beauty and infinite pleasures.

On step five of the descent we are given the gift of counsel. God helps us to consider the means by which we may instil in our neighbor the esteem of God's sweetness. We are led to ponder how we are going to help our neighbor open up the cup of his or her heart to the ocean of God's love?

How will we convey that God is far more lovable, far more desirable than anything in God's good Creation? How are we going to let people know that God is more to be sought after than one's own health, wealth and reputation? These are the questions that preoccupy us on rung five.

Rung four is the gift of fortitude. We receive the gift of courage to overcome the difficulties we will inevitably face in our attempts to share the good news. How do we help a meritocracy, a system based on reward for effort and punishment for lack of effort? How do we help people in this system understand that God's grace is perfectly free, freely given, and there is nothing we can do to earn it?

The gospel is so countercultural that the culture naturally will oppose it. Loving our opponents in sports, politics or business makes no sense. We are supposed to destroy our competitors by out-competing them, not help them out. It takes far more courage to appear naïve and idealistic and love our enemies rather than to trash them. But as Abraham Lincoln said in his wisdom, "Do I not destroy my enemies by making them my friends?"

Step three gives us the Holy Spirit's gift of knowledge. We are now able to preach and exhort souls to follow virtue and flee from sin. We know what motivates people in their particular culture and circumstances and how we can make them see the consequences of whatever paths they find themselves on.

We will see and know how to convey to others what will happen if they continue to pursue the evil spirits: deceit, greed, envy, pride, anger, lust, gluttony, sloth and fear. And conversely, we will be able to communicate the good consequences of honesty, sharing, reconciliation, humility, peacefulness, compassion, self-discipline and trust.

All the negative spirits destroy community and all the positive ones create it. The goal always is to lead people to the Beloved Community, the church, and to the kingdom/queendom/kindom/reign of God on Earth.

Continuing our descent down the ladder of Christ, on the second last rung we are given the Holy Spirit's gift of piety. By the example of living a pious life, we are able to impress upon others the peace and blessings of piety.

The lowest rung of descent is fear of—absolute respect for—God's judgement. We are now ready to step off the ladder and meet our neighbors on the level playing field of Mother Earth.

The gift of fear of the Lord—or absolute respect for God—is, according to scripture, the beginning of wisdom (Proverbs 9:10). We know, but our neighbor does not know, that God does not judge us, and there is nothing to fear from God. But we and our neighbor have to start somewhere, and if with filial reverence as sons and daughters of God, we and our neighbor decide to renounce the false pleasures and promises of our civilization on Earth and begin the arduous ascent toward God together, so be it.

Fear of the wrath of God is the starting point for many on the spiritual journey, and if it gets our neighbor going on their progress towards Supreme Wisdom, and we know their fear will soon be replaced by an unquenchable desire for God as they continue the ascent, so be it.

In healthy Christianity we do not go to God alone. It is all about solidarity with all people. Consequently, as we and our neighbor keep ascending and descending the ladder of Christ, we are always bringing new people back up with us, and our neighbor keeps bringing new people back up with them, so that eventually the whole world will be "saved together," that is, united with all others and with God. This is truly the Beloved Community/Reign of God on the grandest scale.

CHAPTER TWO
THE ROLE OF FEAR IN THE LOVE OF GOD

Even so the divine goodness, wishing to place a great variety of virtues in man's soul, and afterwards to embellish them with his sacred love, makes use of the needle of servile and mercenary fear, with which our hearts are ordinarily first pricked. But still this is not left there, but ever as the virtues are drawn into and laid in the soul, mercenary and servile fear departs, according to the word of the beloved disciple: Perfect charity casteth out fear. 229

While the Divine Providence is about the embroidery of virtues and the work of divine love in our souls, there is always a mercenary or servile fear left in them, till charity comes to perfection. 230

Though the soul comes under the conduct of fear, she does not mean to espouse it; for, in fact, as soon as the soul meets with love, she unites herself unto it, and quits fear. 231

Now although mercenary and servile fear is very necessary for this mortal life, yet it is unworthy to have any part in the immortal, where there will be assurance void of fear, a peace without apprehension, a repose free from anxiety. 232

Servile fear still remains with and aids holy charity, holy love of God, in this life. Here we see through a glass darkly; in eternal life we see God face-to-face and all servile fear is gone. In this present life servile fear, the fear of not loving God enough, protects us from the ten thousand temptations and distractions of life on Earth.

It is natural for us to fear while on this earthly plane. Nature built fear of injury and destruction into us as a chief protective defence mechanism. As embodied beings, like animals, we have to protect ourselves against the elements and against other creatures such as bears, wolves and snakes. Nature's power: lightning, forest fires, volcanoes, tornadoes, earthquakes and tsunamis can turn us toward God out of fear and awe. This natural fear is good and holy.

Besides servile and natural fear there is detestable fear. Detestable fear means obedience to God solely out of fear of damnation. Fear of hell is for many the start of their spiritual journey, which may be necessary, since a person has to start somewhere. However, there is no real love of God in it. We are solely concerned with saving our own skin. It is self-centered fear.

Similarly, although reversed, there is mercenary fear, that is obedience solely out of fear of missing a reward, the supreme reward of heaven. Again, there is no love of God in this fear. We are not interested in God at all but simply in the rewards of God. It is also a self-centered, selfish fear.

Filial fear is similar to servile fear. While servile fear is the fear of not loving God enough due to earthly distractions and temptations, filial fear is born more out of respect for the absolute greatness and glory of God. Filial fear comes from a sense of the absolute privilege of being a son or daughter of the Most High, and fearing that we will not be adequate, we will not live up to this role. It is the fear of not being a worthy child of God, of not living up to all I could be, not being the very best version of myself that I could be, and so disappointing my heavenly Father/Mother. It is the fear children have of not living up to their parents' dreams for them.

While detestable fear and mercenary fear, the fear of divine punishment and of missing the divine reward, have nothing to do with loving God, they may lead into it, and God often uses these fears in this way. In order to avoid hell or obtain heaven, the novice in the spiritual life decides to study scripture and attend church regularly to find out what God wants. He or she gradually gets drawn by the Holy Spirit into a healthy and positive love of God for God's sake alone, not for self-centered reasons.

When starting out in the spiritual life, a mixture of detestable, mercenary, servile and filial fear is normal. Later, as we are becoming more and more immersed in God's love, even the virtues, consolations and seven gifts of the Holy Spirit are not put before love of God. For the saints, love of God comes before everything since God is their All.

Chapter Three
The Role of Sorrow in the Love of God

There is then a sorrow or sadness according to God, which is employed either by sinners in penance, or by the good in compassion for the temporal miseries of their neighbours, or by the perfect in deploring, bemoaning and condoling the spiritual calamity of souls. 233

The worldling is out of temper, uncivil, bitter and gloomy when temporal prosperity fails him; and in abundance he is almost always boastful, foolishly elated and insolent. 234

The sadness of true penitence is not so much to be named sadness as displeasure, or the sense and detestation of evil; a sadness which is never troubled or vexed; a sadness which does not dull the spirit, but makes it active, ready and diligent; a sadness which does not weigh the heart down, but raises it in prayer and hope, and causes in it the movements of the fervour of devotion; a sadness which in the heaviest of the bitternesses ever produces the sweetness of an incomparable consolation. 235

Such is right sadness, which in good sooth is not really sad or melancholy, but only attentive and earnest to detest, reject and hinder the evil of sin for past and for future. 236

In all the sadness which may come upon us, we must employ the authority of the superior will to do all that should be done in favour of divine love. 237

We may be excused for not being always bright, for one is not master of cheerfulness to have it when one will; but we are not excusable for not being always gracious, yielding and considerate; for this is always in the power of our will, and we have only to determine to keep down the contrary humour and inclination. 238

There is holy sorrow and unholy sorrow. Unholy sorrow is centered on our self not on God. Unholy sorrow is self-pity which can lead to depression. It is all about *my* misery, never yours—there is no focus on the suffering others regularly go through. Unholy sorrow is narcissistic, as if we are the only reality.

Holy sorrow on the other hand focuses on God not self. Holy sorrow comes in three varieties: the sorrow of sinners, of the good and of the perfect.

The sorrow of sinners is sadness over and repentance from sin. It may seem self-centered because the focus is on *my* sins, but it is really sadness because we have offended God and others. We have sinned against the love of God and others.

The sorrow of the good involves sadness over the misfortunes of others but focuses on those misfortunes not caused by us. It is sorrow based on the love of God because it comes out of concern for all God's creatures who have had to endure earthquakes, mudslides, hurricanes, floods, droughts, fires, sexual assault, torture, crime, war and the ten thousand other slings and arrows of outrageous fortune.

The sorrow of the perfect is less materially oriented than the sorrow of the good. The perfect are sorrowful over the spiritual calamities of others, their spiritual lostness or aridity, their temptations, sin, confusion and doubt leading to agnosticism or atheism. The perfect are more concerned about spiritual calamities than physical ones as they know spiritual problems have eternal consequences.

Anyone can spiritually survive a physical disaster if they keep their faith intact. As long as we unconditionally trust God, even if we are injured or die, we will be eternally safe.

Those who are perfect in every way actually praise God for trials because they know that challenges make them stronger spiritually. Richard Rohr says that he prays for at least one humiliation a day as he knows many people like him, and he does not want this to swell his ego.

The perfect welcome the challenge of whatever evil people or the random machinations of nature bring them. They are afraid of nothing.

Unholy, worldly sorrow comes from three sources: the devil, the human disposition toward sin, and the hardness of life. All three sources can cause immense suffering which will either lead us away from God or break through our ego's defences and turn us towards the Holy One. Even unholy sorrow can have a role to play in bringing us to charity, the love of God.

People can come to love of God either through great awe, due to the awesomeness of the Creation, or through great fear or great sorrow. The best way to make the most of this initial charity is to develop the lifelong habit of focusing all the energies of our will, intellect, heart and soul on God's unfathomable love in which our love of God and God's love of us constantly deepens.

Chapter Four
The Twelve Fruits of the Love of God

Most holy charity is a virtue, a gift, a fruit and a beatitude.

As being a virtue, it makes us obedient to the exterior inspirations which God gives us by his commandments and counsels, in the execution of which we practise all virtues; whence love is the virtue of all virtues.

As being a gift, charity makes us docile and tractable to interior inspirations, which are, as it were, God's secret commandments and counsels, in the execution of which the seven gifts of the Holy Ghost are employed, so that charity is the gift of gifts.

As being a fruit, it gives us an extreme relish and pleasure in the practice of the devout life, which is felt in the twelve fruits of the Holy Ghost, and therefore it is the fruit of fruits.

As being a beatitude, it makes us repute the affronts, calumnies, revilings and insults which the world heaps upon us as the greatest of favours and a singular honour. 239

He that has love in any abundance, he shall neither have desire, fear, hope, courage, nor joy but for God, and all his movements shall be at rest in this one celestial love. 240

Charity, the love of God, the supreme love, subjects all our will, passions, affections, senses and appetites to itself. Charity grows or dies when it is subjected to trials, rejection and renunciation. It always grows or dies freely. It is always a matter of choice: no matter what is going on externally, we are always free to give up on the love of God or to go deeper. Love of God naturally subjects everything to itself once it is chosen, but God never forces us to love God.

Charity is always offered to us by God, never forced upon us. It is the gift of gifts, the supreme gift, but it has to be freely received by us. Similarly, charity is the virtue of virtues, it crowns and completes all the other virtues, but to be the virtue of virtues, it has to be freely chosen.

Charity is the source of the highest virtues which Jesus outlined in his first major teaching, the Sermon on the Mount. Those supreme virtues are called "beatitudes," the basic values of the Christian faith, the fundamental formulas for Christian living. These values/formulas/beatitudes are simplicity/poverty, humility, meekness/gentleness, purity of heart, hungering and thirsting for righteousness/justice, mercy, holy sorrow over our sins and the sins of the world, and peacemaking. Charity is the beatitude of beatitudes, the Supreme Beatitude.

According to Francis de Sales, charity has twelve properties, the twelve fruits of the Holy Spirit, which are joy, peace, patience, goodness, long-suffering, gentleness, modesty, kindness, self-control, generosity, chastity and fidelity. De Sales has expanded here on the nine fruits of the Holy Spirit given in Galatians 5:22-23: love, joy, peace, patience, kindness, generosity, faithfulness, gentleness and self-control.

All these fruits or virtues mean we live in harmony with our neighbors in kindness, mildness, generosity, self-control, modesty and humility, rejecting every improper behavior in the way we eat, dress and engage in recreation and pleasure. And we live all these external things so that our entire inner being may be given over to joy, peace, patience, long-suffering, goodness and fidelity.

Love of God grows richer in poverty and cannot be quenched by all manner of trials and tribulations. It is exalted when it is despised and humiliated, rejoices in the midst of tears, takes delight in renouncing every sensual and worldly delight, despises temporal grandeur and reputation, grows stronger by all kinds of suffering, and does everything it can to prevent dissension and war.

Love of God, as the virtue of all virtues, makes us obedient to all of God's external inspirations, counsels and commandments. As the gift of gifts, it makes us amenable as well to all of God's interior inspirations which involve the seven gifts of the Holy Spirit identified by the church fathers: wisdom, understanding, counsel, fortitude, knowledge, piety and fear (absolute respect) of the Lord.

Love of God forsakes all other glory except that which comes from the imitation of Christ crucified. We accept all the reviling and insults the world heaps upon us as the greatest of favors and honors. We glory in the debasement, abnegation, and annihilation of our false self, our ego which identifies with worldly glory, so that the glory of our true self, which is rooted and grounded in Christ, may shine forth.

It is important to distinguish here between deserved debasement, authentic criticism and abuse. We only glory in debasement if we have discerned that our ego is getting too wrapped up in and enslaved to worldly glory. Then we welcome comments from others that create more humility in us. We also need to discern if what others are saying is objective criticism of areas we genuinely need to improve in, or just the ego of the other person needing to vent. If it is honest criticism, we welcome it. Otherwise we ignore it. Abuse is criticism that is meant to destroy the person who hears it and should be opposed by the intended victim. In other words, abused or marginalized people need to be supported if they speak out against their perpetrators. And we need to speak out if someone is unjustly abusing us.

For those who are well-advanced on the spiritual journey, the cross of Christ is their only throne, and on it they have more joy, glory and happiness than Solomon, the wisest and wealthiest man of the ancient world. The crosses of the world, if taken with the right attitude, can set us free from the values of the world: pride, lust and violence.

BOOK TWELVE

COUNSELS ON HOLY LOVE

CHAPTER ONE

INTEGRATING HOLY LOVE INTO OUR LIFE

Though souls inclined to love have on the one hand a certain propensity which makes them more ready to desire to love God, they are, on the other hand, so subject to set their affections upon lovable creatures, that their propensity puts them in as great danger of being diverted from the purity of sacred love. 241

It is true that souls of this kind, being once purified from the love of creatures, work wonders in holy loving, as love finds a great facility in diffusing itself throughout all the faculties of the heart. 242

O heart of my soul, created to love the infinite good, what love canst thou desire but this love, which is the most to be desired of all loves! Ah! O soul of my heart, what desire canst thou love but the most lovely of all desires! O love of sacred desires! O desires of sacred love Oh! how have I coveted to long for thy perfections. 243

Those souls that ever abound in desires, designs and projects, never desire holy celestial love as they ought. 244

For this cause the Saints betook themselves to deserts, that being freed from worldly cares they might more ardently apply to heavenly love. 245

They who desire for good and all to love God, shut up their understanding from discoursing of worldly things to employ it more earnestly in the meditation of divine things, and gather up all their pretensions under the sole intention which they have of loving only God. 246

Curiosity, ambition, disquiet, the not averting to, or not consider-

ing, the end for which we are in this world, are the causes why we have a thousand times more hindrance than business, more worries than work, more occupation than profit: and these are the embarrassments, Theotimus, that is, the silly, vain and superfluous undertakings with which we charge ourselves, that turn us from the love of God, and not the true and lawful exercises of our vocations. 247

Necessary employments, according to each one's vocation, do not diminish Divine love, but increase it, and gild, as it were, the work of devotion. The nightingale loves her melody no less when she makes her pauses than when she sings; the devout heart loves no less when she turns to exterior necessities than when she prays: her silence and her speech, her action and her contemplation, her employment and her rest, equally sing in her the hymn of her love. 248

Great works lie not always in our way, but every moment we may do little ones with excellence, that is, with a great love. 249

There are some souls that do many good works, and yet increase but little in charity, because they do them either coldly and negligently, or by natural instinct and inclination rather than by Divine inspiration or heavenly fervour; and on the contrary, others there are who get through little work, but do it with so holy a will and inclination, that they make a wonderful advancement in charity; they have little talent, but they husband it so faithfully that the Lord largely rewards them for it. 250

Let us a hundred and a hundred times a day unite our life to Divine love by the practise of ejaculatory prayers, elevations of heart and spiritual retirements; for these holy exercises, casting and lifting our spirits continually into God, bear also up to him all our actions. 251

The soul who says : "Ah! Lord, I am thine – My beloved is wholly mine, and I, I am all his – My God, thou art my all – O Jesus thou art my life – Ah! Who will do me the favour that I may die to myself, that I may live only to thee – O to love! To advance! To die to self! O to live to God! O to be in God! O God, whatsoever is not thy very self is nothing to me!" – she, I say, does she not continually dedicate her actions to her heavenly spouse? 252

Let us behold how throughout eternity the Divine goodness tenderly cherished us, preparing all suitable means for our salvation and progress *in his love, and in particular the chance of doing the good which now presents itself to us, or suffering the evil which has come upon us.* 253

O blessed tribulation! O holy affliction, how delightful thou art, since thou didst issue from the loving breast of this Father of eternal mercy, who willed thee from all eternity, and ordained thee for my dear people and me! O cross, my heart wills thee, since the heart of my God has willed thee; O cross, my soul cherishes and embraces thee, with its whole affection!

In this sort we are to undertake the gravest affairs, and to meet the sharpest tribulations that can befall us. 254

A natural inclination to love, which we all possess, does not necessarily mean we will love God. Because of our disposition to love whatever is right before us, we can easily be distracted by other loves. It is necessary to fan the flame of our love of God. We can do this in two ways.

First, in order to love God fully, we may have to restrict other desires. Otherwise, it is like too many nursing babies drawing on the same breast—none of them gets fed adequately.

Our vocation or livelihood could be the greatest distraction to loving God, the biggest competing nursing baby of all, since we normally give the lion's share of our waking time to our job or profession. We may have to bracket our desire to spend all our time working on and thinking about our job in order to have more time for God.

On the other hand, our vocation, no matter what it is, if it is indeed a calling from God, could be our greatest vehicle to loving God. The key is to spend every moment of our vocation dedicating it to the Lord. We ought to do every act of service in our daily work as if we were doing it for God, not humans. By this means, many a humble person has become a saint in the church.

St. Andre Bessette (Brother Andre) Is a good example of this. As a doorman, he welcomed every parishioner as if he were welcoming the Lord himself. His humility and simplicity resulted in people loving him and giving him money to build a small chapel. This led, step by step, to the eventual construction of the massive St. Joseph's Oratory on the top of Mount Royal, a Canadian national pilgrimage site in the center of Montreal.

Small acts of charity or love, as Mother Teresa of Calcutta always taught, are greater than great acts done for self-aggrandisement.

However, if our work is not conducive to loving God, we may have to limit the amount of energy we pour into it. We will still need to do our job well in order to survive but need to put some boundaries around it so that it does not become all-consuming. Being at least mentally on the job at all times is a growing modern illness in this age of smart phones where we can be accessed by our supervisor and coworkers at any moment of the day or night.

Secondly, besides restricting other desires, we could fan the flame of our love of God by habitually turning to God in every moment. We saw above how Brother Andre did this. Love of God requires total dedication, becoming a more-than-willing lover of God by constantly meditating on God's greatness.

God is unimaginably great, but here are forty qualities of God that one could meditate on forever. God is infinitely:

Holy: God is utterly pure. There is no sin or evil in God (Leviticus 19:2).

Eternal: God has no beginning or end (Hebrews 9:14).

Real: God is the source, sustenance and goal of all things, the only thing that lasts (Hebrews 1:1-14).

Infinite: The universe is 82 to the 24th power miles in size, that is 82,000,000,000,000,000,000,000,000 miles across—eighty-two septillion miles. God is even bigger. God is unfathomably greater than, and outside of, time and space (Ps. 104:1-6).

Good: All goodness comes from God (I Chronicles 16:34).

Intelligent: God is off the intelligence scales, infinitely more intelligent than Einstein (Exodus 31:3).

Knowledgeable: God knows everything in every academic discipline: art, astronomy, architecture, biology, chemistry, mathematics, medicine, physics, psychology, zoology and so on (Proverbs 2:5-6).

Conscious: God is aware of everything going on inside and outside of us (Luke 9:47). God knows everything in the personal sub-conscious and collective unconscious. God experiences the consciousness of every creature living in the oceans, earth and sky.

Wise: God knows more than all the wisdom of all the great religions and their leaders: Moses, Solomon, Buddha, Lao Tzu, Paul and Mohammed. According to scripture, God's foolishness—Christ crucified—is wiser than human wisdom (I Corinthians 1:25).

True: All truth comes from, points to and leads to God. God is the source of all scientific and religious truth (John 14:6).

Beautiful: God is beauty itself and the ultimate artist, constantly creating all the ever-changing beauty on Earth and unseen beauty on billions of planets (Zechariah 9:17).

Just: God created the law of karma/return/consequences: what you give you receive back in some form or another. God inspired people to create all our justice systems. God motivates us to strive for justice, the proper distribution of love throughout society (Revelation 15:3).

Creative: God is the Creator-Par-Excellence, the Supremely Creative One (Isaiah 40:28). God's unimaginable creativity is seen in the fifty million species of insects, plants and animals on Earth. And there are trillions of planets in the universe with who-knows-what life forms?

Free: God can do anything. In fact, God specializes in doing what is humanly impossible. God leaves what is humanly possible up to us. For God, all things are possible (Mark 10:27). The miracles of Jesus make this point.

Trustworthy: Because God is totally good, God can be totally trusted (Ps. 11:7). God is always there, faithful and loving. God only allows hard things for our growth in depth and wisdom.

Merciful: Think of the mercy of Jesus throughout the gospels: to the blind, lepers, the crippled, Zacchaeus, the woman caught in adultery, the Gadarene demoniac, the good thief crucified beside him. God inspires us to love mercy. All the mercy shown to anyone in history had its source in God (Deuteronomy 4:31).

Kind: All our kindness comes from God. God constantly engages in random acts of kindness toward us (Luke 6:35). Some call these "coincidences" or "synchronicities" but they are really "God-incidences," or as someone said, "God-winks." God is letting us know that God is real.

Personal: God walks beside us and lives inside us always (2 Timothy 1:14). God knows every small detail of our lives. God knows us all by name and feels everything we feel. God is the only one who knows exactly how we feel. God knows us better than we know our self.

Peaceful: God knows the peace of mountain tops and the utter silence of outer space. If we sit quietly, we can experience the peace and silence that is always there behind all human activity. God's language is silence (Colossians 3:15).

Patient: The universe is 13.7 billion years old. After a mere 9.4 billion years, the Earth started to form. God then waited 4.3 billion years for homo sapiens to show up. God has far more than all the time in the world. God is timeless. In fact, God exists outside of time. God knows our present difficulties and the good person we are, the even better person we will become in our later life and the glory we will become in the afterlife. God knows how to wait (2 Peter 3:9).

Joyful: God is pure joy. God rejoices infinitely over the utter all-inclusiveness of the universe—the universe has it all. Although God experiences sadness over the way human sin blights the creation, God knows that it is temporary, that something greater will come out of it, and we will all be with God forever (Nehemiah 8:10).

Glorious: Ten thousand times ten thousand angels surround the divine; ten million times ten million archangels wait upon God. Fire and utterly blinding light continually emanate from God (Revelation 4: 1-11).

Mysterious: Thick darkness conceals the essence of God the Father. God is always beyond us—greater than we can hope for or imagine (Job 11:7-12). However, Jesus the Christ is the Light who reveals to us what the essence of God is truly like.

Generous: God created nature to produce ten thousand seeds to result in one seed growing. God scatters galaxies and planets all over the universe so that some begin to form life. And God has given each of us the whole universe (2 Corinthians 9:8).

Healing: God has created our body in such a way that it can heal itself, created nations to heal themselves and the whole planet to heal itself. Jesus healed people with all manner of illnesses. God is a God of health who created us to be healthy. People who are physically unhealthy are often more deeply spiritual than those who are able-bodied because they know how frail life is and have more of a sense of their need of God. Perhaps God has not healed their body, but their soul has been healed (Psalm 147:3).

Life-Giving: Life pops up everywhere: in artic cold or in thermal vents at the bottom of the ocean. The scriptures say over and over: choose life! Jesus said he came that we might have life and have it abundantly (John 10:10).

Death-Destroying: God is working hard within each of us, motivating everyone to do all they can to live and to prevent and overcome death. The resurrection of Christ overcame death for all who accept it (I Corinthians 15:54-56). Christ came to give us eternal life and he physically raised people from the dead while he was on Earth.

Co-suffering: God knows all our suffering and suffers with us just as a parent suffers when their child is ill. The cross of Christ, the central symbol of Christianity (along with the resurrection), is the great symbol that God suffers with us (and overcomes our suffering) (John 19:1-28 and John 20:3-9).

Humble: God emptied and humbled God's self to the point of becoming human. God was born in a stable—lower than most humans—and died a far lower death than almost all humans—rejected, tortured and nailed to a cross (Philippians 2:5-11).

Helpful: God helps us through every human action that helps another. God gives us our great guide and mentor in Jesus. God is in our parents, relatives, friends and teachers as they help us. God has created us in such a way that our greatest joy lies in helping others. God constantly helps us in hidden ways we know nothing about (Hebrews 13:6).

Compassionate: God knows we are mortal and made of dust.

God knows the craziness and brokenness of human life. God sees all our wounds and how everyone has been sinned against. God understands all this and feels all this with us (Matthew 9:36).

Gracious: God overlooks our sin. God sees that we are foundationally good. God pardons us so that we love God in return. God is the opposite of a judgmental scorekeeper (Joel 2:13).

Understanding: Through having lived as Jesus of Nazareth, God thoroughly understands what it is like to be human. God intimately knows the human heart, soul and will. God understands each of us and supports us all (Hebrews 4:14-16).

Steadfast/Faithful: God was utterly faithful to Israel even when they rejected God and chased other gods. God's love is steadfast. God never gives up on us. God sees us and acts in our whole life from beginning to end (I John 1:9).

Comforting: God gives us to loving parents and to our mother's breasts after the hard work of being born. God is our Comforting Mother. God gives adults the comfort of sex and hugs, cuddling and spooning against the harshness of life (Isaiah 40:1).

Gentle: God showed God's self to Elijah in the gentle breeze, not in the storm, earthquake or fire (I Kings 19:12). God is subtle—the Holy Spirit works quietly within us, so subtly we cannot detect it until the gifts and fruits of the Spirit become visible to us.

Nonviolent: God hates violence of any kind: bullying, abuse, rape, torture, war. Violence mars and destroys God's good handiwork, the Creation. God is a nonviolent warrior calmly fighting for the good in all circumstances (Ezekiel 45:9).

Forgiving: God forgives and forgets our sins as soon as we confess them. Christ said we should forgive seventy-times seven, that is, forever (Matthew 18:21-22). If God did not constantly forgive us, how could any person or nation survive?

Loving: God is Love. Love is what God both *is* and *does*. God loves us with an infinite, absolute, eternal, omnipotent, omnipresent, omniscient and completely unmerited Divine Love (I John 4:7-21).

Lovable: Jesus shows us what God is like (John 14:6-11) and no one is more lovable than Jesus. Nothing and no one is more lovable than God. God has it all—all beauty, wisdom, kindness and so on to infinity. Why would anyone love anything more than God?

CHAPTER TWO
THE NINETY-NINE NAMES OF JESUS THE CHRIST

We have seen throughout this book that nothing is more lovable or more loving than God. Since, for Christians at least, Jesus Christ is considered to be the incarnation of God, nothing and no one is more lovable and loving than Jesus.

In order to prepare for the final chapter on the greatest love of all, let us bask in/contemplate for a few minutes some of the many ways Jesus the Christ is represented throughout the Jewish and Christian scriptures. Here then are the ninety-nine names of Jesus the Christ (in alphabetical order):

—Advocate (I John 2:1)
—Almighty (Revelation 1:8)
—Alpha and Omega (Revelation 1:8)
—Amen (Revelation 3:14)
—Anointed (John 1:41)
—Apostle of Our Confession (Hebrews 3:1)
—Arm of the Lord (Isaiah 53:1)
—Author of Life (Acts 3:15)
—Blessed and Only Sovereign (I Timothy 6:15)
—Branch of the Lord (Isaiah 4:2)
—Bread of Life (John 6:35)
—Bridegroom (Matthew 9:15)
—Chief Shepherd (I Peter 5:4)
—Commander (Isaiah 55:4)

—Consolation of Israel (Luke 2:25)
—Creator of Worlds (Hebrews 1:2)
—Dawn (Luke 1:78)
—Deliverer (Romans 11:26)
—Everlasting Father (Isaiah 9:6)
—Faithful Witness (Revelation 1:5)
—First and Last (Revelation 1:17)
—First Born (Revelation 1:5)
—Forerunner (Hebrews 6:20)
—Gate (John 10:7)
—Glory of the Lord (Isaiah 40:5)
—God Blessed Forever (Romans 9:5)
—God's Beloved (Matthew 12:18)
—God's Chosen (Isaiah 42:1)
—God's Holy Servant (Acts 4:27)
—Good Shepherd (John 10:11)
—Great High Priest (Hebrews 4:14)
—Guardian of Souls (I Peter 2:25)
—Head of the Church (Ephesians 1:22)
—Heir of All Things (Hebrews 1:2)
—Holy and Righteous One (Acts 3:14)
—Holy One of God (Mark 1:24)
—I Am (John 8:58)
—Image of God (II Corinthians 4:4)
—Immanuel (Isaiah 7:14)
—King of the Jews (Matthew 2:2)
—King of Kings (I Timothy 6:15)
—King of Nations (Revelation 15:3)
—Lamb of God (John 1:29)
—Last Adam (I Corinthians 15:45)
—Leader (Isaiah 55:4)
—Life (John 14:6)
—Light (John 1:5)
—Light of the World (John 8:12)
—Lion of Judah (Revelation 5:5)

—Living Water (John 4:14)
—Lord of All (Acts 10:36)
—Lord of Glory (I Corinthians 2:8)
—Lord of Lords (I Timothy 6:15)
—Lord of Righteousness (Jeremiah 23:6)
—Man of Suffering (Isaiah 53:3)
—Mediator (I Timothy 2:5)
—Messenger of the Covenant (Malachi 3:1)
—Messiah of God (Luke 9:20)
—Mighty God (Isaiah 9:6)
—Mighty Savior (Luke 1:69)
—Morning Star (Revelation 22:16)
—Nazarene (Matthew 2:23)
—Only Son of God (John 1:18)
—Origin of Creation (Revelation 3:14)
—Our God (Isaiah 40:3)
—Our Passover Lamb (I Corinthians 5:7)
—Perfecter of Our Faith (Hebrews 12:2)
—Pioneer of Our Faith (Hebrews 12:2)
—Pioneer of Salvation (Hebrews 2:10)
—Prince of Peace (Isaiah 9:6)
—Prophet Mighty in Deed (Luke 24:19)
—Redeemer (Job 19:25)
—Refiner and Purifier (Malachi 3:3)
—Resurrection (John 11:25)
—Righteous One (Acts 7:52)
—Rock (I Corinthians 10:4)
—Root of David (Revelation 22:16)
—Rose of Sharon (Song of Songs 12:1)
—Ruler of Israel (Micah 5:1)
—Ruler of Kings (Revelation 1:5)
—Savior (Luke 2:11)
—Seed of Woman (Genesis 3:15)
—Servant (Philippians 2:7)
—Shepherd of Souls (I Peter 2:25)

—Shiloh (Genesis 49:10)
—Son of David (Matthew 1:1)
—Son of God (Matthew 2:15)
—Son of Man (Matthew 9:6)
—Son of the Blessed One (Mark 14:61)
—Son of the Most High (Luke 1:32)
—Source of Eternal Salvation (Hebrews 5:9)
—Teacher (John 13:13)
—The Way (John 14:6)
—Treasure of All Nations (Haggai 2:7)
—True Light (John 1:9)
—True Vine (John 15:1)
—Witness (Isaiah 55:4)
—Wonderful Counselor (Isaiah 9:6)
—Word (John 1:1)
—Word Become Flesh (John 1:4)
—Word of God (Revelation 19:13)

CHAPTER THREE
THE GREATEST LOVE OF ALL

O Saviour Jesus, when shall it then be, that having sacrificed to thee all that we have, we shall also offer up to thee all that we are? When shall we offer unto thee our free will, the only child of our spirit? 255

O free will of my heart, how good a thing were it for thee to be bound and extended upon the cross of thy divine Saviour! How desirable a thing it is to die to thyself, to burn forever a holocaust to the Lord! Theotimus, our free-will is never so free as when it is a slave to the will of God, nor ever so much a slave when it serves our own will. It never has so much life as when it dies to itself, nor ever so much death, as when it lives to itself. 256

I will sum up those points on which I have touched in this treatise.

The divine goodness considered in itself is not only the first motive of all motives to love God but also the greatest, the most noble and most mighty. For it is that which ravishes the Blessed and crowns their felicity. How can one have a heart, and yet not love so infinite a goodness?

The second motive to love God is that of God's natural Providence towards us, of creation and preservation.

The third motive is that of God's supernatural Providence over us, and of the Redemption he has prepared for us.

The fourth motive is to consider how God brings to effect this Providence and Redemption, giving every one all the graces and assistances required for salvation.

The fifth motive is the eternal glory which the Divine goodness has provided for us, which is the crown of God's benefits towards us. 257

Now to receive from these motives a profound and strong heat of love, it is necessary, that after having considered one of them in a general way, we apply it in particular to ourselves. For example: O how amiable this great God is, who out of his infinite goodness gave his son for the whole world's redemption! Yes, indeed for all in general, but in particular for me, who am the first of sinners. Ah! He hath loved me, yea, I say, he hath loved even me, even me myself, such as I am, and delivered himself to his Passion for me! 258

We must consider the Divine benefits in their first and eternal source. O God! Theotimus, what love can we have sufficiently worthy of the infinite goodness of our Creator, who from all eternity determined to create, preserve, govern, redeem, save and glorify all in general and each in particular? 259

In the day of his Passion, when he offered his tears, his prayers, his blood and his life for all, he breathed in particular for thee these thoughts of love: "Ah! My eternal Father, I take to myself and charge myself with all the sins of poor (your name), to undergo torments and death that (your name) may be freed from them, and that (your name) may not perish but live. Let me die so (your name) may live; let me be crucified so (your name) may be glorified!"

O sovereign love of the Heart of Jesus, what heart can ever bless thee as devotedly as it ought! 260

Choosing to love God above all else then determines all our subsequent choices. It directs or redirects our whole life—everything we think, say, do, believe and hope from that day on.

Love of another person is a choice more than a feeling. There will be times in a marriage or any other close relationship when we are not feeling the love for the other person. But we can still decide to be a loving person and do loving things to them.

It is the same with loving God. Love of God is a choice more than a feeling. There will be times when we do not feel love for God, but we can still choose to do things that increase our knowledge and understanding of God and therefore our love of God.

We could choose to engage in a scripture study course; take theology courses so we have an informed and intelligent faith; go on retreats; pray constantly in many different forms; support our church; in general, simply make God the very first priority in our life. We could plan our whole life around God; constantly strive for justice for everyone; give thanks for all our blessings; teach Sunday school; start a spiritual reading group; volunteer to work at our church's soup kitchen; talk to friends, family and co-workers about God and so on.

Taking action to love God when we are not feeling love for God continually points us in the right direction. Engaging in little acts like saying to the Lord "I am all yours" can help us surrender our whole life to God.

All the above things help us raise our heart and mind to God, and to accept whatever happens as God's providence.

The greatest act of love is to give up what we love the most out of love for God.

The greatest example of this in the Jewish scriptures was when Abraham was willing to sacrifice his only son Isaac out of obedience to God.

The story of Abraham and Isaac is an illustration of the point that we are all called to embrace, out of love for God, any cross that God allows to happen to us, even if it makes absolutely no rational sense. We are called to embrace our greatest challenges out of unconditional trust, hope and love of God.

Again, love of God is the Virtue of all virtues, the Beatitude of all beatitudes, the Sacrament of all sacraments. When asked what the greatest commandment was, Jesus replied "You shall love the Lord your God with all your heart, and with all your soul, and with all your mind" (Matthew 22:37). All else in Christianity, Judaism, and all the world's great religions, is simply an elaboration on this fundamental command.

There are six basic motives for loving God.

First of all, we could love God for God's providence in this life. This is not a bad motive: to be thankful for being taken care of by God while on Earth. Life is hard, and to appreciate and give thanks for all of God's help in coping with life, surviving and even thriving, is a good motive.

Every great sage knows that God is so loving, that even if we just said "thank you" for whatever level of prosperity God gave us, it would be enough: whether it was for having a large family or just a single friend; for being robustly healthy or just having few health complaints; for having great wealth or just a few dollars.

Beyond that, it would be an even better motive of being thankful for God's providence if we thanked God for giving us rejection by others, ill health and poverty. Then we would be thanking God for just being, for just being allowed to exist.

Another basic motive for loving God, beyond God's providence, is God's redemption. God has given us not just life but God's saving love. God has pulled our life out of the pit and set our feet on the solid ground of God's love, which never passes away. We are now on the right path, the highway that leads to the kingdom/queendom of heaven.

We may have chosen to love God because God got us out of the ultimately meaningless hell we were living in. We may love God because we have woken up to the fact that, even though we had all the world has to offer, our heart was not with God, and we were not at peace, it was not ultimately satisfying because we knew in our heart of hearts that it was all passing away. We knew that in spite of having everything we were still poor and blind and naked because we did not have God. Our motive for loving God was God's redemption from all this.

A third basic (but not base) motive for loving God is the desire for eternal life. Our most basic drive while on earth is to survive. We will do anything and everything to avoid death. The desire to not die underlies everyone's thoughts and actions.

It is no wonder then that we desire to live forever. This is simply a projection of our most basic desire, survival, into life beyond the grave. God put in our hearts the desire to survive and the desire for eternal life.

We know that when we return the love God has showered on us, we accept God's offer of a place in heaven forever. It is not that God will not grant eternal life to everyone who wants it, but returning God's love brings us into communion with God and prepares us to live in the place God has prepared for us in heaven.

Beyond the desire for eternal life, another related motive for loving God would be the desire for eternal glory. God does not want us just to survive, God wants us to be fully alive, completely fulfilled. And just as the desire to survive leads to the desire for eternal life, so the desire for fulfillment in this life leads to the desire for complete fulfillment in the afterlife.

Just as a baby in the womb has no idea how glorious life on Earth will be, we on Earth have no idea how much more glorious the afterlife will be. We begin the process of learning about eternal glory by beginning to love God while we are on Earth. Once we start loving God, the Holy Spirit draws us with cords of love ever more deeply into the mystery of God. We begin to taste what eternal glory might be like.

All the above reasons or motives for loving God: God's providence, redemption, eternal life and eternal glory may seem self-centered, and that is somewhat true, but remember, God wants to be loved by us and has planted these desires in us so we might love God back. God has programmed these motives into our DNA.

Of course, we can always refuse to love God, resist all this, or get distracted and put our most inspired motives on the back burner as we scramble to just survive in our super-competitive, materialistic, individualistic world.

God never forces anyone to do anything. But God hopes we will put God first, make God our first and foremost priority so that God can show us the never-ending riches of God's glory, which then becomes our glory. Our glory is to have the inestimable blessing of participating in God's glory. This is our true inheritance.

The far better motive of course would be to love God not for anything we could receive in return, but to love God for God's self alone. God is far more loving and lovable than anything else: what riches on Earth can compare to God's riches? What wise man or wise woman can compare to the wisdom of God? What holy person can hold a candle to the exploding sun of God's holiness? What lover has ever loved us the way God loves us?

God simply has, and is to the maximum, every virtue and value: kindness, peace, justice, patience, forgiveness, truth, beauty, goodness, gentleness, understanding, consciousness, knowledge, mercy, freedom, friendship, trustworthiness, joy, generosity, mystery, healing, humility, compassion, graciousness, steadfastness, faithfulness, comfort and on and on. Why would anyone love anything or anyone more than God?

The most compelling of all motives for loving God is that the unimaginably majestic God, the God of the ninety-nine names, became incarnate in Jesus of Nazareth, lived and died for you alone.

If we want to develop a fiery love of God, let us make the universal personal: Christ lived and died for all, yes, but if there had been no one else on Earth except you, Christ would have come and lived and died just for you. Jesus the Christ suffered the slings and arrows of life just for you, he lived just for you. And he was brutally tortured and died a gruesome death just for you alone.

God has no favorites, everyone is God's favorite. You are God's favorite. And God, the Creator, Sustainer and Goal of the entire universe, came to Earth, and lived and died and rose again just for you alone. Jesus did not just suffer and die for you. By his resurrection he lives in you always and you live in him always. This is true life, your life, your resurrected life!

The unimaginably glorious Jesus the Christ of the ninety-nine names did all this just for you. This is as good as it gets. There is no better reason to love God in return. This is the supreme motive for loving God: nothing and no one has ever, nor will ever, nor could ever, love you more than Jesus the Christ loves you!!

Alleluia!!!

EPILOGUE

Dear Reader,

If you enjoyed reading this book, and found it helpful in increasing your awareness and love of God, would you be so kind as to help me help others love God by writing a review of the book?

What the world needs now is love, sweet love, particularly God's sweet love, so please spread the word about this book, tell your friends and family about it, and write a review of it.

If you would like a free digital copy of *God's Ecstatic Love* that you can email to your friends and family, email *btallman@rogers.com* with "Send free copy of *God's Ecstatic Love*" in the subject line or body of your email, and I will send it to you right away. Feel free to share your free copy with as many people as you want. It makes a great gift.

If you want to write a review, just visit your favorite online book seller, then search for the title of the book and scroll down to where it says "Review this product." Writing a review will really help to get the word out about *God's Ecstatic Love.*

Thank you very much!
Bruce Tallman

SCRIPTURE CITED

Genesis 1:31

Genesis 3:15

Exodus 31:3

Leviticus 19:2

Deuteronomy 30:19-20

I Kings 19:12

Nehemiah 8:10

Job 19:25

Psalm 1:6

Psalm 3:3

Psalm 4:3

Psalm 7:1

Psalm 9:4

Psalm 10:14

Psalm 11:7

Psalm 16:2

Psalm 16:6

Psalm 17:6

Psalm 18:6

Psalm 18:35

Psalm 21:7

Psalm 23:1-2

Psalm 24:10

Psalm 27:1

Psalm 28:8

Psalm 31:4

Psalm 32:5

Psalm 33:6

Psalm 34:8

Psalm 37:5

Psalm 40:11

Psalm 42:8

Genesis 2:2

Genesis 29:15-30

Exodus 34:14

Deuteronomy 4:31

2 Samuel 11:2-5

2 Kings 2:11

Job 1:12

Job 33:4

Psalm 2:11

Psalm 3:8

Psalm 5:6

Psalm 7:9

Psalm 9:7

Psalm 10:17

Psalm 13:6

Psalm 16:3

Psalm 16:7

Psalm 18:1

Psalm 18:28

Psalm 19:1

Psalm 22:5

Psalm 23:5

Psalm 25:6

Psalm 27:3

Psalm 30:2

Psalm 31:19

Psalm 32:8

Psalm 33:20

Psalm 34:16

Psalm 37:37

Psalm 40:14

Psalm 44:6

Genesis 2:7

Genesis 49:10

Exodus 34:29-35

Deuteronomy 6:5

I Kings 9:12

I Chronicles 16:34

Job 11:7-12

Psalm 1:1-2

Psalm 2:12

Psalm 4:1

Psalm 6:9

Psalm 8:3

Psalm 9:18

Psalm 11:4

Psalm 16:1

Psalm 16:5

Psalm 16:11

Psalm 18:2

Psalm 18:30

Psalm 19:9-10

Psalm 22:24

Psalm 24:8

Psalm 25:21

Psalm 28:7

Psalm 31:3

Psalm 32:2

Psalm 33:4

Psalm 34:4

Psalm 37:3

Psalm 40:10

Psalm 42:2

Psalm 44:26

Psalm 46:1	Psalm 46:4	Psalm 46:7
Psalm 46:10	Psalm 47:2	Psalm 47:7
Psalm 48:14	Psalm 49:15	Psalm 50:1
Psalm 50:6	Psalm 51:1	Psalm 51:8
Psalm 51:17	Psalm 52:1	Psalm 54:4
Psalm 54:7	Psalm 55:19	Psalm 55:22
Psalm 56:1	Psalm 56:8	Psalm 56:13
Psalm 57:1	Psalm 57:3	Psalm 57:10
Psalm 62:6	Psalm 62:7	Psalm 64:5
Psalm 65:5	Psalm 65:13	Psalm 66:20
Psalm 94:19	Psalm 95:4	Psalm 96:12
Psalm 104:1-6	Psalm 104:24-25	Psalm 139:14
Psalm 147:3	Proverbs 2:5-6	Proverbs 4:3
Proverbs 9:10	Proverbs 23:26	Proverbs 30:8-9
Song of Solomon 2:1	Song of Solomon 2:16	Song of Solomon 3:1
Isaiah 4:2	Isaiah 7:14	Isaiah 9:6
Isaiah 40:1-5	Isaiah 40:28	Isaiah 42:1
Isaiah 53:1	Isaiah 53:3	Isaiah 53:5-10
Isaiah 55:4	Jeremiah 23:6	Ezekiel 45:9
Joel 2:13	Micah 5:1	Micah 6:8
Haggai 2:7	Zechariah 9:17	Malachi 3:1-3
Matthew 1:1	Matthew 2:2	Matthew 2:15
Matthew 2:23	Matthew 4:5-7	Matthew 5:3-12
Matthew 5:13-14	Matthew 5:16	Matthew 5:17
Matthew 5:42-45	Matthew 6:3-4	Matthew 6:19-21
Matthew 6:24	Matthew 6:25,33	Matthew 7:1
Matthew 7:8	Matthew 9:15-16	Matthew 9:36
Matthew 10:30,31	Matthew 11:30	Matthew 11:25
Matthew 12:18	Matthew 13:9-17	Matthew 14:22-33
Matthew 16:24	Matthew 18:3	Matthew 18:6
Matthew 18:21-22	Matthew 19:16-26	Matthew 20:1-16
Matthew 22:37-40	Matthew 23:2-3	Matthew 23:12
Matthew 25:40	Matthew 26:25	Matthew 27:3-5
Matthew 27:46	Mark 1:24	Mark 8:35
Mark 9:24	Mark 10:27	Mark 10:47
Mark 12:30	Mark 14:61	Luke 1:32-33
Luke 1:42-43	Luke 1:69	Luke 1:78
Luke 2:11	Luke 2:25-35	Luke 2:52
Luke 6:35-38	Luke 9:20	Luke 9:47
Luke 9:51	Luke 12:32	Luke 22:17-20
Luke 23:34	Luke 23:39-43	Luke 24:19
John 1:1	John 1:3	John 1:5
John 1:9	John 1:14	John 1:18

John 1:29   John 1:41   John 4:14
John 6:35   John 6:68   John 8:12
John 8:32   John 8:58   John 10:7
John 10:10-11   John 11:25   John 13:13
John 14:6-11   John 14:27   John 15:1
John 15:13   John 19:1-28   John 20:3-9
John 21:15-17   Acts 3:14-15   Acts 4:27
Acts 7:52   Acts: 8:1   Acts 9:1-19
Acts 10:36   Acts 16:22-34   Romans 5:20
Romans 8:6   Romans 9:5   Romans 8:28
Romans 11:26   Romans 12:11   Romans 15:13
I Corinthians 1:25 I Corinthians 2:8   I Corinthians 2:14-16
I Corinthians 3:2   I Corinthians 8:1   I Corinthians 10:4
I Corinthians 11:23-26 I Corinthians 13:1-8 I Corinthians 15:45
I Corinthians 15:54-56 2 Corinthians 3:18 2 Corinthians 4:4
2 Corinthians 5:7   2 Corinthians 8:15 2 Corinthians 9:6
2 Corinthians 9:8   2 Corinthians 9:12 Galatians 2:11-14
Galatians 2:19-20   Ephesians 1:4   Ephesians 1:22
Ephesians 3:20-21   Ephesians 4:13   Philippians 2:5-11
Philippians 4:7   Colossians 1:15-17 Colossians 3:3
Colossians 3:14-15 I Timothy 2:5   I Timothy 6:15
2 Timothy 1:7-8   2 Timothy 1:14   Hebrews 1:1-14
Hebrews 2:10   Hebrews 3:1   Hebrews 4:14-16
Hebrews 5:9   Hebrews 6:20   Hebrews 9:14
Hebrews 11:1   Hebrews 12:2   Hebrews 13:6
I Peter 2:25   I Peter 5:4   I Peter 5:7-8
2 Peter 3:9   I John 1:9   I John 2:1
I John 4:7-21   I John 5:2   Revelation 1:5
Revelation 1:8   Revelation 1:17   Revelation 3:14
Revelation 4:1-11   Revelation 5:5   Revelation 12:1
Revelation 15:3   Revelation 19:13   Revelation 22:16

FOOTNOTES

TREATISE ON THE LOVE OF GOD

1. Treatise, p. 24-25
2. Ibid. p.25
3. Ibid. p.28
4. Ibid. p.28
5. Ibid. p.28
6. Ibid. p.29
7. Ibid. p.29
8. Ibid. p.154
9. Ibid. p.154
10. Ibid. p.37
11. Ibid. p.54
12. Ibid. p.57
13. Ibid. p.57
14. Ibid. p.57
15. Ibid. p.176
16. Ibid. p.176
17. Ibid. p.58
18. Ibid. p.60
19. Ibid. p.73
20. Ibid. p.74
21. Ibid. p.75
22. Ibid. p.75
23. Ibid. p.76
24. Ibid. p.76
25. Ibid. p.76
26. Ibid. p.78
27. Ibid. pp.81
28. Ibid. p.83

29. Ibid. p.84
30. Ibid. p.85
31. Ibid. p. 86
32. Ibid. p.87-88
33. Ibid. p.95-96
34. Ibid. p.95
35. Ibid. p.102-103
36. Ibid. p. 103
37. Ibid. p.103-104
38. Ibid. pp.134
39. Ibid. p.134
40. Ibid. p.145-146
41. Ibid. p.146
42. Ibid. p.144
43. Ibid. p.144
44. Ibid. p.92
45. Ibid. pp.92
46. Ibid. p.146
47. Ibid. p.1113
48. Ibid. p.114
49. Ibid. p.96
50. Ibid. p.96
51. Ibid. p.97-98
52. Ibid. p.116
53. Ibid. p.115
54. Ibid. pp.116
55. Ibid. p.123-124
56. Ibid. pp.138

57. Ibid. pp.124
58. Ibid. p.128-129
59. Ibid. pp.129
60. Ibid. p.129
61. Ibid. p.139
62. Ibid. p.138
63. Ibid. p.141
64. Ibid. p.231
65. Ibid. pp.232-233
66. Ibid. pp.235
67. Ibid. p.236
68. Ibid. p.236
69. Ibid. p.239
70. Ibid. p.240
71. Ibid. p.240
72. Ibid. p.244
73. Ibid. p.245
74. Ibid. p.246
75. Ibid. p.249
76. Ibid. p.250
77. Ibid. p.255
78. Ibid. p.255
79. Ibid. p.255
80. Ibid. p.256
81. Ibid. p.258
82. Ibid. pp.258
83. Ibid. pp.259
84. Ibid. p.260

85. Ibid. p.264
86. Ibid. pp.267
87. Ibid. p.270
88. Ibid. p.272
89. Ibid. p.274
90. Ibid. p.274
91. Ibid. p.277
92. Ibid. p.279
93. Ibid. p.151-152
94. Ibid. p.152-153
95. Ibid. p.153
96. Ibid. p.358
97. Ibid. pp.358
98. Ibid. p.358
99. Ibid. p.307
100. Ibid. p.309
101. Ibid. p.310
102. Ibid. p.310
103. Ibid. p.311
104. Ibid. pp.311
105. Ibid. p.311
106. Ibid. p.334
107. Ibid. p.334
108. Ibid. p.335
109. Ibid. p.336
110. Ibid. p.336
111. Ibid. p.337
112. Ibid. p.337
113. Ibid. pp.337-338
114. Ibid. p.338
115. Ibid. p.339
116. Ibid. p.340
117. Ibid. p.342
118. Ibid. p.342-343
119. Ibid. pp.343
120. Ibid. p.345
121. Ibid. p.346
122. Ibid. p.347
123. Ibid. p.347
124. Ibid. p.347
125. Ibid. p.349-350
126. Ibid. p.350
127. Ibid. pp.351
128. Ibid. p.352
129. Ibid. pp.354
130. Ibid. p.355
131. Ibid. p.356
132. Ibid. pp.357
133. Ibid. p.361
134. Ibid. p.361
135. Ibid. p.367-368
136. Ibid. p.368
137. Ibid. p.368
138. Ibid. p.369
139. Ibid. p.370
140. Ibid. p.371
141. Ibid. p.373
142. Ibid. p.373-374
143. Ibid. pp.374-375
144. Ibid. p.375
145. Ibid. pp.378
146. Ibid. p.376
147. Ibid. p.379
148. Ibid. p.379
149. Ibid. p.380
150. Ibid. p.381
151. Ibid. p.382
152. Ibid. p.391
153. Ibid. p.391-392
154. Ibid. p.392
155. Ibid. p.393
156. Ibid. p.394
157. Ibid. p.397
158. Ibid. p.398
159. Ibid. p.407
160. Ibid. p.409
161. Ibid. p.410
162. Ibid. p.410
163. Ibid. p.413-414
164. Ibid. p.417-418
165. Ibid. p.422
166. Ibid. p.423
167. Ibid. p.423
168. Ibid. p.426
169. Ibid. p.426
170. Ibid. p.429
171. Ibid. p.430
172. Ibid. p.437
173. Ibid. p.437
174. Ibid. p.437
175. Ibid. p.438
176. Ibid. p.438
177. Ibid. p.439
178. Ibid. p.440
179. Ibid. p.441
180. Ibid. p.442
181. Ibid. p.442
182. Ibid. p.442
183. Ibid. p.443
184. Ibid. p.443-444
185. Ibid. p.444-445
186. Ibid. p.447
187. Ibid. p.447
188. Ibid. p.449
189. Ibid. p.449
190. Ibid. p.450-451
191. Ibid. p.451
192. Ibid. p.451
193. Ibid. p.452
194. Ibid. p.455
195. Ibid. p.455
196. Ibid. p.456-457
197. Ibid. p.458
198. Ibid. p.460
199. Ibid. p.460
200. Ibid. p.460
201. Ibid. p.460-461
202. Ibid. p.461
203. Ibid. p.462
204. Ibid. p.462
205. Ibid. p.463
206. Ibid. p.468
207. Ibid. p.468
208. Ibid. p.469
209. Ibid. p.470
210. Ibid. p.470
211. Ibid. p.471
212. Ibid. p.472
213. Ibid. p.472

214. Ibid. p.473
215. Ibid. p.474
216. Ibid. p.483
217. Ibid. p.486
218. Ibid. p.486-487
219. Ibid. p.488
220. Ibid. p.488
221. Ibid. p.489
222. Ibid. p.490
223. Ibid. p.491
224. Ibid. p.499
225. Ibid. p.499
226. Ibid. p.508
227. Ibid. p.510
228. Ibid. p.510
229. Ibid. p.513
230. Ibid. p.514

231. Ibid. p.514
232. Ibid. p.516
233. Ibid. p.528-529
234. Ibid. p.530
235. Ibid. p.530
236. Ibid. p.531
237. Ibid. p.531
238. Ibid. p.532
239. Ibid. p.523
240. Ibid. p.525
241. Ibid. p.533
242. Ibid. p.534
243. Ibid. p.535
244. Ibid. p.536
245. Ibid. p.537
246. Ibid. p.537
247. Ibid, p.538

248. Ibid. p.540
249. Ibid. p.541
250. Ibid. p.542
251. Ibid. p.546
252. Ibid. p.546
253. Ibid. p.547
254. Ibid. p.547-548
255. Ibid. p.550
256. Ibid. p.550
257. Ibid. p.551-552
258. Ibid. p.552
259. Ibid. p.552
260. Ibid. p.553

HEART, MIND, AND SOUL BIBLIOGRAPHY
BOOKS TO STIMULATE LOVING GOD
WITH TOTAL PASSION, INTELLECT AND DEPTH

à Kempis, Thomas. *The Imitation of Christ*. Translated by Betty I. Knott. Glasgow: William Collins and Sons, 1963.

Augustine. *The Confessions of St. Augustine*. Translated by John K. Ryan. Garden City, New York: Doubleday, Image Books, 1960.

Bell, Rob. *Love Wins: A Book about Heaven, Hell, and the Fate of Every Person Who Ever Lived*. New York: HarperOne, 2011.

Bonhoeffer, Dietrich. *Christology*. Translated by John Bowden. New York: Harper and Row, 1966.

_____. *The Cost of Discipleship*. Translated by R. H. Fuller. New York: MacMillan, 1963.

_____. *I Loved This People*. Translated by Keith R. Crim. Richmond, Virginia: John Knox Press, 1966.

_____. *Life Together*. Translated by John W. Doberstein. New York: Harper and Row, 1954.

Borg, Marcus. *Jesus: Uncovering the Life, Teachings, and Relevance of a Religious Revolutionary*. New York: HarperOne, 2006.

_____. *Meeting Jesus Again for the First Time: The Historical Jesus and the Heart of Contemporary Faith*. New York: HarperSanFrancisco, 1994.

_____. *Reading the Bible Again for the First Time: Taking the Bible Seriously Not Literally*. New York: HarperSanFrancisco, 2001.

Buber, Martin. *Between Man and Man*. Translated by Ronald Gregor Smith. London: William Collins and Sons, 1947.

_____. *I and Thou*. Translated by Walter Kaufmann. New York: Charles Scribner's Sons, 1970.

Campbell, Joseph. *The Hero with A Thousand Faces*. Novato, California: New World Library, 2008.

_____. ed. *Myths, Dreams, and Religion*. New York: E. P. Dutton, 1970.

_____. *Myths to Live By*. New York: Bantam, 1972.

Carretto, Carlo. *Summoned by Love*. Translated by Alan Neame. London: Darton, Longman and Todd Ltd., 1977.

Chauchard, Paul. *Teilhard de Chardin on Love and Suffering*. Translated by Marie Chêne. New York: Paulist Press, 1966.

Clift, Wallace B. *Jung and Christianity: The Challenge of Reconciliation*. New York: Crossroad, 1985.

Crosby, Michael. *Spirituality of the Beatitudes: Matthew's Challenge for First World Christians*. Maryknoll, New York: Orbis Books, 1981.

de Caussade, Jean-Pierre. *The Sacrament of the Present Moment*. Translated by Kitty Muggeridge. Glasgow: William Collins and Sons, 1981.

de Chardin, Teilhard. *Hymn of the Universe*. London: Collins, 1965.

_____. *Le Milieu Divin: An Essay on the Interior Life*. London: Collins, 1957.

_____. *On Suffering*. Glasgow: William Collins and Sons, 1975.

_____. *The Phenomenon of Man*. Translated by Julian Huxley. London: William Collins and Sons, 1959.

de Lubac, Henri. *The Religion of Teilhard de Chardin*. Translated by René Hague. London: Collins, 1967.

de Sales, Francis. *Introduction to the Devout Life*. Translated by John K. Ryan. New York: Harper and Brothers, 1952.

_____. *Treatise on the Love of God*. Translated by John K. Ryan. Rockford, Illinois: Tan Books and Publishers, 1975.

de Mello, Anthony. *Sadhana, A Way to God: Christian Exercises in Eastern Form*. New York: Doubleday, Image Books, 1978.

_____. *The Song of the Bird*. New York: Doubleday, Image Books, 1982.

_____. *Taking Flight: A Book of Story Meditations*. New York: Doubleday, Image Books, 1988.

Dourley, John P. *The Psyche as Sacrament: A Comparative Study of C. G. Jung and Paul Tillich*. Toronto: Inner City Books, 1981.

Finley, James. *Merton's Palace of Nowhere: A Search for God through Awareness of the True Self*. Notre Dame, Indiana: Ave Maria Press, 1978.

Fox, Matthew. *The Coming of the Cosmic Christ*. San Francisco: Harper and Row, 1988.

_____. *Original Blessing: A Primer in Creation Spirituality*. Santa Fe, New Mexico: Bear and Company, 1983.

_____. *A Spirituality Named Compassion*. Minneapolis, Minnesota: Winston Press, 1979.

_____. *Wrestling with the Prophets: Essays on Creation Spirituality and Everyday Life*. New York: HarperSanFrancisco, 1995.

Fromm, Erich. *The Art of Loving*. New York: Harper and Row, 1956.

Haring, Bernard. *Love Is the Answer*. Denville, New Jersey: Dimension Books, 1970.

Griffiths, Bede. *The Marriage of East and West*. Springfield, Illinois: Templegate Publishers, 1982.

John of the Cross. *Dark Night of the Soul*. Translated by E. Allison Peers. New York: Doubleday, Image Books, 1990.

_____. *Spiritual Canticle*. Translated by E. Allison Peers. Garden City, New York: Doubleday, Image Books, 1961.

Johnston, William. *Arise My Love: Mysticism for a New Era*. Maryknoll, New York: Orbis Books, 2000.

_____. *Christian Mysticism Today*. San Francisco: Harper and Row, 1984.

_____, ed. *The Cloud of Unknowing*. New York: Doubleday, Image Books, 1973.

_____. *Mystical Journey: An Autobiography.* Maryknoll, New York: Orbis Books, 2006.

Jung, Carl. ed. *Man and His Symbols.* New York: Dell Publishing, 1964.

_____. *The Undiscovered Self.* Translated by R.F.C. Hull. New York: New American Library, Mentor Books, 1957.

_____. *Modern Man in Search of a Soul.* Translated by W. S. Dell. New York: Harcourt Brace, Harvest Books,1933.

Keating, Thomas. *The Heart of the World: An Introduction to Contemplative Christianity.* New York: Crossroad, 1981.

_____. *The Mystery of Christ: The Liturgy as Spiritual Experience.* New York: Continuum, 1987.

_____. *Open Mind, Open Heart: The Contemplative Dimension of the Gospel.* Warwick, New York: Amity House, 1986.

Lewis, C. S. *The Four Loves.* Glasgow: William Collins and Sons, 1960.

_____. *Mere Christianity.* Glasgow: William Collins and Sons, 1952.

_____. *The Problem of Pain.* Glasgow: William Collins and Sons, 1940.

Lawrence, Brother. *The Practice of the Presence of God.* USA: Fleming H. Revell Company, 1958.

Marcel, Gabriel. *Being and Having: An Existentialist Diary.* New York: Harper and Row, 1965.

_____. *Mystery of Being*. Chicago: Henry Regnery Company, 1960.

McBrien, Richard P. *Catholicism*. Minneapolis, Minnesota: Winston Press, 1981.

Merton, Thomas. *The Ascent to Truth*. New York: Harcourt Brace, 1951.

_____. *Contemplation in a World of Action*. New York: Doubleday, Image Books, 1965.

_____. *Contemplative Prayer*. New York: Herder and Herder, 1969.

_____. *Life and Holiness*. New York: Doubleday, Image Books, 1963.

_____. *Love and Living*. Editors: Naomi Burton Stone and Brother Patrick Hart. New York: Bantam Books, 1980.

_____. *Mystics and Zen Masters*. New York: Dell, 1961.

_____. *The Seven Storey Mountain*. New York: Harcourt Brace, 1948.

_____. *Thoughts in Solitude*. New York: Doubleday, Image Books, 1956.

Moore, Robert L. ed. *Carl Jung and Christian Spirituality*. New York: Paulist Press, 1988.

Moore, Thomas. *Care of the Soul*. New York: HarperCollins, 1992.

_____. *Soul Mates: Honoring the Mysteries of Love and Relationships*. New York: HarperCollins, 1994.

Niebuhr, H. Richard. *Christ and Culture.* New York: Harper and Row, 1951.

Niebuhr, Reinhold. *Moral Man and Immoral Society.* New York: Charles Scribner's Sons, 1932.

_____. *The Nature and Destiny of Man.* New York: Charles Scribner's Sons, 1943.

Nolan, Albert. *Jesus Before Christianity.* Maryknoll, New York: Orbis Books, 1976.

_____. *Jesus Today: A Spirituality of Radical Freedom.* Maryknoll, New York: Orbis Books, 2006.

Nouwen, Henri J. M. *Following Jesus: Finding Our Way Home in an Age of Anxiety.* Edited by Gabrielle Earnshaw. New York: Random House, 2019.

_____. *The Inner Voice of Love: a Journey Through Anguish to Freedom.* New York: Doubleday, Image Books, 1996.

_____. *Intimacy: Pastoral Psychological Essays.* Notre Dame, Indiana: Fides Publishers, 1969.

_____. *Life of the Beloved: Spiritual Living in a Secular World.* New York: Crossroad, 1992.

_____. *The Return of the Prodigal Son.* New York: Doubleday, Image Books, 1992.

_____. *The Way of the Heart.* New York: Ballantine Books, 1981.

_____. *The Wounded Healer: Ministry in Contemporary Society.* New York: Doubleday, 1972.

Otto, Rudolf. *The Idea of the Holy*. London: Oxford University Press, 1923.

Powell, John. *Fully Human, Fully Alive*. Niles, Illinois: Argus Communications, 1976.

_____. *Unconditional Love*. Niles, Illinois: Argus Communications, 1978.

_____. *Why Am I Afraid to Love?* Chicago: Argus Communications, 1972.

Rahner, Karl. *Grace in Freedom*. Translated by Hilda Graef. Montreal: Herder, Palm Publishers, 1969.

_____. *The Love of Jesus and the Love of Neighbor*. Translated by Robert Barr. New York: Crossroad, 1963.

_____. *On Prayer*. New York: Paulist Press, 1968.

Rohr, Richard. *Everything Belongs: The Gift of Contemplative Prayer*. New York: Crossroad, 1999.

_____. *Immortal Diamond: The Search for Our True Self*. San Francisco: Jossey-Bass, 2013.

_____. *The Naked Now: Learning to See as the Mystics See*. New York: Crossroad, 2009.

_____. *Simplicity: The Art of Living*. New York: Crossroad, 1991.

_____. *What the Mystics Know: Seven Pathways to Your Deeper Self*. New York: Crossroad, 2015.

Rolheiser, Ronald. *The Holy Longing: The Search for a Christian Spirituality*. New York: Doubleday, Image Books, 1998.

_____. *Sacred Fire: A Vision for a Deeper Human and Christian Maturity*. New York: Penguin Random House, Image Books, 2014.

_____. *Wrestling with God: Finding Hope and Meaning in Our Daily Struggles to Be Human*. New York: Penguin Random House, Image Books, 2018.

Steindl-Rast, David. *Gratefulness, the Heart of Prayer: An Approach to Life in Fullness*. Ramsey, New Jersey: Paulist Press, 1984.

Teresa Of Avila. *Interior Castle*. Translated by E. Allison Peers. New York: Doubleday, Image Books, 1961.

Thérèse of Lisieux. *Prayers and Meditations of Thérèse of Lisieux*. Edited by Cindy Cavnar. Ann Arbor, Michigan: Servant Publications, 1992.

_____. *The Story of a Soul*. Translated by Michael Day. Charlotte, North Carolina: Saint Benedict Press, Tan Books, 2010.

Tillich, Paul. *The Courage to Be*. Glasgow: William Collins and Sons, 1952.

_____. *Dynamics of Faith*. New York: Harper and Row, 1957.

_____. *The Eternal Now*. New York: Charles Scribner's Sons, 1956.

_____. *The New Being*. New York: Charles Scribner's Sons, 1955.

_____. *The Shaking of the Foundations*. New York: Charles Scribner's Sons, 1948.

_____. *Systematic Theology: Three Volumes*. Chicago: University of Chicago Press, 1950, 1957, 1963.

Tolle, Eckhart. *A New Earth: Awakening to Your Life's Purpose*. New

York: Penguin Group, 2005.

_____. *The Power of Now: A Guide to Spiritual Enlightenment*. Novato, California: New World Library, 1999.

Underhill, Evelyn. *Mysticism*. New York: New American Library, 1974.

Wilber, Ken. *A Brief History of Everything*. Boston: Shambhala, 1996.

_____. *Integral Spirituality: A Startling New Role for Religion in the Modern and Postmodern World*. Boston, Shambhala, Integral Books, 2006.

_____. *The Integral Vision: A Very Short Introduction to the Revolutionary Integral Approach to Life, God, the Universe, and Everything*. Boston: Shambhala, 2007.

_____. *The Marriage of Sense and Soul: Integrating Science and Religion*. New York: Random House, Broadway Books, 1998.

ABOUT THE AUTHOR

Bruce Tallman is a lover of God who lives in London, Ontario, Canada with his wife Grace. They have three adult children: Hailey, Brandon and Alana.

Bruce was the director of two adult religious education centers for 14 years for the Roman Catholic Diocese of London, Ontario. He has a Doctor of Ministry degree in Spiritual Direction and has worked since 2002 as a spiritual director, religious educator of adults and writer.

He is the author of three other books and has had hundreds of articles published on spirituality, religion, theology and ethics.

Dr. Tallman's book *Finding Seekers: How to Develop a Spiritual Direction Practice from Beginning to Full-Time Employment* is a best-seller in the field of spiritual counselling.

For more information see *www.brucetallman.com*
or email *btallman@rogers.com*

CPSIA information can be obtained
at www.ICGtesting.com
Printed in the USA
LVHW021114010921
696600LV00011B/500

9 781955 821568